Web–Based Supply Chain Management and Digital Signal Processing:
Methods for Effective Information Administration and Transmission

Manjunath Ramachandra
MSR School of Advanced Studies, Philips, India

BUSINESS SCIENCE REFERENCE

Hershey · New York

Director of Editorial Content:	Kristin Klinger
Senior Managing Editor:	Jamie Snavely
Assistant Managing Editor:	Michael Brehm
Publishing Assistant:	Sean Woznicki
Typesetter:	Sean Woznicki, Mike Killian
Cover Design:	Lisa Tosheff
Printed at:	Yurchak Printing Inc.

Published in the United States of America by
Business Science Reference (an imprint of IGI Global)
701 E. Chocolate Avenue
Hershey PA 17033
Tel: 717-533-8845
Fax: 717-533-8661
E-mail: cust@igi-global.com
Web site: http://www.igi-global.com/reference

Library of Congress Cataloging-in-Publication Data

Ramachandra, Manjunath, 1970-
  Web-based supply chain management and digital signal processing : methods for effective information administration and transmission / by Manjunath Ramachandra.
       p. cm.
  Includes bibliographical references and index.
  Summary: "This book presents trends and techniques for successful intelligent decision-making and transfer of products through digital signal processing, including research in supply chain management with examples and case studies useful for those involved with various levels of management"-- Provided by publisher.

  ISBN 978-1-60566-888-8 (hbk.) -- ISBN 978-1-60566-889-5 (ebook) 1.
Business logistics--Data processing. 2. Signal processing--Digital
techniques. 3. Management information systems. 4. Data transmission systems.
I. Title.
  HD38.5.R35 2010
  658.500285--dc22
                         2009025031

British Cataloguing in Publication Data
A Cataloguing in Publication record for this book is available from the British Library.

Table of Contents

Section 1
Introduction

Chapter 1

Section 2
Signal Processing for Information Supply Chain

Chapter 2

Section 3
Information Acquisition and Processing

Section 4
Information Storage

Section 5
Information Retrieval

Section 6
Information Transmission

Preface

WHAT IS INFORMATION MANAGEMENT?

Information management basically refers to the administration of information that includes acquisition, storage and retrieval of information. In the process, the information modified and cleaned. James Robertson writes in his article, *10 principles of effective information management*, as:

'Information management' is an umbrella term that encompasses all the systems and processes within an organization for the creation and use of corporate information. Professor T.D. Wilson, Högskolan i Borås, Sweden, *defined Information management as: "The application of management principles to the acquisition, organization, control, dissemination and use of information relevant to the effective operation of organizations of all kinds".*

Information Management is the administration of information, its usage and transmission, and the application of theories and techniques of information science to create, modify, or improve information handling systems.

IMPORTANCE OF SUPPLY CHAIN MODEL

Supply chain is a self contained and self sustained system. It is a reflection of the inequality wherein a component with surplus "commodity" transfers a portion of the same on to a component which requires it. It is this demand for the commodity and the supply of the same that ensures stability of the supply chain.

Innumerable examples exist for both natural and artificial supply chains depending on what the components are and what gets transfers across them. It spans contrasting players like the farmers growing wheat and the Bakers; the steel industries and the automobile industries; the forest and the tigers; finally authors and the readers binding them in fine unseen fabric. The last example stands as a candidate for information flow from the author to the readers. This book peeps in to this sustained unseen relation and provides the better understanding and alternate mechanisms for information management based on signal processing and web technologies to shape the same. In this book, the information life cycle is linked to the information supply chain management.

Information Technology is the acquisition, processing, storage, manipulation and dissemination of digital information by computing or telecommunications or a combination of both.

The book also provides an insight in to information supply chain- the end-to-end flow of information in an organization. Although enterprise resource planning centralizes transaction data and ensures transaction consistency, it was never designed for semantic persistence. However, because master data is embodied in transactions, it is not possible to achieve enterprise information management without Enterprise Resource Planning (ERP). For the same reason, the book contains examples from the enterprise information supply chain though no assumption has been made on the nature of the enterprise.

The information required to maintain a successful supply chain is the core of the supply chain management. Here an attempt has been made to integrate the two proven work systems. Information management is used as a tool for the realization of the supply chain management. This book is wound around the same with a specific emphasis to the web based information management for the supply chain. Further discussion on other components of the supply chain is out of scope of this book.

Organizations, data warehouses, business units, enterprises repeatedly used in this book are all different implementations and parts of a supply chain. Focus is on the study and shaping of the characteristics of each one of these components. No specific supply chains are assumed although the examples, descriptions and interpretations point to the "information" supply chain. Along with any supply chain, the 'data' supply chain has to be present for its successful management. The book is written in a user centric way with more emphasis to the interaction among the players of the supply chain.

NEED OF SIGNAL PROCESSING

Digital signal processing (DSP) is a growing area invaded in to all walks of life starting from consumer products to database management. In this book the DSP application for the effective information management will be covered. Although it is possible to digest the essence of this book at the level of the application layer or as the end user without a prior exposure to DSP, it is recommended to get an overview of the topics such as Statistical (Bayesian) estimators, Neural networks etc before implementing the solutions or architecting the designs. In each chapter, references are provided as appropriate.

The data as such will be useless unless it carries some information. Interestingly, the data carries information only when some one needs and uses the same. So, all round efforts are required for the proper handling of the data so that it bears the relevant information. In this book, the sophisticated techniques borrowed from signal processing are applied for effective management of the information.

ORGANIZATION OF THE BOOK

Objective of this book is to bring out the effective management of the information system accessible to the reader at one place. The book is wound around the theme of **managing authorized information from a single facility.** The present trend is to automate the information management that calls for effective electronic techniques involving DSP for handling transduction, intelligent decisions etc. The objective of this book is to provide the latest and complete information with examples and case studies. The entire flow of information handling along the supply chain, from retrieval to application, will be covered.

The book is wound around the concepts developed in the introductory chapter. Here the solutions based on differential feedback are introduced. Though there is no restriction on the sequence to be followed after the introductory chapter, it is advisable to cover the first two chapters before getting in to any of the chapters of the other sections.

All the chapters are interlinked in one-way or the other. It provides continuity and comfort feel for the reader. The book covers the interests of a wide range of readers from the new entrants to the field up to the advanced research scholars perusing research/courses in DSP, IT and management. The examples, without any bias in the order, include but not limited to:

- Industries, Executives and managers of large organizations: The book gives guidelines and methodology for managing information supply chain in a large organization like IT industries, library, e-learning, banking, information systems, financial systems, Bio informatics, multimedia, fleet management, manufacturing industries, storage systems, avionics etc. Information supply chain management strategies have been successfully used in various applications as diverse as the hydraulic plant control in China.
- Academics, Business school students and researchers in the field of management: Now a day there is an increasing demand from all corners to have the information supply chain management from one integrated platform. Courses on information supply chain management are being taught in leading business schools. They'll find the new approaches described in this book extremely useful. The techniques may be included in the curriculum.
- E-libraries, E-publishers: This book also looks at the software aspects such as hyper documents, XML etc. Hyper documents are nonlinear documents made of linked nodes. The content of each node is text. Picture, sound or some mix of these in a multimedia hyper documents. That makes a convenient and promising organization for rich classes of sets of documents used in an electronic encyclopedia, computer-aided learning (E-library), software documentation, multi-Author editing, e-publishing etc. The book will be extremely useful in these areas.

In this book, novel features such as knowledge based expert systems are introduced. The advanced results obtained in the research of the other areas of DSP are projected to be useful for information supply chain management. Adequate effort has been made to bring the different dimensions of management under one platform with numerous live examples and case studies. The topics such as hierarchical organization, feedback neural network and shifted feedback etc are uniquely covered in this book.

A lot of customization has been made to the available literature and references in the information management area to fit in to the book. Numerous examples are provided appropriately.

There are a good number of papers available on supply chain management. Some of them address the signal processing techniques with restricted scope for information management such as data storage, retrieval, data mining etc. They are scattered across the different journals. The good points from these papers have been included in the book

A major part of the book is devoted for data management. A chapter at the end is reserved for knowledge management systems. Data mining concepts will be addressed along with the information storage. A separate chapter will explain machine learning, XML, hypermedia engineering etc. Control, access, and sharing of the metadata in one centralized location will be explained.

The book provides insight to the various activities taking place along the information supply chain. No assumption has been made on the size and nature of the information supply chain. The first step in dealing with the data or information is to acquire the same and represent it in a way compatible for subsequent usage. The acquired information would be subjected to cleaning to ensure the data quality and represented in such a way that it would be easy store and retrieve the same. It calls for a brief description on the data that happens through metadata.

In an enterprise data would be stored in distributed environment. For the effective usage the requisite data from different units are to be brought and integrated. In order to search the required data from the archive, efficient searching algorithms are required. The efficiency of searching once again depends up on how the data is organized and described with metadata. Once the requisite data or information is available from the search engine, it has to reach the recipient. Two aspects play a major role during the transmission of this data- Service quality and security. The service quality ensures that the right time data is available from the heterogeneous sources in the distributed environment while the security protocols assure only the intended recipient gets the data.

To use the data effectively and to extract some useful information out of the stored data, various tools are required. These tools help the end user, the human being in identifying the requisite patterns in the vast ocean of data and spread the knowledge across.

All these transactions are mapped on to different chapters in this book. In a way all these chapters are interlinked and represent the information flow along the supply chain.

In addition to the introduction, there are five parts in the book reflecting the lifecycle of information supply chain. The first part provides an introduction and insight in to the subject matter. The activities in the information supply chain management including information acquisition, storage, retrieval and transmission are covered in rest of the chapters.

In each chapter a substantial part is devoted to the issues and solutions in the subject matter followed by the future trends and expected changes. These sections are covered keeping the title of the book in mind. The solutions provided are intended to solve the issues highlighted. These problems are typically encountered in various organizations that get involved in the life cycle of the information. Fine tuning of these solutions may be required to adapt to any specific application. The future trends are intended to provide insight on the upcoming technologies and to help in ramping up accordingly. It also provides a good topic for research. A spectrum of products and projects may be derived from these tips.

The other half of each chapter introduces the topic and provides adequate background material and references to understand the issues faced and the emerging trends.

Information supply chains exist since ages in various forms and shapes. The Multistoried libraries of ancient India and china archiving the palm leaf books stand as a good example for information system. The issues in handling such a system bear some commonalities with the issues in a present day digital library although the solutions are different. Information management can still exist without signal processing. Other forms such as we technology can provide the solution. For example, web technology can provide the required distributed storage medium to archive a large data. Signal processing techniques however insist on using small size memory and keep the data in compressed form to reduce the data transfer latencies. The signal processing solutions need not be seen as a separate technique. They provide the requisite algorithms and designs to aid the existing techniques and result in substantial saving of time and cost. The logical extension of any information management technique points to Digital signal processing.

Signal processing technology is matured, advanced and meant to handle any problem in a simple way. However, the mathematics and reasoning behind every solution is highly complicated. The flip side is that the solution would be ensured, as it would be simple. Often it would be unthinkable by other means at the end. The proposed solutions and the future trends make use of digital signal processing in one way or the other. Though other solutions are feasible and in place, the signal processing based solutions provide a list of advantages over the others as mentioned below:

The DSP based solutions and algorithms may be directly implemented with dedicated processors. As the cost of the processors are coming down, the solutions and the trends discussed in each chapter extensively make use of DSP algorithms. Typical example is the compression technology where the algorithms make use of complicated mathematics and the solution provides attractive results. But for signal processing, such a solution would not have come up.

The advanced signal processing technique mentioned in this book is unique of its kind. It provides a broader opportunity to explore the new ideas and novel techniques to venture in to the competitive market. Most of the commercially available software, tools and techniques used for resource planning, data acquisition, processing, cleansing, achieving, storage, security, rights management, transmission, servicing, searching, knowledge management, data mining, pattern recognition, artificial intelligence and expert systems. The solutions include wireless, mobile, satellite and fixed infrastructure domains.

Another attraction with signal processing solution is the modularity and reusability. The solution in one enterprise can be customized and used in the other enterprise. That is how relatively unthinkable organizations are linked today. The modular approach in the design and the transducers permits to apply the signal processing tools and techniques at any part of the flow. The generic nature of the solution permits mass production as reusable components. It is interesting to see that most of the Intellectual property (IPS) originating today involves signal processing in one way or the other.

The generic nature of signal processing roots back to the initial stages of the design. The mathematical model describing the problem, irrespective of the domain or organization, can be directly implemented with signal processing techniques. Hence the signal processing algorithms work with a problem in economics such as financial time series much the same as they do with a problem in communications such as data compression. The power of signal processing hence depends up on the availability of a strong and stable model and representation of the problems in the form of mathematical models. In this book the second chapter extensively covers data representation through a new modeling technique based on a feedback from the output to the input.

Meeting the customer requirements with quality in time requires stringent requirements on the flow of data (information) and the control signals over the information supply chain. To make it happen, the minimum requirement is that:

1. The supplier has to pump in the information at the required rate.
2. Ensure the security of information till it reached the customer premises.
3. Ensure that the authorized person or organizations and it would not fall in to the wrong hands. Resending the information for the intended customers will not nullify the consequences.
4. The information should reach the customer in agreed time.
5. Transmission corruptions are to be strictly avoided.

These points are discussed in the subsequent chapters.

In the first half of the book, extraction, transformation and loading of the data from multiple platforms and sources will be explained. It effectively covers the information administration. The technology for the retrieval and transmission of the information is provided in the second half of the book.

A separate introductory chapter is provided to bind the four important concepts of information administration, supply chain, signal processing and web based technologies.

The first section of the book provides the introductory chapter for the web based supply chain. The second section is about the advanced information technology. It may be noted that the intention of this book is not to cover the breadth and depth of information theory. Only the relevant and powerful concepts required for information supply chain are highlighted here. The new concept of differential feedback representation of the information is given here. The focus is on the information administration and management. It provides framework for rest of the book. Section 2 has 4 chapters:

Chapter 2 gives the basics of information modeling and measurement. A good methodology is required for the scientific measurement of the information. It is required to ascertain the value of the information that gets transported or sold. The important model called feedback neural network model for the information is provided. The model comes with tons of interesting properties that are used subsequently in rest of the book.

Chapter 3 provides basics of information representation. The data or information needs to be put in an appropriate form the end user can understand. In between the source and the destination, it has to be put in a form convenient for storage and transmission. The chapter explains the syntax and semantics for information representation. The raw stream of data as such carries no meaning. It attains a meaning only when the user is able to interpret. Depending up on the context and rendering device, the string takes meaning when fed to appropriate application. Ontology plays an important role in the interpretation of the information depending on the context. The raw DataStream would be called as information only when a certain meaning is derivable from the same.

Chapter 4 introduces the information systems. It is basically a self sustained framework involving the entire life cycle of the information. The activities include acquisition, processing, storage and retrieval. Each of these activities forms a separate section in the book. There are various examples for information systems used in day to day life including World Wide Web, data mart, data warehouse etc.

Chapter 5 is about information management. It goes with a part of the title of this book. The material covered in this book is introduced here. The information management includes supervising all the activities of the information system. Specifically it includes identifying information needs, acquiring information, organizing and storing information, developing information products and services, distributing information, and using information.

The third section is about acquisition and processing of the information. The data acquired has to be appropriately cleaned before being processed. It is only then the data would be called information. Associated with the information is the metadata that has to provide adequate meaning and relevance for the information.

Chapter 6 covers the information acquisition and presentation techniques. Care has to be taken to ensure optimal data acquisition. Too much or too little data would result in confusion along the supply chain. An optimal amount of data is required to be collected. The user interface couples the end user i.e. human being with the machine. To make the interaction highly effective, the interface has to be specially designed. It also indicates the requirement of an intelligent machine, addressed in a different chapter.

Chapter 7 explains the processing techniques for the data. The data acquired from the sources would generally get mixed with noise, under or over sampled or distorted. To make it useful and meaningful, it is first cleaned and then subjected to transformations. Quality constrains are imposed on the cleanliness of the data to make sure that it meets the industry standards. Some of the useful transformations required in the industry are Fourier transform, averaging, curve fitting etc. The transformed data would be stored.

Chapter 8 explains the compression techniques in detail. The information acquired from the sources would have some redundancies. By removing these redundancies, it would be possible to store the data effectively with minimum space. The concepts of compression are derived from Shannon's information theory and coding. Various compression techniques are explained.

Chapter 9 is about the Metadata. Metadata is the information about the information. It binds the data with the meaning. A good metadata description for the data is extremely important in operations while searching. The different metadata schemes are explained.

The fourth section is about storage of the information. The information would retain its value only when it is possible to capture the same. The storage of information has grown in to a big industry with billions of dollar transactions. In this section the data storage, archival mechanisms are explained. The stored data needs to be maintained with security. The security and rights concepts are fused while storing the data. The integration of heterogeneous data is an additional chapter in this section.

Chapter 10 is about data integration. The data integration is required at various levels. The data along the supply chain would be organized in different levels of hierarchy and at various levels of abstraction. Integration of the data has to consider the service quality. The service oriented protocol and its impact on the data integration are discussed

Chapter 11 deals with the storage mechanisms being practiced in various enterprises. Planning is required for the storage and subsequent utilization of the data. Examples of the data warehouse and data mart are provided. The mechanism to handle the heterogeneous data has been explained.

Chapter 12 is about the archival of the information. Back up and archiving are the important activities in any enterprise. The various standards and mechanisms existing for digital archiving are discussed.

Chapter 13 explains the access and security mechanisms associated with the stored data. In the digital era, it is possible to assign permissions selectively in the sense that, a particular target group can use the intended section of the data. The rights are fused as a part of the content creation. The different rights management standards are discussed.

The fifth part is about the retrieval of the information after it is acquired and stored. The rest of the activities are there for the effective usage of the information. The raw data would be called information by finding some meaning in it. The information would be called knowledge together with a collection of similar data or data base. Such a data base is called expert system that is intended to provide answers to user queries in a specific field. As one move from data to information and information to knowledge there is a change in the abstraction and visibility of the things.

The usage of this huge knowledge base calls for the assistance of intelligent elements. Automated intelligence is required for assisting the user in identifying the requisite hidden patterns in the data, quantitative prediction based on the previous history or knowledge etc. Tools are also required for searching the knowledge or information that is useful for a large section of people. Knowledge management addresses all these issues including acquisition, interpretation, deployment and searching of the knowledge.

Chapter 14 deals with the data retrieval techniques and standards and provides good input for the search engines. For the Searching of the data various algorithms including parallelization of search and fusion of the results are discussed.

Chapter 15 explains how machine intelligence can be used to identify the patterns hidden in the data. These patterns are generally invisible for a human user, but helpful for the search engines to retrieve the data.

Chapter 16 gives an overview of a knowledge base system towards providing the required information for the end user. Building and effectively using such a system is challenging. It calls for machine intelligence to achieve the same. The inferences and interpretations of such a system will have far reaching effects.

Chapter 17 is about the data mining. Artificial neural networks are extremely useful in learning the known patterns in the data and start giving inferences when they are provided with unknown patterns.

Chapter 18 is about the knowledge management. The knowledge management includes effective acquisition, processing, storage, retrieval and decimation of the knowledge. It follows the similar cycles of information management but at a different level of abstraction. The tools and techniques used are a bit different and calls for more intelligence in the present case. Knowledge based systems provide the required expertise for the end customers to interpret the data and aid in the retrieval of the required information.

The last part is about the transmission of the data over the supply chain. The data stored has to reach the end user to serve the purpose. It calls for effective and secure means for the transmission. The enterprises require the right time data rather then the real time data. To meet the same good data searching algorithms are required. Weightage has to be given for the real time data transmission with quality. The data transmission has to adhere to the agreed quality of service. Another factor to be considered during the data transmission is the security. The communication channels are prone to attacks from the intruders. Adequate security measures are to be in place during the transmission of the data.

Chapter 19 is about data streaming. Streaming is a special way of data transmission adhering to the streaming protocols. Streaming is done to transfer live actions be it a live sports or a stored advertisement. Streaming has its attraction in simplified storage constraints and live display of contents. The attractive feature of streaming over the other data transfers such as FTP is that the entire data need not be stored before use. i.e., the streamed data may be decoded and displayed on the fly without waiting for the entire data to be transferred. Small buffering may be required to provide a smooth output.

Chapter 20 gives the data transmission under service quality constraints. In an enterprise, the data sources are distributed and carry heterogeneous data. The priorities and data availability constraints on each of them would be different. They all contend for the common resources such as buffer all along the way. This calls for the usage of an intelligent element to schedule the resources so that they are utilized effectively and the service quality of the transmitted data is met.

Chapter 21 is about the secure transmission of the data. The different data encryption standards are discussed and suggestions are provided to speed up the process so that timing constraints of the service quality are met.

Acknowledgment

The author is thankful for the IGI Global publishers and the editors in helping to convert the manuscript in to a beautiful book

The documents available on the Internet have provides a rich source of references for this book. Thanks to the authors, who have made these documents available on the web. Although care has been taken to quote these references, some of them may be missing when the list is too exhaustive.

The author is thankful for the friends and reviewers for providing the valuable feedback to enhance the quality of the book.

Sincere thanks to the family members who could put up with the absence of my attention and being supportive while preparing the manuscript.

Manjunath Ramachandra
Author

Section 1
Introduction

Chapter 1
Web Based Model for Information Supply Chain

ABSTRACT

Advances in the web technologies and signal processing have resulted in their extensive usage in all walks of life. Although independent, these great technologies often cross each other when it comes to the realization of applications suitable for the current requirements. The present day requirements for information have changed drastically in terms of time, quality and quantity. In this chapter, the usage of these technologies for information supply chain management is explored. It forms the foundation for the rest of the chapters in this book.

INTRODUCTION

Electronic supply chain, often called e-supply chain integrates the e- commerce with the supply chain. The supply chain spans a source, distributor, retailer and the end customer. With the evolution of the World Wide Web, the components of the supply chain often referred as 'players' in the book, exchange vital information over the internet, leading to the paradigm of i-supply chain. The 'i' factor is absorbed throughout this book.

Before placing the aforementioned vital information or the data over the internet, it is required to process the same in to a useable form. It requires a spectrum of data processing techniques introduced in different chapters of this book. To start with, this chapter blends the distinct technologies of World Wide Web and the signal processing. Rest of the chapters in the book extensively makes use of the concepts introduced here.

DOI: 10.4018/978-1-60566-888-8.ch001

Figure 1. Information supply chain.

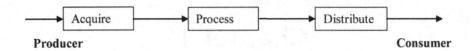

INFORMATION SUPPLY CHAIN

Information Administration

Today, data is being used as a commodity. Like any material such as fruits and bricks, there is a producer and a consumer for the data. Before reaching g the consumer, the data gets processed much similar to the production stage in a supply chain. Like cloths in a ware house, the data or information also gets auctioned over the internet. Finally, information or data has become an integral part of commodities that gets travelled along the supply chain.

The process of organization and transfer of information that enables it to be stored, archived, located and retrieved is called information administration. Together with the information transfer, it forms an important component of the information supply chain

A supply chain spans acquisition, processing and distribution of commodities and involves the producer and the consumer at its two ends. Throughout this book, the paradigm of supply chain is used in two independent contexts, both of them being focused equally.

Supply chain with information in the forward path: Today, the growing demand for information has turned it in to a commodity. The data or information required by the consumer flows from the suppliers all along the supply line like any other material in the physical sense. Digital libraries, video on demand etc numerous applications stand as good examples. Here the end user gets the "digital content" as the commodity in return for the money paid. The involvement of the internet in these applications is evident. Figure 1 shows the linear flow of information along the supply chain.

Supply chain with information over the feedback path: One of the issues with the supply chain is the flooding of the commodity that gets transferred down the line. It means more than excess commodity flows through the supply chain pipe. This is a typical problem in open loop system. However, if the status of the players in the supply chain is made known through a feedback mechanism well ahead of time, the flow of commodity gets regulated. If the data on the status of the commodity are made available on the web, it would be possible to predict the same for the near future and take appropriate measures. For the success of the supply chain, availability of the data over the web and right usage of the same for prediction and planning hold the key. Figure 2 shows how the supply chain works with its players communicating through the internet.

The effective organization of this data is required for access permissions, meeting the need of real time availability, security etc. The chapters of this book are wound around the best utilization and management of the web based technology and signal processing to handle this data.

For handling the data at various stages in the supply chain, collaboration is becoming increasingly important. A set of web based data and knowledge sharing tools are introduced in the last chapter.

Figure 2. Players of supply chain exchanging control information over the internet.

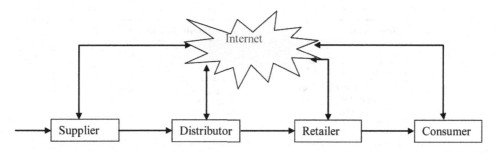

Supply Chain Management

Supply chain management refers to the integration of the business process from the customer to the supplier, spanning all the intermediate players. It ensures smooth flow of the commodity over the supply chain. The role of feedback signals for effective supply chain management is evident from the above section. The listing 1 shows the requirements for a good supply chain management. The techniques to address them are based on the feedback signals from one end of the supply chain to the other end. All these techniques would be discussed in detail in the subsequent chapters.

Supply chain management refers to the automation of the demand and supply forecasting (Raschid Ijioui, Heike Emmerich, Michael Ceyp, 2007), as well as control. In addition to demand and supply, it also includes Inventory where the item to be supplied to the end user is stored (Michael H. Hugos, 2006) and the transportation of these items down the supply chain (James B. Ayers, 2006). Backbone of the supply chain management is the information management that binds the different components of the supply chain together. It is important to make sure that the inventory is managed to meet the demand-supply requirements. The inventory management is a tough task. Too much of products in the inventory make it maintenance costly. On the other hand, empty inventory fails to meet the demands of the consumer. It is required to maintain an optimal inventory.

Case Study: Vendor Managed Inventory

The purchasing pattern of the end user may be analyzed to get crucial information for the inventory management. The vendor has to get the feedback of the purchaser regarding the flow of the commodities and alter the rate of this flow depending up on the foreseen or predicted demand. This calls for the growth or shrinkage of the inventory. The vendor can put constraints on the high and low levels of the inventory and reduce the fluctuations. The model provides a very helpful tool for the vendor. The model is generic, applicable for the supply of information as the commodity and explained in depth in a separate chapter in the book. The data buffers take the role of the inventory managed by the vendor or the content provider.

Signal Processing Techniques

When a feedback is provided to a system in general, the output turns oscillatory depending up on the damping factors of the system. The oscillatory output may be thought of as the different representation

Figure 3. Requirements for supply chain management

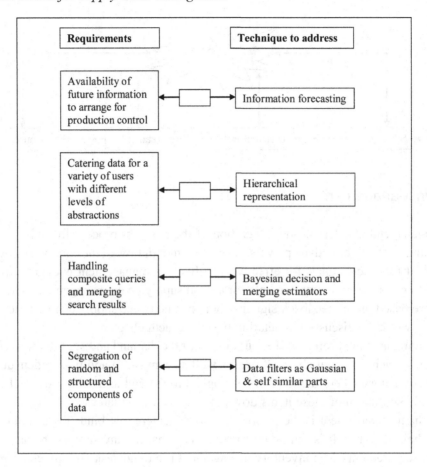

of the stable output, at different resolutions. Although this explanation is less useful in the analog world, it provides a new understanding for the activities spanning a digital system and therefore used for the illustrations here. The digital systems have the advantages of providing delayed versions of feedback that is also equal to the different orders of differentials of the output.

In a digital system, a feedback on the output available at the input shapes the output. The output now takes a different form. The different outputs for all combinations of degrees of feedback form a hierarchy of outputs with different levels of information.

Just like the different outputs of an analog oscillatory system have a stable value that is the average of different undershoots and overshoots in some statistical sense, the stable output of a digital system happens to be the weighted average of the manifold of outputs.

For different damping indices, the output of an analog system contains a stable part and an infinite set of oscillatory parts. The same way, in a digital system, output contains a fixed part and self similar variable parts. Any of the variable part, arising as a result of feedback, may be obtained from any other variable part by convolving with a Gaussian pulse.

The information associated with a system is expressible as a sum of a fixed part and the weighted sum of variable parts. This feature makes the hierarchical representation of the data possible and provides scalable and extensible features. This representation will have implications on the commercial as well as the data acquisition models. The incremental data acquisition will be feasible with these models.

Example of Supply Chain Management

The simple hypothetical supply chain with a book author publishing and selling the book on line is provided here. It involves the following steps.

1. First, the author acquires the required material from different sources. The internet provides a major source of up-to-date information.
2. The information gets 'cleaned' at the earliest to prevent the pile up of junk folders. Otherwise, the whole of internet would get in to the author's computer.
3. In addition to the information gathered from the web, the experience of the author in writing books is very important. The author basically works as an 'expert system' updating the 'knowledge' after every book or paper contribution. The updation of knowledge can happen through a variety of collaboration tools. The author at this stage is equipped with the 'knowledge' to write a book.
4. The author now starts drafting the book in a language acceptable for the readers.
5. Finally the book would be sold to the distributors and retailers who adds some 'metadata' tags for short description, puts it under the class "supply chain" and/or "information transmission" and keeps the same in an achieve of books. It so happens that the same distributor can supply any of the several books on "supply chain management" depending up on the requirements of the reader. The metadata plays a crucial role in matching with the requirements of the reader. Thus, the archive contains the books from multiple sources.
6. The individual chapters of the book are compressed and stored.
7. Different packages are carved out based on the user 'demand'. Ie as individual chapters, as the abstract of all chapters, as a cluster of information transmission and retrieval, as a cluster of information supply chain life cycle including acquisition, storage, retrieval and transmission and so on. One can see the degree of abstraction in the packages.
8. To cater for the requirements of the readers, when a query is made on 'information supply chain' this book should pop up. Once the user requests for the required package, the data is to be transferred over a secure connection in time.
9. The reader, when subscribes for online reading should not be made to wait especially during page turnovers. A minimum interactivity is to be supported.

All these steps are covered under information supply chain management and map on to different chapters of the book.

Producer Consumer Model

Supply chain comprises of all activities in down the line between the producer and the consumer. Data representation spans the online interaction of the end customer to get the invoices, data reports, real time status of payment, invoice delivery, placing of the purchase orders and bidding. The report is to be accessible at each stage of the supply chain as appropriate. It demands a standard representation of the data for the easy readability and rendering. One of the advantages of integrating the steps of supply

Figure 4. Information value due to fluctuations in an open loop supply chain.

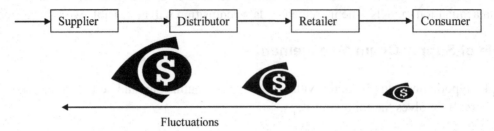

Figure 5. Information value due to fluctuations in a closed loop supply chain.

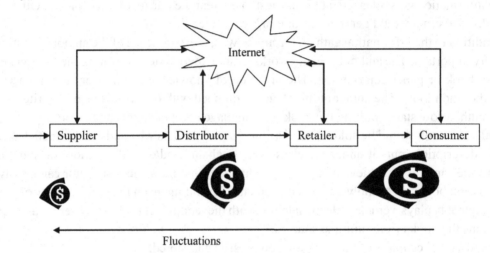

chain is to generate the reports authoritatively. It also helps to forecast the demand supply balance at each stage and take the appropriate measures well in advance.

A supply chain supports one or both of the business models: Built to stock (BTS) and built to order (BTO). The BTS is basically a push model that works on the basis of anticipated customer demand while the BTO is a pull model driven by the customer requirement. A crucial balance between the two is required for effective supply chain management. In (Takahashi, K., Nakamura, N, 2004) Takahashi and Nakamura propose the usage of both these models. It is often called hybrid system. The push mechanism can dictate the degree of pull and vice versa, forming a closed loop.

Bullwhip Effect

A small fluctuation in the demand at the customer end gets amplified as it passes over the supply chain. It attributes to the major issues in the supply chain management. One of the reasons for this effect to creep in is that the players in the supply chain have limited global vision and constrained by the limited data that gets propagated upwards. The effective mean to contain this effect is to share the information at each stage down the supply chain and arrest the fluctuations rather than allowing it to propagate. The Figures 4 and 5 show how it may be contained.

Figure 6. DSP algorithms.

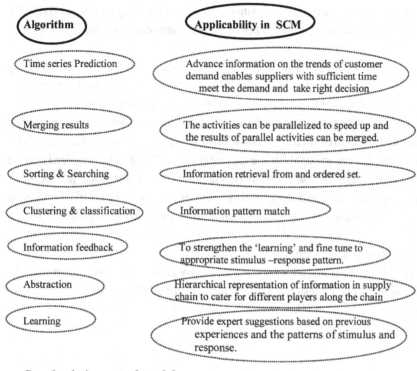

Supply chain control model

Integrated Supply Chain Management (SCM)

In order to integrate the data available on the web from the different players of a supply chain, it is required that the data structures and the data elements adhere to a standardized format. The metadata describing these data formats therefore plays a crucial role in the integration. XML is one such standardized format for the metadata description. To run the business transactions, the use of XML goes beyond the data description and spans the entire frame work consisting of document description, business process description and messaging. The reference (Kotinurmi, 2003) provides how XML based data integration brings in supply chain integration

Realization of Information Supply Chain

The following listing provides a couple of examples for how advanced algorithms are used in SCM. The web happens to be an important component of these algorithms. The subsequent chapters in the book address how a handful of powerful signal processing tools can be repeatedly used towards the implementation of these algorithms and solve various issues in SCM. Important signal processing algorithms for supply chain management are provided in Figure 6.

Various models exist for the supply chain control. All of them make use of signal processing to different degrees. A good introduction to model based supply chain control is found in (Perea-Lopez, E.,

B. E. Ydstie, and I. E. Grossman, 2003). The models are often required for the data prediction (P.H.Lin, S.S.Jang, D.S.H.Wong, 2005).

The linear models make use of conventional Auto Regressive Moving Average (ARMA).

They fail to catch the nonlinearities in the supply chain dynamics. The non linear models however use apparatus such as neural networks.

The producer consumer model is a self sustained control model. When the producer pumps in mode commodity on to the supply chain than the demand at the consumer end, it would get rejected automatically (equivalently, the value drops at the receiving end) prompting a reduction in the production. This self sustained model fits with the paradigm of differential feedback wherein the previous experience works as the dampener or the control factor for the rate of production. Throughout this book, the producer consumer model goes synonymous with the differential feedback. The required feedback signals get transferred over the internet (web based control). The chapters of this book are wound around the generation, transfer and usage of this control signal. It is this control signal that influences all activities of the information supply chain, including data acquisition, definition, abstract representation, hierarchical storage, secure transfer etc. The hierarchical representation of data maps on to the natural abstractions in the supply chain, such as supplier's supplier, customer's customer etc.

The various factors to be considered in information supply chain are provided in the Figure 7. The data from sources encounter more or less the flow before reaching the customer. The book is roughly organized in the same order.

Decision Making in SCM

The decision making has to happen in real time to absorb the dynamics and fluctuations in the market. The customers and suppliers dynamically attach and detach in to the chain. The decision support system includes planning, forecasting and dynamic decision making. The usage of neural networks for data forecasting is provided in (Murat Ermis, Ozgur Koray Sahingoz and Fusun Ulengin, 2004).

Figure 7. Factors to be considered in information supply chain.

- Information acquisition,
- Information processing,
- Information compression,
- Information description,
- Information modeling,
- Information representation,
- Information storage,
- Information integration,
- Information archiving,
- Information distribution rights & access permissions,
- Information quality,
- Information transmission,
- Information retrieval,
- Information security,
- Information patterns,
- Information translation (to knowledge),
- Information mining

Data Forecasting

The data forecasting in a supply chain often helps in the control of inventories. The size of inventories, that work as buffers along the supply chain can be reduced. Prediction of the demand is required for optimal inventory. Excess production leads to increased investment as well as inventory maintenance.

Supply Chain Management extensively makes use of data forecast. e.g. Future demand, future prices. The models are however static. The model is computed once and not updated thereafter. In reality, the data patterns change rapidly calling for a periodic re-evaluation of the model. It is to be updated with the availability of the new data sets. A feedback from the output to the input, however, can reflect the fluctuations in the data over the model.

Web Based Supply Chain Management

With an increased accessibility of the internet for the end users, they tend to make choices on the suppliers at the last minute anticipating the latest data for comparison. Manual handling of the transactions obviously result in losses especially when the customer changes the orders. The round trip communication would turn out to be costly. As a result, the suppliers are forced to switch over to the web based transactions with the customers providing the latest data and get their instant response. The usage of internet for supply chain management is described in (Lawrence, 2002)

Apart from the data, the customers often request for intelligent solutions for their problems. It involves the support of decision making tools for the databases resulting in the expert system architecture. Migration to web based approach is required for maintaining a consistent and predictable quality of service and controlled distribution of the data which is otherwise not possible to achieve. The various activities involved in web based supply chain before the data reaches the customer are shown in the flow chart in Figure 8. Each of them roughly map on to a separate chapter of the book.

CONTROL MECHANISM IN WEB BASED SUPPLY CHAIN MODEL

Need of Collaboration among the Players in a Supply Chain

Conventional supply chain is more centralized and restricted to handle specific requirements of the customer. Here there is less scope for the sharing of available data over the entire supply chain. This poses the challenge for the effective management of the supply chain in terms of planning, control and distribution.

To overcome this difficulty, an integrated view of the data down the supply chain is required. The right data is to be accessible at the right time calling for the collaboration within a supply chain.

In order to make sure that the supply and demand get balanced out with in a supply chain, it is required to keep the two ends informed about each other. While the data as a commodity moves from the producer to the consumer, the status of the connecting supply chain as well as the degree of demand from the consumer move in the opposite direction.

This information would be extremely useful for the producer end towards the production and distribution control along the supply chain. In a sustained supply chain, it is often necessary to predict this information several steps ahead of time to take the appropriate measures.

Figure 8 Information flow

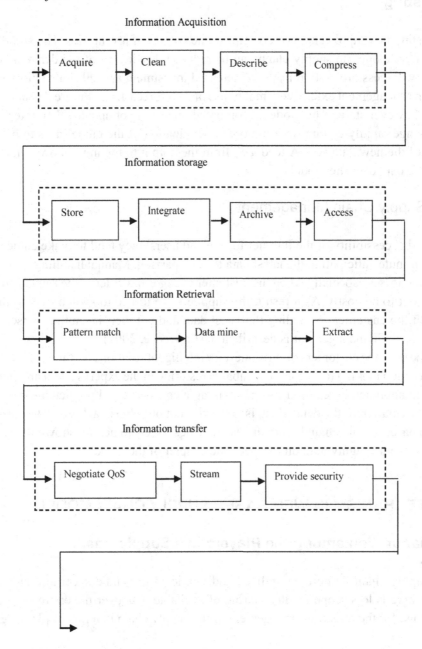

TRANSFER CONTROL MECHANISM

Need of Transfer Control: The Bottleneck Effect

Transportation is an important part of the supply chain and logistics strategy. In spans the movement of materials, products, information, and finances to cater for the requirements of the customers. Apart from the internet, the other media used for the communication of signals (and/or data) along the supply chain include GPS, MMS and Wireless etc.

Figure 9. Resource contentions in supply chain.

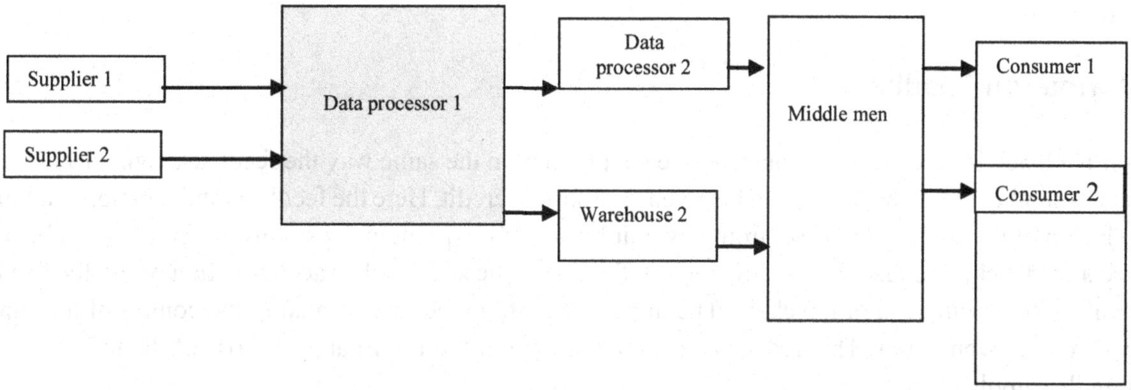

Consider the supply chain shown in the figure. It involves a series of intermediate players apart from the supplier and the consumer. The middle men include the retailers and distributors.

At each player, there will be more than one input flow. It is expected that the players have the resources to handle these distinct flows. If any of the flows need a considerable attention of the player at the cost of the other flows, it leads to a bottle neck among these flows leading to a slow down in supply and requires to be regulated at the supplier end to ensure a smooth handling. To make it happen, the information on the available resources at each stage in the supply chain are to be provided to the suppliers. It requires a considerable collaboration among them. Internet provides a powerful infrastructure to connect them as it is easily accessible for all the players to take a decision on the rate of supply along the chain. Limited resources in one of the players of the supply chain block the flow of information and thereby affect the performance of the system. Here it is referred as bottleneck effect.

The internet provides the required feedback path of the information flow. The information is all about the status and load on the supply chain, that provides a valuable input for the suppliers to take the right action at the right time.

Another input to be made available to the suppliers on the same lines is the demand from the consumers. A reduced demand requires a proportionally reduced supply for the consumers.

The internet supports accessibility for a variety of devices with different capabilities from across a globe through a set of well defined standards (W3C). Thus, the stationary as well as the mobile players from land, sea or air can access the data on the internet through the satellite phones. Figure 9 shows the resource contention.

Optimal Transfer of Information along Supply Chain

The information system may be modeled as a supply chain involving the sequences acquisition, processing, storage and retrieval by the end user. These activities are discussed in the subsequent chapters of this book.

In the process, with various players along the supply chain in place, the model that translates individual behavior to the collective behavior of the group will play an important role. With information feedback, the system can merge the individual behaviors in to an abstract global behavior that controls the information flow along the chain. The merging unit is often referred as Bayesian merger and shown in figure 10.

Information Feedback

User feedback is given due weightage in the supply line. In the same way the feedback signal from one level to another along the line would be given appropriate credit. Here the feedback information is about the health of the supply chain. So, from any point to any other point in the supply chain, it is possible to have a feedback. The feedback at any point in the line is the sum total or accumulation of the feedback signals in the tailing end of the chain. The importance of the feedback signal in the control of the supply chain is given below. This reduces the stranded time of the information or loss of the information along the supply chain.

It is quite possible that the supply chains from the various producers to the consumers criss-cross or intersect each other calling for a kind of contention for the resources. The contention could be in various forms, in terms of financial investment or storage space.

The first step towards resolving this contention and optimizing the supply chains is to define service classes for each of the chains passing through the intermediate agents or the brokers. In addition, for each of the service classes, a set of quality parameters is defined. Both the absolute value and the relative values of the parameter are important for optimization. It is required to keep the absolute parameters with in a certain agreed limit and the relative parameters at a pre specified constant value. Various algorithms and implementation schemes exist considering the optimal utilization of resources.

Maintaining a constant agreed ratio of defects or losses, i.e. quality of service in the information supply chain is often tricky. The problem gets further complicated when the chain contains multiple source streams which is often the case. In this book, an information feedback based model has been introduced to predict the defects or losses of information along the supply chain. Any data or information not meeting the requirement may be thought of as not meeting the quality of service (QoS).

Figure 10. Bayesian merging of individual behavior.

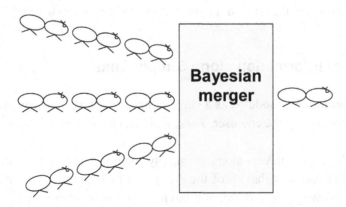

Feedback Signals in the Supply Chain

The outlet monitoring system provides information on the current inventory and demand. The supplier or the source extrapolates the changes in the supply chain based on the available demand and the material. A decision to this effect may be taken by the central supply chain administrator shown in figure 11. Some of the functions of the administrator include

- Update the inventories
- Take the purchase order (PO) and route the same to the next level
- Provide alternative source/supplier
- Provide alternative customer
- Shortest delivery route
- Delivery status
- Forecast demand/decision to supply

Shifted Feedback

A shifted version of the loss of information as seen by the destination will be used as feedback signal. The number of defects observed at a point in the supply chain gets reduces with the shifted feedback signal. It happens because the system performance would be made known through a prediction by several steps providing ample time for the source to adjust the information transfer rates to meet the prescribed quality of service parameters. With the defects getting reduced, for a given demand at any point down the supply chain, the quantum of input may be reduced with shifted feedback to achieve the same performance

Because of abstraction and redundancy, even if a portion of the information is lost or if it is required to predict the future uncertainties with minimum available information, it can be repaired or re-synthesized using the available information. The wrong or corrupted information is more harmful than the loss of information. It calls for stringent quality of service constraints on the wrong information. The prediction probability as mentioned in the second chapter is self similar with the addition of more and

Figure 11. Players of supply chain exchanging control information over the internet.

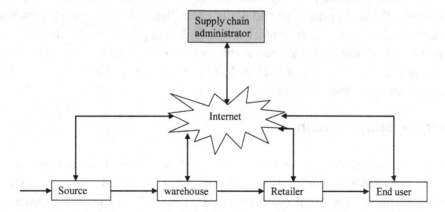

more estimators. The statistical properties happen to get scaled proportionally with the addition of more feedback terms.

The self-similar property of the component induces interesting properties in to the system. This property may be used as lead-lag components in controlling the information transfer along the supply chain. The feedback may iterate along the members of the chain. Closed loop feedback is utilized to control the signals transferred over the network. Intermediate self-similar structures or switches may modulate the feedback signals and control the system behaviour. In a separate section, the extension of the supply chain for knowledge management will be discussed.

Several independent communication paths are involved in the information supply chain from the information source to the input buffers of the data acquisition transducers, from the data acquisition system to the storage system, from the storage system to the end user's display buffer and from the display buffer to the display device or the output transducer. In addition, the stored information gets mirrored and archived with the help of storage area network. In all these scenarios and communications, lot of resource contention is involved posing a great challenge for the quality of the information received in time.

Feedback from the destination of the information to the source may be used to enhance the quality of the communication although the implementation methodologies vary. The different techniques are considered appropriately in the subsequent chapters.

The broker model where by the intermediate agents along the supply chain apparently shield the actual source from the destination and often act as virtual sources down the line, may be taught of as an extreme case of the supply chain. In such a scenario, the service quality constraints are to be met by all the agents in between.

Decision Systems in the Feedback Path

When a feedback neural network is inserted in a supply line, interesting properties may be observed. The neural network as such exhibits self similarity. The different estimators exhibit similar characteristics but for scaling. All the estimators arising from feedback are similar but for the information abstraction. This self similarity is because of the long range dependency arising as a result of the usage of historical data in the generation of each of the estimators. When such an element is introduced in to a system, the whole system turns self similar. Logically this is because of the forced usage of the self similar data. In the supply chain, the whole of the chain would exhibit self similar property. Any segment of the chain would also exhibit the self similar property with respect to the signals that move up and down along the chain. This makes the chain predictive and easily controllable. By changing the parameters of the neural network, it would be possible to control whole of the supply chain. The information flow in a supply chain is shown in figure 12. Data flows in the forward path while the user or intermediate agent feedback on the data flows along the feedback path. The feedback may be from the directly connected node or from any other node down the line

Signals over the Supply Chain

The signals that move over the supply chain in the feedback path or from the destination to the source can be predicted in advance by a neural network. The predicted signal reflects the availability of the resources in future over the line and hence useful to control the transfer rate in the forward path. It ensures that the chain would be used optimally and maximum transfer of the commodity or information takes

Figure 12. Information flow in a supply chain.

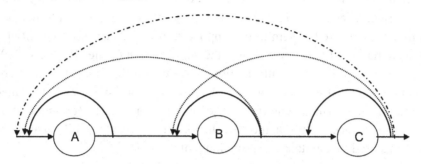

place over the chain. The Neural network controller here works as a scheduler, congestion controller and the traffic shaper. The role of a neural network in shaping the quality of the information that flows down the line is explained in the chapter Information Transmission with quality of service

In this context, a closed loop feedback mechanism is assumed. Multiple bits are used as feedback control signal with the bits representing the predicted version of the status of the available resources along the path as it evolves. Here the notification signal or feedback signal is time shifted to get better performance. A general feedback based control mechanism is popularly used in systems that require a precise adaptive control. The feedback systems are often prone to instability. With a feedback neural network, there is a feedback and an accurate model is not needed (only one that captures the 'dominant' behavior of the system). Only careful design of the controller is required.

Supply chain model bears a reasonable degree of similarity with the data propagation over a network and the concept may be borrowed for further analysis. Basically the data network is a particular form of the supply chain. The relative service parameters come in to picture when the different classes of the flow contend for the common resources such as the operating path, docking space etc that tend to get choked and required to maintain a fixed ratio of the flows or members.

Various enterprise models are used for representation of static and behavioral system aspects. It results in the issues with integration and conflicts. However, a feedback neural network acting as a Bayesian estimator can merge the various models and rules with different syntactic, semantic and pragmatic dependencies.

The information transfer across the hierarchies is limited by the channel capacity. The workaround for the transfer of maximum information in minimum time without sacrificing the quality for the underlying channel noise is to allocate minimum number of bits for the information to be transferred over the channel. This is achieved by content adaptive arithmetic coding scheme where a certain symbol would be represented with variable number of bits depending up on the context and the probability of occurrence of the symbol with in the data set. The same symbol could take fewer bits in a different context. Such an adaptive change provides very good information transfer rate. A feedback system may be used to achieve the same. It happens because with differential feedback the source entropy gets reduced and helps in providing noise immunity.

The different information sub systems in an organization could often compete. This results in a kind of unsupervised learning and happens to be beneficial for the organization. At the end, with the competition, one of them happens to be the winner and the others get configured around this. It provides maximum information.

Supply chain management refers to the automation of the demand and supply forecasting (Raschid Ijioui, Heike Emmerich, Michael Ceyp, 2007), as well as control. In addition to demand and supply, it also includes Inventory where the item to be supplied to the end user is stored (Michael H. Hugos, 2006) and the transportation of these items down the supply chain (James B. Ayers, 2006). Backbone of the supply chain management is the information management that binds the different components of the supply chain together. It is important to make sure that the inventory is managed to meet the demand-supply requirements. The inventory management is a tough task. Too much of products in the inventory make it maintenance costly. On the other hand, empty inventory fails to meet the demands of the consumer. It is required to maintain an optimal inventory.

CONCLUSION

In this chapter,

- The players along the information supply chain are introduced.
- The importance of web based technologies for information management is discussed.

Information transfer for the end user involves substantial signal processing as well as the intervention of the World Wide Web. The signal processing algorithms are being used all along the lifecycle of the information. For an efficient transfer, supply demand relation is to be considered along the supply chain through the information feedback.

QUESTIONS

1. Who are the players in a supply chain?
2. What is the importance of web technologies for the supply chain management?
3. How does the signal processing help in the supply chain management?
4. How are the players in a supply chain related?
5. What is the relevance for the feedback path in a supply chain?

REFERENCES

Ayers, J. B. (2006). Handbook of supply chain management, (2nd Ed.). Boca Raton, FL: CRC Press.

Ermis, M., Sahingoz, O. K., & Ulengin, F. (2004). *An Agent Based Supply Chain System with Neural Network Controlled Processes*, (LNCS). Berlin: Springer.

Hugos, M. H. (2006). *Essentials of supply chain management*, (2nd Ed.). Chichester, UK: John Wiley and Sons.

Ijioui, R., Emmerich, H., & Ceyp, M. (2007). *Strategies and Tactics in Supply Chain Event Management*. Berlin: Springer.

Jankowska, A. M., Kurbel, K., & Schreber, D. (2007). An architecture for agent- based mobile Supply Chain Event Management. *International Journal of Mobile Communications, 5*(3), 243–258. doi:10.1504/IJMC.2007.012393

Kotinurmi, P., Nurmilaakso, J. M., & Laesvuori, H. (2003). Standardization of XML-based e-business frameworks. In J.L. King, K. Lyytinen, (Eds.), *Proceedings of the Workshop on Standard Making: A Critical Research Frontier for Information Systems*, ICIS 2003 Pre-conference Workshop, December 12-14, Seattle, WA, (pp. 135-146).

Lawrence, E., Corbitt, B., Newton, S., Braithwaite, R., & Parker, C. (2002). *Technology of Internet Business*. Brisbane, Australia: John Wiley & Sons.

Lin, P. H., Jang, S. S., & Wong, D. S. H. (2005). Predictive control of a decentralized supply Chain unit. *Industrial & Engineering Chemistry Research, 44*, 9120–9128. doi:10.1021/ie0489610

Perea-Lopez, E., Ydstie, B. E., & Grossman, I. E. (2003). A model predictive control Strategy for supply chain optimization. *Computers & Chemical Engineering, 27*, 1201–1218. doi:10.1016/S0098-1354(03)00047-4

Takahashi, K., & Nakamura, N. (2004). Push, pull, or hybrid control in supply chain management. *International Journal of Computer Integrated Manufacturing, 17*(2), 126–140. doi:10.1080/09511920310001593083

Section 2
Signal Processing for Information Supply Chain

Chapter 2
Information Model and Measurement

ABSTRACT

Accurate modeling and measurement of digital information is very important to ascertain the commercial value for the same. The value and demand for the information fluctuates all along the information supply chain posing a challenge for the players of the supply chain. It calls for a dynamic supply chain model. In this chapter, a predictive model based on information feedback is introduced to exploit the dynamism.

INTRODUCTION

In the last chapter, the need of web technologies for the supply chain management is explained. The different players of the supply chain need to exchange a lot of "meaningful" and "useful" data along with the commodities. The meaning and use of the data may be enhanced by knowing how to measure the same. Here, the model for measuring the information associated with the data is provided. The various properties of this model that may be used for enhancing the information are discussed.

The intention of a good communications system (Bekenstein, Jacob D, 2003) is to transfer meaningful data from the source to the destination. Although the meaning associated with the data is subjective, it is possible to measure the same in the statistical sense. This chapter addresses the popular queries like, what exactly is information (Luciano Floridi, 2005) and how the transferred information may be parameterized and measured. A new approach for the information measurement using classifiers is provided. It provides a foundation for the better understanding of the book. Throughout this chapter and to some extent in the entire book, the example of estimators or classifiers is considered. The concepts

DOI: 10.4018/978-1-60566-888-8.ch002

are introduced through the example of statistical estimators. For business and purchase departments, it provides a technique to ascertain the value for the data source such as libraries, albums, online games etc based on the information content.

The degree of information content in a message, measured in the unit "bits", is dictated by the choice of the source in the selection of the message. If the selection of the message is as likely as not selecting the same, the message carries one bit of information. This selection of messages imparts a kind of randomness in to the message, making it ambiguous. The degree of randomness or ambiguity associated with the message is called entropy, a term borrowed from thermodynamics. The randomness associated with the message decreases with more information associated with the message. E.g. "I am crying" is more ambiguous then "I am crying for a chocolate" as the latter carries more information and reduces the randomness.

The information from the source requires a physical medium to reach the destination. For a given channel or medium, there is a theoretical maximum capacity or rate at which it can carry the information. This is called "Shannon limit" named after its inventor. It is defined and expressed in the units of bits per second. To transfer more information over the loaded channel, in general, it is necessary to process the information before transfer by a way of encoding. Transmission of information in a compressed form over a band limited channel is the topic of discussion for a chapter in the next part.

Amari.S has provided the geometric interpretation of the information that is of a great theoretical importance. Like "bits" in the Shannon's description of information, another interesting measure of information is "Kullback divergence". The kullback divergence between a pair of probability distribution functions is the information distance between the two estimators in the family of feedback neural networks.

Shannon's theorem on data coding also infers that, if a data source with certain entropy pumps information in to a channel with a limited capacity and if the entropy of the source is less than the channel capacity, there exist a coding scheme that can reduce the errors to the desired rate. However, the coding scheme fails to help if the channel capacity is less than the source entropy.

According to the theory, there can be a mismatch between the received signal and the transmitted signal as a result of the channel impairments such as the noise and random disturbances. Channel noise reduces the capacity of the channel to transfer the information. (Raymond W. Yeung, 2002). By providing adequate redundancy for the message, it is still possible to recover the same without errors.

Throughout this book, an approach supplement to Shannon's information would be followed.

BACKGROUND

The quantitative measurement of information started with Shannon in 1948. The amount of information buried in the data is measured by the impact or reaction it creates up on first reception from the recipient. If the recipient already has the same data, the reaction would be cold! On the other hand, if it is beyond one's imagination or guessing, it would evoke a warm response. Thus, the degree of information present in the data is linked to the ability of the recipient to guess the same, throwing the measurement in to the probabilistic space. Although it is subjective and individual specific, information measurement is possible in the statistical sense.

This led Shannon to define the information I as:

$$I = \log\left(\frac{1}{p}\right)$$

(1)

p being the probability of getting the data as seen by the recipient. It is measured in the units of bits. Thus more probable messages carry less information and vice versa. It goes well with the perception.

Need of Measurement

Measurement of information is required for various purposes. Present day commercialized services like library, web services and information centers of organizations call for the effective measurement of the information flow. Days have come where billing is done for the amount of information rather than for the data flow. For the end user, it also provides a mechanism to evaluate different alternatives that give different amount of information for the same price. The techniques are especially useful in the acquisition of databases, digital content, knowledge wealth or libraries.

Measurement of information is important especially to ascertain its market value. Precise measurement of information is required for fixing value for the database. The availability of a spectrum of security products in the market, both for storage and transfer of the information, needs to be evaluated on the same basis. The security of information is related to the ease with which a portion of the data may be tapped or tampered and impact information contained in the data (without being detected). This throws light on the weightage to be assigned to the different confidential databases in the organization.

Randomness in the Data

According to the definition from Shannon, the amount of information in the data or message is the degree of uncertainty or surprise in the message. Thus the quantitative measurement of information is the measure of the uncertainty in the data (Alan Chmura, J. Mark Heumann, 2005). The uncertainty in the data gets reduced with the subsequent transfer or availability in the information.

The uncertainty associated with the data is also called as entropy. The entropy represents the average information in statistical sense. Larger the uncertainty associate with the data, more would be the explanation required to provide better clarity and vice versa (Thomas M. Cover, Joy A. Thomas, 2006). This factor gets reflected on the representation of the information. The qualitative concepts like variety, choice, disorder etc take a quantitative measure with the Entropy of the data and the associated information. Mathematically, it is expressible using the probabilities. Let *P(s)* represent the probability distribution of a system S to be in the state *s*. The associated choice C can then be expressed as the entropy *H* of the system, a term frequently used in statistical mechanics.

$$H(p) = -\sum_{s \in S} P(s) . \log P(s)$$

(2)

By differentiating equation 2 with respect to *p* and equating the same to 0, it is possible to show that entropy of a system reaches its maximum when all the states of the system are equi- likely. As a result, the preference or choice over the states would be difficult. The entropy H represents the degree

Figure 1. Components of data.

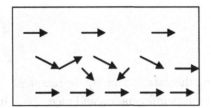

of uncertainty or randomness associated with the state of the system. The equation also shows that, the entropy becomes 0 when the probability of a certain state is 1 and that of all other states is 0. This is because, under this condition, the complete information about the state of the system is available with full certainty and no additional information is required. The presence of noise in the data increases its randomness.

When the entropy of a symbol gets reduced, the clarity on the same increases and the importance of the symbol in conveying the information gets reduced. With this, it is affordable to lose the symbol in the worst case without much of a penalty.

Data, in general, has two components- a deterministic part and a random part. Alternative classification is 'known part' and 'unknown part'. Figure 1 illustrates the classification.

The figure also shows the different levels of abstractions in the data. The amount of information varies over the different abstractions of the data.

Information of Noisy Data

In the presence of noise, the message gets corrupted. A transmitted symbol x would get corrupted as and received as y at the receiver. By measurements on y or by observing y along with the previous history of the received symbols, the information content of x may be deduced.

There are two well known approaches for this measurement. Both of them require a relationship between the symbols x and y.

Mutual Information

The first one is mutual information. It is defined as

$$I(x,y) = H(x) - H(x \mid y)$$ (3)

The corresponding conditional entropy is defined as

$$H(x,y) = -\sum_{x,y} P(x,y) \log_2 P(x,y)$$ (4)

The conditional entropy is also called equivocation and it represents the amount of uncertainty about the transmitted message x, give that the received message is y.

Kullback Distance

The other approach is using the divergence or Kullback distance. The Kullback divergence between a pair of distribution functions p and q is given by

$$D = p * \log(p \big/ q)$$

(5)

In the above formula, each occurrence of a symbol is taken as a statistically independent event. In reality, the probability of the occurrence of one symbol often depends up on (or affects) the occurrence of the other symbols. The sources emitting such symbols are called Markov sources. Due to the dependency, they require extended formulae for the representation of the entropy

How Effectively the Language Represents Information?

The information content of a string of symbols is measured using Kolmogorov-Chaitin Complexity. It is defined as the smallest size of the program that can generate the string. It is used as a parameter to prove some important concepts in information theory. However, it is not widely used and assign a meaningful number to a string, like what Shannon's formula can do. It is not a standard yardstick as it largely depends up on the language (like the complexity of the book depending up on the author!)

Information Prediction

The data from a source would carry maximum price only if the associated information is not known apriori (David J. C. MacKay, 2003) to the intended recipients. However, if there is a mechanism to know what the next message from the source would carry, the recipients would welcome the same. E.g. an investor would be extremely happy if a method is provided to know the share prices after an hour or so. Although the precise information is anticipated, the one generated with the guesswork would also help. In general, all the investments are made based on the anticipation and predictions.

Prediction of the information or future data finds wide spread applications including the share markets, weather forecasting etc. If not for the actual data, the trends in statistical sense are also good enough for some applications. For Prediction to be accurate, background or historical data associated with the source is required to be used. A good predictor has to generate the approximate values of the future data based on the previously generated values, the present and the previous data from the source. One such predictor model is the auto regressive moving average model (ARMA). In this chapter, the characteristics of ARMA and its variants are thoroughly examined.

In a typical Autoregressive moving average (ARMA) model, the output and input are related through

$$y(n) = a_0 * x(n) + a_1 * x(n-1) + \ldots + b_1 * y(n-1) + \ldots$$

(6)

Here $a_0, a_1, \ldots b_1, \ldots$ are the model parameters. x is the input, y is the output. The present output is being expressed as the weighted sum of the previous outputs and the inputs.

Figure 2. Information prediction model.

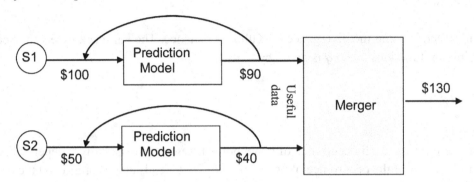

Information Prediction Model

Here, the information life cycle including the generation (Burnham, K. P. and Anderson D. R., 2002), transfer and reception would be interpreted in the light of feedback signals and system. When the input data in a system change (Len Silverston, W.H.Inmon, Kent Graziano, 2007), the output data also changes in the same way. The error in the output is found to be minimal when there is a differential feedback from the output to the input. The differential feedback may be easily generated by providing the historical data. By increasing the order of the differential or providing more historical data, the error can be made arbitrarily small.

When a predicted signal, based on the past history, is provided as the feedback signal to the source, the system would find useful applications. The shifted feedback signal may be used to achieve improved quality of service for the transferred data, such as the absolute delay guarantee, fraction of the services lost etc. The usage of shifted signals can reduce the attenuation of the information in the path (due to non availability of the resources and time outs), reduce the choke in the loop and improve the service in terms of overall successful operations in a given time.

Figure 2 shows the information prediction model. With the availability of the sophisticated tools, the information may be predicted in advance reducing its potential value. The merger integrates the predictions from different models as explained in the next sections.

Consider the information or data as a time varying signal. A feedback from the output to the input results in the increased stability. When this feedback signal is used in the decision-making process, the system turns auto regressive with enhanced predictability. This model of the feedback neural network is applicable for the information prediction as well.

Quantitative Measurement of Information

The major issue with information measurement (Christoph Arndt, 2004), is the degree of anticipation or prediction by the end user. Each human being will have a different perception of the information resulting in a huge difference. It will have impact on the market value of the content or the information source. Once the probability of occurrence of the message is fixed, the information content can be quantified with Shannon's formula in equation 1. However, quantifying this subjective probability is not an easy task. Is there a scientific way to model the probability?

The probability associated with a message consists of two components - the absolute probability and the conditional probability. The absolute probability is the one a user perceives for the first time in an unbiased state, like the initial response to the fact that a comet would collide with the earth in 2011. By and large, the initial response of every one remains the same. When the same message is repeated the response would be different and biased by the judgment of the user.

The conditional probability is predominant in interactive communications such as Browsing. The browser pops up results depending up on the user queries. For example, for a keyword "solar system" one can definitely expect a result with a mentioning about the earth. This is the known part of the result (depending up on our knowledge on the solar system and the browser characteristics). The unknown part would be the exact wordings about the earth.

In the limiting case, where there is no knowledge about the message being received (or retrieved), the conditional probability turns out to be zero and the total probability would contain the contribution from the source.

The feedback neural network models the above issue. It nonlinearly relates the output with the inputs of the model and plays a pivotal role in the accuracy of the prediction. The nonlinear function relating the prediction with the current (instantaneous) as well as the historical data may be expanded using Taylor series as:

$$y(n) = y(0) + n \frac{dy}{dt}_{t=0} + \frac{n^2}{2!} \frac{d^2y}{dt^2}_{t=0}$$

(7)

The prediction *y(n)* indicates the probability associated with the predicted message at a future instant '*n*' based on the available message and the historical data (differentials) at present. i.e. at *t*=0.

The probability associated with the available message, $y(0)$ represents the absolute probability that is instantaneous unbiased component of the total probability. The differentials represent the conditional probabilities that depend up on the previous experience with similar messages. Since probability is a non negative value, more historical data certainly reduces the information content or the value of the message.

Each of the end user would have different exposure and weightages for the historical data.

Each of the information users may be modeled by a statistical or probability estimator corresponding to different degrees of differentials in the model. Alternatively, each of the information measurements based on the different conditional probability terms may classify the message differently. The issue is to combine these estimators or classifiers and provide a single number based on the predictions and the appropriate weightages for the different users. Further discussion on the estimators is available in (J. A. Starzyk and F. Wang, 2004)

The equation (7) provides enough input for the effective data organization. Data from a source may be organized in to multiple abstractions or different lengths of history each of which map on to an estimator. The abstraction levels form a hierarchy of information prediction. The quality of prediction in turn depends up on the level of abstraction used. In addition, the members of the hierarchy would have different resolutions.

In the measurement of information, error creeps in if the prediction of the message is not accurate. Hence, the error itself contains two components, a fixed part or a bias term due to the absolute probability and the variable part or variance term(s) due to the conditional probability associated with the different number of terms in the equation (7).

With more terms getting added in the equation (7), the associated information gets reduced. The entropy starts decreasing as the distribution tends towards Gaussian. The knowledge on information source increases. As the information source starts responding to the feedback from the end user, it would be possible to predict the information more precisely at the receiving end. The importance of entropy in the context of neural networks model is provided in (H.L.Tsai and S.J.Lee, 2004).

The probabilities associated with the estimators of different degrees of feedback may be mapped on to the wavelet coefficients resulting in different resolutions of the interpreted information.

A neural network trained with Bayesian learning (Bolstad, William M, 2004) algorithm outputs entire distribution of probabilities over the hypothesis set rather than a single hypothesis. In the present context each hypothesis corresponds to one estimator i.e., a different order of feedback. Each of the classifier has an associated probability density function. Interestingly, any of the classifiers may be modeled from any other classifier by adding or deleting certain terms. Such a classifier is repeatedly referred in this book as Bayesian classifier or Bayesian neural network. The degree of belief is the lowest when there is no historical data or the differential term and increases towards 1 for infinitely large number of terms or when all the classifiers merge. In a classifier with infinite historical data, the actual output may be thought of as the superposition of beliefs (hypothesis). It is often referred as ideal classifier or estimator as it happens to be idealistic. If each of the classifier outputs a certain prediction (of information) subjected to a certain rule mapping with the associated historical data, a Bayesian neural network merges the learning rules. This property is valid for any number of differential terms in the equation. I.e. there exists an estimator that can effectively replace all other estimators. In this book, it is referred as equivalent principle.

The learning algorithms of the feedback neural network model described above resemble Bayesian learning algorithms (Radford Neal, 1996) that are resistant to over fitting. I.e. it provides the advantage of learning with a minimum experience or dataset. Additional information on the over fitting is provided in a separate section below.

ISSUES AND SOLUTIONS

Data Prediction

Information or data prediction has a lot of commercial importance. However, the accuracy of prediction and the time taken for the prediction are the issues calling for optimization. A conventional ARMA is a linear model that fails to capture the non-linearity associated with the data. However, in general, the predicted value is to be nonlinearly related to the ingredients used for the prediction. The requirement of a large historical data is an additional drawback with this model.

Artificial neural networks are generally used to overcome this limitation. A good introduction to neural networks is found in (Bigus, J.P., 1996). They have built in capability of learning and adaptation. With some training, they are able to learn to simulate and predict the non linear relations in the data. It happens because, the system consists of a nonlinear transfer function (such as a sigmoid) as the output unit. However, in a conventional neural network, unlike ARMA, there is no work for the historical data after training. There is no scope for learning from the immediately previous predictions. Hence the

Figure 3. Information predictions through estimators

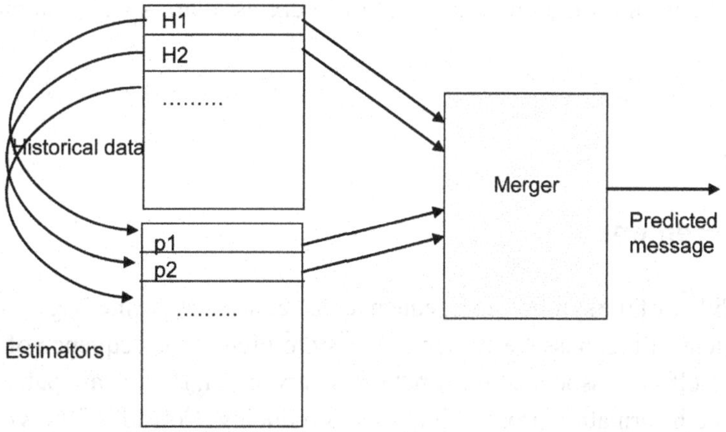

training required has to be exhaustive and lengthy. In addition to increasing the computations and the deployment time, the lengthy training sets often drive the system in different directions resulting in the change of system parameters (also called weight) every time. Finally the neural network would be over trained and results in erroneous predictions.

The solution is to combine both these models resulting in a non-linear ARMA or feedback (a feature of ARMA) neural network. This model can learn non linear functions or relations with reduced training period and reduced prediction error. The model is resistant for over fitting or over training. In this book, the same model is repeatedly used.

This small change to the artificial neural network or any system that does similar operations brings out major changes in the output. Even for a dumb system, a certain degree of intelligence would get added with the feedback. This is primarily because the system would have learnt or in possession with the "history" embedded in the input. I.e. a part of the information content is already known or anticipated.

Although models exist with user feedback in the transfer of the information, few models consider the rate of change and time evolution of the feedback. The model described here can make use of a set of 'N' previous samples of the weighted output as the additional inputs resulting in n^{th} order feedback.

Data Over-Fitting

When more data or information is available on the response of a system, it is often difficult to find a single relationship valid over the entire set, leading to over fitting of the data. Modeling of such a system would be difficult.

From the above paragraphs, it is clear that the posterior or probability associated with the predicted message has two components-a current-data independent Gaussian prior part and a current-data dependent term (impulsive part). They correspond to the two components of the probability described earlier. Logically, the Gaussian part may be attributed to the previous or differential terms of the prediction since the weighted sum of any probability distribution function in general turns to be Gaussian. Such a Gaussian classifier is known to be resistant for over-fitting and goes well with a similar feature of the feedback neural network model.

The information prediction through estimators that make use of previous or historical data is shown in figure 3. The merger combines the outputs of the different estimators and generates the predicted information.

FUTURE TRENDS

Information Measurement

The degree of predictability of the symbols in a sequence that constitute the message provides a measure of the information content of the message. When it is easy to predict the sequence of the symbols and therefore the message itself, the associated information is very small. If a certain pattern is found in the sequence of symbols, the information progressively starts reducing. Consider following sequence:

A B C D E F G H I J K L

As one starts reading the symbols, it would be clear that it is a sequence of English alphabets. The interest in reading the sequence further gets reduced as the reader is familiar with the alphabets and the sequence bears no information.

However, when the information of each of the symbol is measured stand alone without considering the previous symbols, it contributes equally for the information content of the message.

The effective measurement of information is required for the development of new coding standards that reduce the bits required to represent the information as well the transmission errors (Roger L. Freeman, 1998). The errors in the data transmission may be reduced by decreasing the entropy per bit. This reduction in the entropy can be brought in by providing a kind of dependency in the bit stream i.e. by making each of the coded bits as a function of the data bit being coded as well as the previous data bits. A feedback neural network may be directly used to incorporate this kind of dependency. The associated properties of abstraction, hierarchies etc may be used. It calls for the use of new channel coding standards.

The dependency in the data while coding is used in all brands of channel coding. A feedback neural network can easily implement any of them as a pattern map. The scheme may be implemented by filtering the bit stream. A variant of the method called down sampling is in place in the compression of images.

Entropy Reduction

With increase in the order of feedback, it has been observed that the entropy gets reduced. Hence a strong dependency over the previous data bits can result in better error resistance to the code.

The sub partitions of the message in to chunks of data actually reduce the entropy (Trevor Hastie, Robert Tibshirani and Jerome Friedman, 2001). Specifically, if the relation among the chunks is known, the entropy gets reduced further. The total entropy of the message is equal to the sum of the entropies of the individual chunks and it can never exceed the entropy when all the symbols belong to the same chunk. Each chunk here is assumed to carry a different probability of occurrence. The clustering problem is defined as: Given there are a certain symbols N, how do we cluster them in such a way that the messages or words generated out of the symbols from these chunks carry minimum entropy? The usage of an artificial neural network for clustering is given in the chapters intelligent information processing and information mining.

In a specially designed feedback neural network, it is possible to have equal weightage for all the estimators. I.e. each of the estimators would be realized by the same number of other estimators. Equivalently, each of the symbols would be generated by the same number of weighted sum of the other symbols. This scenario represents the Block codes that operate over stored messages rather than over a stream. Here the properties, however, are a bit different.

All codes would be at the same level of abstraction. The abstraction may be increase by moving more messages in to the cluster or equivalently in to the weighted sum of the probabilities. Any of the code may be obtained from any other code through a simple convolution with the appropriate polynomial. These polynomials would be the entries of Generator/parity matrix. Thus, the code generated by a general differential feedback network does not have separate data and parity bits. Instead they are scattered over the various levels of abstraction. It provides more resistance for the errors. This way, it resembles the convolution code. If the channel response has a multiplicative or convolving noise, such a coding scheme would be effective, as the message from each of the estimators that are prone for this convolution are separately coded. The other particular case of coding is the source coding wherein there will be no dependency between the present input and the previous outputs.

Information Value

The value of information for an organization or for an individual consumer depends up on the information content in the data (Leon W. Couch II, 1997). Though there is a mathematical framework for the measurement of the information, it would be often subjective. If the client for the information can generate the requisite data on his own by guesswork or otherwise, the information content for the data drops down substantially irrespective of what the mathematics says. The relevance of information for the end user and the appropriate response play a pivotal role.

It attains importance especially in the commercial models of the information or data transfers. The information technology adds to billions of dollars of transactions. This calls for a new model of information in particular and signals in general where the feedback from the output or end users are given due credit.

In the above model, the flow of information or data is unidirectional. Independent of what the end user feels, the data transfer takes place. The amount of information as well as its commercial value remains invariant for the user.

If the users' feedback is provided as an additional input or the controlling input for the data, the total information content gets altered depending up on what the user feels. From the marketing perspective, if the user is very much in need of the data, its information content increases. Alternatively, if the user shows little interest or already in possession of a similar data, the information content as seen by the user gets reduced dramatically.

CONCLUSION

In this chapter,

- The mathematical formalism for the information is given.
- The formalism of feedback neural network model for the information is provided.

With a feedback from the end user to the source of an information system, the interpretation of the information at the user end gets modified. The entropy of the output of the estimator gets reduced with increase in the order of the feedback.

The feedback, when applied over a set leads to a manifold estimators. The classifier represented by a certain prediction or distribution is the weighted sum of all other classifiers. This model provides a mechanism for representing the data in to multiple levels of abstraction.

QUESTIONS

1. What is the difference between information and data?
2. How does signal processing help in information management?
3. What are the advantages of the feedback networks?
4. What are the properties of a feedback neural network?
5. What is the impact of data over prediction on the supply chain management?

REFERENCES

Amari, S. (1998). Natural gradient works efficiently in learning. *Neural Computation, 10*, 251–276. doi:10.1162/089976698300017746

Amari, S., & Nagaoka, H. (2000). *Methods of information geometry*. New York: AMS and Oxford University press

Bekenstein, J. D. (2003, August). Information in the holographic universe. *Scientific American.*

Bigus, J. P. (1996), *Data Mining with Neural Networks: Solving Business Problems--from Application Development to Decision Support*. New York: McGraw-Hill.

Bolstad, W. M. (2004). *Introduction to Bayesian Statistics*. Mahwah, NJ: John Wiley.

Burnham, K. P., & Anderson, D. R. (2002). *Model Selection and Multimodel Inference: A Practical Information-Theoretic Approach*, (2nd Ed.). New York: Springer Science

Couch, L. W., II. (1997). Digital and Analog Communication Systems. *International Joint Conference on Neural Networks, 4*, 79-84.

Cover, T. M., & Thomas, J. A. (2006) *Elements of information theory*, (2nd Ed.). New York: Wiley-Interscience.

Dovrolis, C. (2000, December). *Proportional differentiated services for the Internet*. PhD thesis, University of Wisconsin-Madison. Arndt, C. (2004). *Information Measures, Information and its Description in Science and Engineering*. Springer Series: Signals and Communication Technology.

Floridi, L. (2005). Semantic Conceptions of Information. E. N. Zalta (ed.), *The Stanford Encyclopedia of Philosophy* (Winter 2005 Edition).

Freeman, R. L. (1998). *Telecommunications Transmission Handbook*. Chichester, UK: John Wiley & Sons Inc.

Gibson, J. D. (1997). *The Communications Handbook* (pp. 224-235). Boca Raton, FL: CRC Press, Inc.

Harnmut Guting, R., Papadias, D., & Lochovsky, F. (1999). *Advances in Spatial Databases: by - Computers 6th International Symposium*, Ssd'99, Hong Kong, China.

Hastie, T., Tibshirani, R., & Friedman, J. (2001). *The Elements of Statistical Learning*. Berlin: Springer.

MacKay, D. J. C. (2003). *Information Theory, Inference, and Learning Algorithms*. Cambridge, UK: Cambridge University Press.

Meinicke, P., & Ritter, H. (1999). *Resolution based complexity control for Gaussian mixture models*. Technical report, Faculty of Technology, University of Bielefeld

Neal, R. (1996). *Bayesian learning in neural networks*. Berlin: Springer verlag.

Silverston, L., Inmon, W. H., & Graziano, K. (2007). *The Data Model Resource Book*. Chichester, UK: Wiley.

Sklar, B. (1998). *Digital Communications*. Upper Saddle River, NJ: Prentice Hall Inc.

Starzyk, J. A., & Wang, F. (2004). Dynamic Probability Estimator for Machine Learning. *IEEE Transactions on Neural Networks*, *15*(2), 298–308. doi:10.1109/TNN.2004.824254

Tsai, H. L., & Lee, S. J. (2004). Entropy-Based Generation of Supervised Neural Networks for Classification of Structured Patterns. *IEEE Transactions on Neural Networks*, *15*(2), 283–297. doi:10.1109/TNN.2004.824253

Chapter 3
Information Representation

ABSTRACT

The data from the supplier of the supply chain provides relevant information for the customers only when presented in the appropriate form. The data is to be modeled for to be meaningful and make sense. In this chapter, the semantic web is introduced to bring out the meaning for the data. Hierarchical organization is proposed for the data to provide meaning for different players along the supply chain.

INTRODUCTION

The last chapter provides the definition of the information and explains how it is modeled and measured using signal processing tools. The qualitative and the quantitative measurement of the information may be enhanced with a structured representation of the information. It consists of two components: the syntax and the semantics. Here, the data representation and organization for maximizing the value of the information is discussed.

Inside a storage device as well as during the transmission over a channel, digital data from any source, including the video, audio or machine data, is represented as a string of well demarcated logic levels. Depending up on the context, application and the rendering device, the string gains the appropriate meaning. A group of bits, called "code word" would provide the appropriate meaning to the program.

The representation of data (Chu, 2005) is closely linked to the storage and retrieval devices. The data storage pattern on a magnetic disc available today will be binary with a specific magnetic orientation representing the logic "high" and another orientation representing the logic "low". If the device can

DOI: 10.4018/978-1-60566-888-8.ch003

afford, a multi valued logic symbol can be stored. In a 'qbit' memory based on quantum mechanical principles, the spin of electrons represents various logic levels making the storage density very high.

Bit is the unit for the measurement of information. In the context of digital information, it represents the binary values "0" or "1". A bit must be either a "0" or a "1" at a time. However, a 'qbit' can be "0" or "1" or a combination of both (i.e. weighted sum of "0" and "1"). A discussion on qbit is found in (David Mermin.N, 2003).

Information models provide a vital clue on the type of the information to be included in a particular information product. Information models are to consider all the possible scenarios with the users of the information. Hence it is required to understand the need of the users of the information down the line, well in advance.

An alternative architecture of information representation as multiple abstraction levels is provided in this chapter. The information system (IS) architects and IS managers would find it useful to put the content in multiple abstraction levels as explained here. It provides a firm footing for the enterprise data integration, data marts etc. The concepts discussed here are expected to handle semantic web and natural language processing as well.

BACKGROUND

The goal of information representation is to use minimum space or symbols for representing maximum data and convey maximum meaning. Often, it is in the form of familiar icons that the user can easily interpret and understand. E.g. Symbols used to distinguish ladies and Gents toilets. Especially, in dialog boxes, it conveys instant message to the user compared to the associated text. A picture is worth thousand words. For the same reason, interactive software GUI make use of icons very frequently. In the digital world, the representation of information is in the form of bits. In the analog world, it can be a graph, a picture, number etc.

Information representation has a say on the information lifecycle comprising of storage, retrieval and rendering of the information. The information serves no purpose unless it is rendered to the intended user in the anticipated format. The figure 1 shows how the data is organized in to information and knowledge.

Systems making use of artificial intelligence for knowledge or information representation (Gleb Frank, Adam Farquhar, and Richard Fikes, 1999) employ symbolic languages. The usage of intelligent elements is explained in detail in a separate section of this book.

Figure 1.

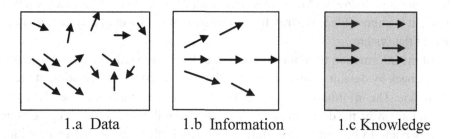

| 1.a Data | 1.b Information | 1.c Knowledge |

A high level language program running on a digital computing machine supports several data types such as integer, floating point, double precision and character. The number could be signed or unsigned, big Endean or little Endean. In all these cases the basic data is still in binary form. The interpretation will be different and appropriate to the context. Information systems follow either or a combination of the following approaches:

- **Logic based:** Here the relationship between the objects and the structures is well defined. E.g. database representation, knowledge representation (O'Leary, D. E., 1998).
- **Text based:** Here the data is stored as raw natural language text. It is used where the applications can afford less structured information.

There are two classes of information representation:

1. **Structural information:** It turns the bit sequence in to high level structures, a data type that a computer can understand, through a set of rules.
2. **Semantic information:** It adds (Geroimenko, 2003) the meaning associated with the elements of structural information, operations on the data type and the relation among the data types. It also tells what the data object is. The representation is recursive through the mapping rules that map the information.

Information is basically a pattern-a signal connecting known objects or patterns. E.g. In the sentence "Atlanta attacked Asbesta", for a person not aware of Atlanta or Asbesta or 'attack' action, the statement is absurd and carries no meaning. For those who are aware of the vocabulary, the term attack connects the objects Asbesta and Atlanta and makes sense or informative. Information is represented by the signal. The reverse statement carries much more information making the signal totally directional.

In the coarse form, the communication signal or the data flowing down from the source to the destination is the information. If a part of this signal is tapped at the destination and fed back to the source and collated with the source data, the information content would be more. E.g. Asbesta and Atlanta are attacking each other carries much more information and surprise than either of the sentence.

A signal is basically multidimensional with components as 'object' and 'context' mapped with the 'degree of binding'. The degree of binding is also called 'information. Context of publishing information is also important. When the list of 2009 Nobel Prize winners in chemistry appears in the newspapers for the first time, it is news. When it appears every second day, it will not bear any useful information as it would have already reached the destination.

The information provided by a system or the data source is associated with the randomness exhibited by the system. The direct relationship between the information and the entropy or randomness of the system may be understood using the Maxwell's demon experiment. One of the interesting results of the experiment is that it is impossible to destroy the information thrown out of a system without increasing the randomness of the system.

A feedback of the information from the destination to the source reduces the information flow. This is because the feedback by default is not random and depends up on the information of the source available at the destination. The information thrown out by the source would make use of the feedback from the destination and in a way, the destination would be able to tell, with in some degree of accuracy, the information that is going to be sent by the source. As a result, the entropy increases with feedback of

Figure 2. Flow of information

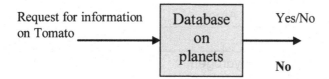

the information. The technique may be used in the future information systems. The example of query over a database is shown in Figure 2. The user makes a request for information on Tomato on a database of planets. After getting a null response and using this as a feedback input for another query, the user modifies the query as shown in Figure 3. While this query is being made, the user has some information about the database.

Information represents the relationship among the data. The relationship itself exhibits abstract levels of hierarchy in the presence of feedback. As there are communications back and forth among the data, each source would adjust itself to other source or it will be able to predict what the other source gives out. That results in the information to turn abstract. It is just scaling in the log domain (information measure) or convolution with an abstraction function such as Gaussian signal of various degrees of abstraction in the time or spatial domain.

Information modeled as a collection of known patterns present in the data. The known patterns include the repetitions in the structure of the data. The patterns so discovered are applicable to specific context and represent the knowledge specific to a domain. Since it is tied to a specific domain, it is difficult to maintain. The usage of a neural network for pattern identification in the information is given in a separate chapter.

Ontology

Ontology is the mechanism for modeling the data, used to represent the concepts and the relation among them. The relation is based on reasoning making it an ideal modeling tool for machine intelligence and programmable. An ontology (B. Chandrasekaran, John R. Josephson, and V. Richard Benjamins, 1999, Fluit et.al, 2005) is the unique way of modeling the information representation.

Ontology is used for the modeling the concepts in the application areas comprising of artificial intelligence, genetics, semantic web, knowledge representation, software engineering etc. It consists of four major players:

- **Individuals:** The elementary objects or the leaf nodes
- **Classes or sets:** Set of similar individuals

Figure 3. Flow of information

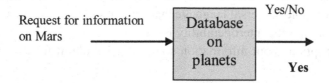

Figure 4. Ontological representations of Hydrogen isotopes

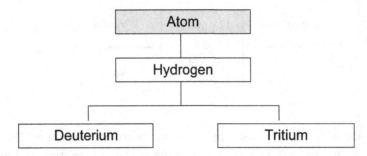

- **Attributes:** The properties or characteristics of the individuals in a set
- **Relations:** Binds the individuals and classes through the attributes.

The example of representation of deuterium and tritium, the isotopes of Hydrogen is considered here to demonstrate the ontological representation. Here "Atom" is the individual. "Atom" is also the class. In practice the hierarchy level 'individual' is not required. However, ontology supports the same to classify the individuals, even if they are not with the ontology. The class 'Atom' includes the atoms. Now the class 'Atom' branches in to two parts, each with a minimum of one different attribute. The attributes include atomic number, atomic mass etc. The relation is such that by colliding deuterium with a neutron, one can get tritium. It is expressed as:

Successor: Tritium

The tree structure in Figure 4 depicts how the objects are related to one another.

Ontology details the categories (William Swartout and Austin Tate, 1999) and entities of information system.

From the computational perspective, ontology is the definition of the data hierarchy in a specific domain of knowledge (Missikoff, M., R. Navigli, and P. Velardi, 2002) that contains the set of relevant terms, the relationships between them and the rules within the domain. It is also referred as the 'information systems' in communication science. The usage of ontology for information representation would be discussed in this chapter.

Semantic Web

Semantic Web is a technique for information representation (S. Kinsella, J.G. Breslin, A. Passant, S. Decker, 2008) in large scale. The Semantic Web (Davies, J. Fensel. D, 2003, Swartz, A, 2005) is meant for the machines rather than the human beings. The machines 'browse' the required information automatically and interpret the same. So, the information is to be stored in a machine processable form instead of readable text. A variety of information models like XML may be used for this purpose. XML is the extensively used freely available universal language that supports the machine readable syntax to represent the information and handles the interoperability issues.

Metadata provides the description about information sources. It is helpful for the organization of information resources and management of their contents. Metadata also helps in the discovery, browsing, searching and navigation of the content. The usage of Metadata for information representation is provided in a separate chapter.

In order to help the end user while retrieving the information, similar information may be sorted in to clusters. The abstraction in the cluster makes it possible to treat the large information space as one unit, without revealing the details of its contents.

Data Model

A data model provides visual representation of the nature of the data (Teorey, T. J., S. Lightstone and T. Nadeau, 2006), organization of the data in the database and business rules applicable over the data. Data models are extremely useful for the design of information systems. This type of software typically uses a database management system (DBMS).

A data model consists of two parts- logical design and physical design. The logical design provides an understanding of the structure of the information while the physical design gives the data type and the related details used by the query engine.

The data models bind the functional team and the technical team of the projects. First, the data objects provided by the functional team are to be reflected in the model. Later, the technical team makes use of the model in the design of the physical database. In addition the data model provides the requisite information to define the relational tables, primary and foreign keys for encryption, stored procedures etc.

Interoperability of Data

There is a large number of data modeling tools available commercially to transform business requirements into the realizable physical data model through the intermediate logical data model. Often the physical model is used to generate the required query language code to generate the database.

The translation of logical model in to physical model may result in conflicts in the two domains such as the excess in the length of the table or column name than the allowed value for the database. Often it requires renaming and manual editing to conform to the database standards. During the translation,

In order to support interoperability, the data model is to be standardized. The same attributes are repeatedly used in the entities. It calls for the standardization of the attribute names and the data types used in different programs. The data in several files are connected through the attribute that is standardized. The data structure nomenclature is to be consistent across. To make it happen, an abbreviation document is to be maintained.

The data modeling helps in developing a single view of the data elements and their relationships across the information supply chain. This type of data modeling provides and requires access to information scattered throughout the supply chain under the control of different players all along, with different databases and data models.

Information Model

An information model represents high level information on the data sources or entities such as their properties, the inter relationship and the possible operations on them. The entities include a wide vari-

Figure 5. Hierarchical representation of the information

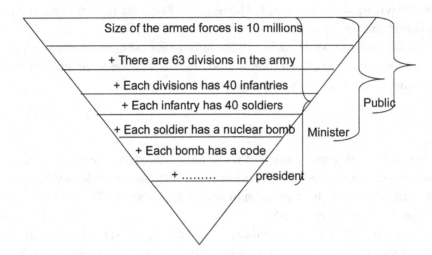

ety of objects such as devices on a network, agents in a supply chain etc. The models are applied over a specific domain that is self contained with a set of entities, properties, relationship and operations. Larger the problem size, larger would be the abstraction.

The description of the information model enjoys full freedom of providing the techniques independent of the implementation. The information mappings composed of Object Models, Entity Relationship Models or XML schemas.

The Distributed Management Task Force (DMTF) was working on a information model to be interoperable across the industries. It comprises of domain specific information models for the domains under Common Information Model (CIM). Next, the information model specific to a project or functionality or domain is derived from the CIM.

Hierarchical Representation of Information

The book (Ting Chu, 2005) provides good introduction to the quality of information representation. Hierarchical representation of information with different degrees of granularity at each level in the databases caters to the intentions of different classes (Runkler. T, 2000) of users as explained in Figure 5 and billing for information may be done accordingly. The interest as well as the requirements of the different people shown in the figure is different. It opens up new commercial horizons for selling the information. To make it happen, the keyword used for query is to be entered at different levels in the structure.

The retrieval of information has to be linked to the user behavior. Users prefer intermittently and interchangeably searching and reading. The commercial angle of redundancies in information representation may also be considered.

ISSUES AND SOLUTIONS

Data Representation

Compared to its digital counter part, analog representation suffers with problem of precision or scaling. This problem is frequently encountered in the digital representation of multimedia data such as audio, video etc. The precision of data representation is largely dictated by the analog to digital converters that provides a certain number of bits for the digital representation. However, due to the limitations on the human perception of audio or video data, it is still affordable to lose some precision. The eyes and ears have a limited resolution for different parameters of audio or video.

While human eye can accurately differentiate the pictures with 4 bits and 8 bits representation, they cannot do the same for 22 bit and 24 bit representation. I.e. beyond a certain precision that happen to be the characteristic threshold, it is of no use to represent the information accurately. Also, the eyes are more sensitive for intensity than for the colors. So the right number of bits may be allocated for both.

Analog form of data representation provides a unique advantage of pictorial representation. The data may be linked with appropriate icons, bar graphs, charts etc that convey maximum information for the user. It may be recalled that one picture is worth thousand words.

Representation of multimedia data is challenging. The data types used to represent video, still image call for new and sophisticated data models. The practical feasibility, affordability and the market demand call for storage of the data on DVD or CDs.

Multiple Logic Levels

For better compression, the information may be represented with multiple logic levels. In the place of 0 & 1 of binary, multiple voltage levels may be used to map on to the logic levels. However, such a representation faces interface problems. In addition, the logic levels are not well demarked. This poses a serious threat, especially in noisy environment where the data is prone to get corrupted.

One of the solutions to isolate the multiple logic levels and prevent them getting changed with noise is to go for 'qbit' representation. Here the electron spin states map on to the distinct levels and the commonly encountered noise does not change one logic level to the other.

The additional advantage is that the qbit representation easily map on to the hierarchical representation of the data in to multiple levels of abstraction, where the spin states correspond to the estimators of various levels of abstraction.

FUTURE TRENDS

Structured Representation

Extensible markup language (XML) is popularly used for storing structured information. It is more flexible than hypertext markup language (HTML), allowing the users to create their own customized mark-up languages for storing the data and the associated semantics. Based on the application in hand, different markup language representations are possible, spanning the protein synthesis to the chemical composition of a compound. XML happens to be a subset of Structured General Markup Language

Figure 6. Components of information

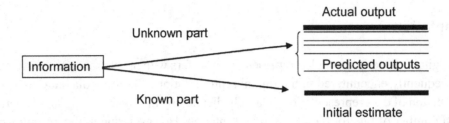

(SGML), a powerful and popularly used language.

There are specific languages for information representation. Symbolic languages such as Prolog and Lisp are highly coupled to the artificial intelligence data representation. A more generalized language is the Word-based Information Representation Language (WHIRL) that enjoys the features of Logic based and text based representation systems. The article in (William W. Cohen, 2000) provides a good discussion on WHIRL.

The information representation language should support simple retrieval mechanism, integration of the data with the heterogeneous information sources, text classification etc.

Semantic Representation

Semantics provide the meaning for the syntactic elements. A semantic engine takes the syntax of an element as the input and generates the semantic representation of the elements as an output. The output has to consider the fact that the same concept might be named differently to maintain a certain degree of redundancy. The same output has to be generated along with the synonyms. Semantics express the meaning to a term and places it in the concept hierarchy. Often, concept is the specialized or generalized version of the other concepts. It can be a part of other concepts.

The feedback neural network model of information allows mapping of the syntax to the estimator with zero feedback and the semantics hierarchy to the estimators originating as a result of more feedback.

The information contains known and unknown components as shown in Figure 6. The predictions are made based on the known parts. The predictions made with the estimators throw a hierarchy of outputs.

Figure 7. Semantic distance

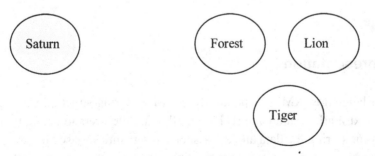

Figure 8. Semantic distance

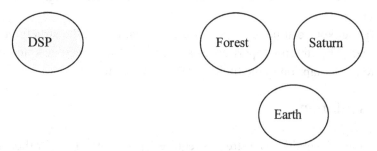

More the number of terms considered for prediction, better would be the prediction.

The hierarchical representation of the semantics exhibits different levels of abstraction. Like the semantics, the information is physically placed in multiple servers hierarchically. This architecture of the servers enable distributed search and browsing in the sea of information. The browsers will be able to provide specific results for the user queries. In addition, the entire information system would be scalable and extensible with scope for adding additional in as well as the metadata at any point of time.

Cluster Maps

Cluster maps provide the visual and hierarchical representation of the information. They provide a visual indication of how the information resources are distributed over the supply chain. In the representation, the classes or objects that are semantically or physically close are grouped together. More information may be extracted by applying a different ontology on the same set of information.

Cluster maps may be used for comparison of objects or services. The same ontology is to be applied over the different data sets to find the semantic differences. Eg. This technique may be used to find the difference in the services from different institutions. The cluster maps are useful for data retrieval. It provides a selected set of items in a large collection through the keywords and Booleans for the search. Accordingly, the search result may be too large or empty. When the results do not match with the search criteria, it calls for a contextual optimization.

Semantic distance between the objects plays a major role in clustering. Figures 7 & 8 shows the clustering based on the semantics of the data. The clustering is context dependent as evident from the figures. The usage of a neural network for clustering applications is given in a separate chapter of the book.

While rendering the results, visualization techniques may be used to provide alternative solutions to the users in iteration, each time relaxing a certain criterion. Another approach is to refine the query based on the ontological nature of the data.

Since Ontologies define (Schreiber. G, 2005) a rich semantics of complex objects, they are useful for the description of the heterogeneous information resources. They play a key role in the realization of the semantic web. The usage of a neural network for handling heterogeneous data sources is given in section 4. Appropriate weightages are given to the heterogeneous sources. The information from these sources may be merged with a Bayesian network implemented through the neural networks.

Ontologies (Van Heijst, G, 1995) provide the generic representation of the domain descriptions through a model. Information is derived from the raw data. The data in its original form is unstructured, random, redundant and often irrelevant. To convert this data in to meaningful information, lot of analysis and processing has to be done and the meaning for this data has to be brought out. It is challenging to represent these activities.

A feedback neural network can be used as a sieve to separate out the structured and unstructured components of the data. The structured part arises as a result of zero feedback and contributes for the bias. The unstructured part maps on to the higher order feedback terms.

Metadata Representation

He metadata representing the multimedia streams requires special attention for the content description. The data is often represented in a hierarchical, scalable and time dependent form. The MPEG-7 provides the required support for the Metadata representation of such content. In order to automate the handling of the content, the descriptors span the semantic definitions, indexing etc and enable smart retrieval.

Increasingly, the components of an information system are being modeled and represented with XML. The universality of XML makes it possible to represent all the components of the information system in a single language and get rid of the interoperability issues. It is possible to optimize the information representation in XML further, by providing a built-in intelligence of reconfiguration in the absence of a centralized intelligent element i.e. by exposing the system to unsupervised learning, The usage of XML for information representation is provided in the next section of the book.

Information servers are required to support interleaved searching and browsing activities of a wide range including, a well-defined search for a specific document to a query on what information is available, leading to a non-specific set of documents. To support these activities, systems make use of the metadata information or content labels. It helps in providing services that can refine user queries to focus a search and automatically route the queries to the relevant servers and cluster the related items before rendering the result.

Hierarchical representation of information maps on to the hierarchical representation of the metadata and merges the same to respond to the queries.

CONCLUSION

In this chapter,

- The two components of information namely, syntax and semantics are introduced and explained.
- The Hierarchical representation of the data is introduced

The part of supply chain involving information acquisition at the source to rendering at the user terminal is dictated by the techniques and models used for information representation. But for the precision loss during the conversion and the transformations, the digital representation of data should be exactly retained throughout the chain.

QUESTIONS

1.   What are the differences between syntax and semantics?

2. How does hierarchical representation of the data help in the semantic representation of the data?
3. How does XML provide a structured representation of the data?
4. What are the applications of cluster maps?
5. What are the different ways for representing the digital data?

REFERENCES

Chandrasekaran, B., Josephson, J. R. & Benjamins, V. R. (1999). What Are Ontologies, and Why Do We Need Them? *Intelligent Systems & their applications, 14*(1).

Chu (2005). Information Representation and Retrieval in the Digital Age.

Cohen, W.W. (2000). {WHIRL}: A word-based information representation language. *Artificial Intelligence, 118*(1—2), 163-196.

Davies, J., & Fensel, D. (2003). Chapter 9. F. van Harmelen, (Eds), *Towards the Semantic Web*. Chichester, UK: JohnWiley & Sons.

Fluit, C., et al. (2005). *Ontology-based Information Visualization*. http://www.cs.vu.nl/~marta/papers/VSW02Book.pdf

Framework, R. D. *(RDF) Schema Specification* (1999). WD-rdf-schema-19990218, W3C Working Draft. *Resource Description Framework (RDF) Model and Syntax Specification*, (n.d.). W3C. Retrieved from http://www.w3.org/TR/PR-rdf-syntax/

Geroimenko (2003). Chapters 3 and 4. V., Chen, C. (Eds), *Visualizing the Semantic Web*. London: Springer-Verlag.

Gleb, F., Farquhar, A. & Fikes, R. (1999). Building a Large Knowledge Base from a Structured Source. *Intelligent Systems & their applications, 14*(1), January/February.

Haynes, D. (2004). *Metadata for Information Management and Retrieval*. London: Facet Publishing.

Karpuk, D. (2004). *Metadata: From Resource Discovery to Knowledge Management*. Westport, CT: Libraries Unlimited.

Kinsella, S., Breslin, J. G., Passant, A., & Decker, S. (2008). Applications of semantic web Methodologies and Techniques to Social Networks and Social Websites. In *Proceedings of the Reasoning Web Summer School (RWSS 2008)*, (LNCS vol. 5224, pp. 171– 199). Berlin: Springer.

Knowledge Management through Ontologies (1998). U. Reimer (ed.) *PAKM 98 Practical aspects of Knowledge Management. Proceedings of the Second International Conference,* Basel, Switzerland *MPEG-7 Requirements Document V.7* (1998). Doc ISO/IEC JTC1/SC29/WG11 MPEG98/N2461, MPEG Atlantic City Meeting.

Melnik, S. (2000). *A Layered Approach to Information Modeling and Interoperability on the Web*. Stefan Decker Database Group, Stanford University, CA.

Mermin, N. D. (2003). From Cbits to Qbits: Teaching computer scientists quantum mechanics. *American Journal of Physics, 71*, 23. doi:10.1119/1.1522741

Missikoff, M., Navigli, R., & Velardi, P. (2002). *Integrated Approach to Web Ontology Learning and Engineering, Computer. METS (Metadata Encoding and Transmission Standard)* (n.d.). Retrieved from http://www.loc.gov/standards/mets/

O'Leary, D. E. (1998). Using AI in Knowledge Management: Knowledge Bases and Ontologies. *Intelligent Systems, 13*(3), 34-39. *International Journal of Human-Computer Studies, 52*(6), 1071–1109.

Resource Description Framework (RDF) Model and Syntax Specification. (1999). [Recommendation.]. *REC-rdf-syntax, 19990222*, W3C.

Runkler, T. (2000). *Information Mining*. Vieweg Verlagsgesellschaft.

Schemafor Object-Oriented XML (SOX), (1998). NOTE-SOX-19980930, Submission to W3C.

Schreiber, G. (2005). *The making of a Web Ontology Language a chair's perspective*. Retrieved from http://www.cs.vu.nl/~guus/public/2004-webont-zeist/all.htm

Swartout, W. & Tate, A. (1999). Guest Editors' Introduction. *Ontologies Intelligent Systems & their applications, 14*(1).

Swartz, A. (2005). *The Semantic Web In Breadth*. Retrieved from http://logicerror.com/semanticWeb-long

Topic Maps, X. M. L. (2005). Retrieved from http://www.topicmaps.org/xtm/1.0/

Van Heijst, G. (1995). *The Role of Ontologies in Knowledge Engineering*. PhD thesis, University of Amsterdam.

XML (2005). Retrieved from http://www.w3.org/XML/

XML Schema Working Group XML-Data (1998). W3C Note.

Chapter 4
Information Systems

ABSTRACT

The activities of information administration in an organization are wound around the information system. It forms the gate for the organizational information lifecycle and the supply chain that enables the information to be shared across. In this chapter, the model of information system for successful sharing of information is provided.

INTRODUCTION

In the last chapter, representation of information in to syntactic and semantic components is provided. This representation is has a say over various transactions with the information and subsequently with a large system. Here, the architecture of information system that makes use of this representation is introduced.

As the system complexities evolved from a child crying for milk to the updating of invoice records in a billion dollar company, from the sharp and blunt tools of a caveman to the PDAs, the processing devices also evolved metamorphically.

All information systems have three inseparable components - the creator of information, the flow of information and the user of the information. The creator and the consumer of the information should have a common understanding and must be in the same plane to make the information more useful. The creator, also called massage source, formats the information accordingly.

The transmitter puts this message over the channel or the physical medium. It can be in the analog or the digital format, real time data or the archived information. It calls for various methods for the

DOI: 10.4018/978-1-60566-888-8.ch004

transfer or storage of information as appropriate. The transmitter takes the responsibility of conveying the information to the receiver in a secure way. The medium over which the information gets transferred would be shared by a large number of transmitters and the corresponding receivers. Adequate wrappers providing the address and other information are required to be put around the message so that it reaches only the intended recipient. The receiver in its turn takes out these wrappers and presents only the required message to the end users for further processing.

Information systems (IS) exist exclusively within the organizations (Anita Cassidy, Keith Guggenberger, 1998), to support their work, and to cater for their information and communication requirements. It would be unique to the organization.

These concepts are brought out in a separate chapter. Information systems are responsible for the usage of information by the different resources in the organization making use of the computer based systems. They are closely tied to the usage of the information in the organization. To understand the information system, it is therefore required to understand the organization. The accurate representation and modeling of the information requires the right interpretation of the needs of the organization.

Information systems are required for the processing of data generate as well as consumed in the technical, financial, strategic, HR and other groups of the companies. A well designed information system in the organization facilitates decision-making, making it useful for long-term planning and investments. It is very useful as the redesigning of computer systems every now and then turns out to be costly.

The objective of this chapter is to allow the readers to gain the skills and methods required for the overall design and management of information systems. The architecture is introduced through the example of web based transactions. It is expected to be useful in exploring alternative designs for the data organization and web based management. The focus of the solution is to use syntax for the representation and structuring of the information. This unified approach of the Semantic Web is provided in (Wand, Y. and Weber, R, 1995). The usage of semantic annotation for decision making is explained here. To day, there is a drift in the solution based on semantics, from data and information to services and processes.

The Semantic Web is the generalization and extension of the existing World Wide Web. The Web is treated as a large-scale information system, although most of the transactions on the web take place in the areas other than the database and the information systems. This chapter has been organized to explore the web based enterprise information system and the relation they enjoy with the organization of the database and information systems.

Publishing data over the web is often the easy approach to make the information available to a large number of users. It can be done easily and economically done with the help of the tools available today. The usage of web creates enormous impact. In this chapter, the architecture and the issues arising out of information system are provided.

BACKGROUND

An information system may be roughly defined as the information processing mechanism (Beynon-Davies P, 2002) involving the important stages in the life cycle of the information: i.e. capturing, transmitting, storing, retrieving, manipulating and display of information

These topics are examined in detail in the next sections of the book. The activity of an information system (Sloan Career Cornerstone Center, 2008) touches up on the following points:

Figure 1. Informational system

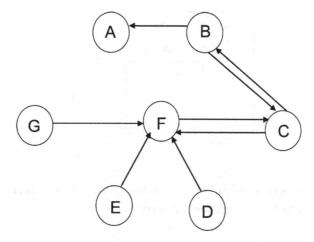

- **Planning:** It involves the choice of the concepts and development of theories relevant to the planning, analysis, design and evaluation of information systems;
- **Development:** It requires the development of languages, tools and techniques for supporting the development activities such as planning, specifications, requirements analysis, design, validation of the information systems and their verification and certification.
- **Process:** It covers the guidelines for the analysis, validation, and selection of information systems development alternatives.
- **Practices:** One of the requirements of an information system is to reuse the similar modules and application from the related areas as appropriate; It includes computer science, software engineering, knowledge engineering, cognitive science, management science, organization theory and systems theory - and applying the advancements for the development of information systems

Architecture

An information system (Lindsay, John, 2000) in an organization takes care of communication and information related issues of an organization. It connects the different components of an organization as shown in the figure 1. The connectivity could be unidirectional or bidirectional, forming a network of components.

The information system architectures (Weber, R, 2002) support heterogeneity of semantics and interoperability. The Semantics of the data (Weber, 1997, 2002) are useful for data interpretation, retrieval, schema integration etc. The semantic heterogeneity requires expertise in several domains among the database and the IS community. It is required for maintaining a high performance semantic web, information management, information retrieval and database management. The semantic web supports automation of data retrieval and processing.

Enterprise Information System

A class of information systems that provides the requisite data to carryout the business of an organization is the enterprise information system (EIS) (Dimitris N. Chorafas, 2001), (Warboys, B., Kawalek,

Figure 2. Hierarchical relations among the different levels of integrations

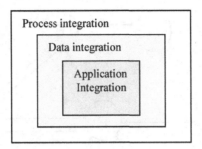

P., Robertson, I., and Greenwood, R. 1999,2000) of an enterprise. The EIS is composed of the enterprise resource planning (ERP), data bases, Relational databases etc.

Features of EIS

The enterprises are fast adapting to the present day technologies. There is a large scale migration towards the web based architectures (Weber, R, 1997) and web services to manage the data transactions over the supply chain. However, the legacy infrastructure and the databases need to be supported. The new applications need to be interoperable and coexist with the legacy applications. Today, the application development in EIS covers more of the integration activities than the development from the scratch. Such applications are readily available, reducing the turn around time and call for customization before integration. EIS integration is a part of the enterprise application integration problem that targets applications and enterprise data sources to share the common business processes and the data.

The integration process in enterprise information systems is explained in detail in the Information storage part. The different hierarchical levels of integration are given below. The detailed description is provided in a separate chapter. Figure 2 provides the hierarchical relation among these integrations.

- **Application integration**: It involves the seamless connection of the:
  - existing applications being used in the enterprise,
  - procured applications
  - The applications developed in-house.

The applications are required to support the customized utilities developed in the organization. The existing applications should go well with the future applications. Typical applications are Supply chain management, customer relation management, inventory management etc.

- **Data integration**: In order to supply a variety of applications, an organization has to maintain databases in different formats such as hierarchical, relational, object oriented etc. Another source that puts data in different formats is the support for multiple customers who generate and provide the data in their own formats. Data integration ensures seamless usage of the databases across different applications as appropriate.
- **Process integration**: Another important component in information system apart from the application and the data is the process or the driving mechanism that uses them.

Figure 3. Two tier model

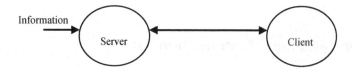

Information System Modeling

Various tools and techniques are available for the information system modeling (Warboys, B., Greenwood, R., and Kawalek, P, 2000). Handling of a large scale data for business process and planning (Warboys, B., Kawalek, P., Robertson, I., and Greenwood, R, 1999) require a strategic Information Systems across the supply chain (Walker, K.B. and E.L. Denna, 1997). The Information System Model and Architecture Generator (ISMOD) provides the required automation and architecture to carryout the same.

Case Study: Internet

Internet may be modeled as a major information system. For the internet based information system, client-server architecture is extensively used. It is based on the typical two-tier client server system modeling shown in figure 3. The client requests the server for the data or service through the browser. It is not equipped with a powerful processor for computing, as it predominantly performs UI operations and less of data processing, providing the interface to the end user. The server supports the information service. It provides the required data and service to the end user through the client. Depending up on the operating system, it is implemented as the Tomcat, Apache, Web Server, Internet Information Server (IIS) or Java Web Server (JWS).

The two tier model is more relevant for static information System and not for handling the service data. It helps to distribute the predefined information, data or message over the internet to run the business.

The three-tiered model is the natural extension of the two-tier one. It deals with the increased complexity in the functionalities and the data processing. The three-tier model shown in figure 4 consists of

Figure 4. Three tier model

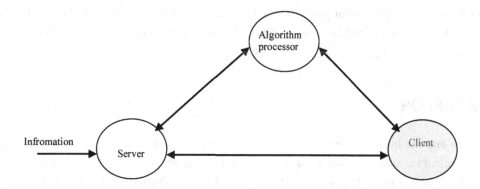

the algorithmic tier for the information system to perform the additional functionalities supported by a database management system.

Hierarchical Representation of Information

There is a level of abstraction from the information representation to the information model and from the information model to the information system and from system to the organization. The same logic may be used across all the levels of abstraction.

A kind of self similarity in the information and its variations may be seen across the different levels of abstraction of the hierarchies. This is because of the presence of the long range dependencies in the data across the hierarchies arising out of the usage of historical data. It may be seen that the amount of information in the raw representation of the data would be less, though the physical space occupied is very large. Next in the hierarchy is the model whose output carries some relevant information. This is going to happen after filtering tons of data and arranging in the relevant order.

If the data in the raw representation exhibits self similarity, it continues to do so in the next level of the hierarchy. The information content at any level in the hierarchy may be thought of as the scaled version of the lower levels. I.e. the autocorrelation of the information or the mutual information across these levels exhibits self similarity. It is true with any pair in the hierarchy.

As the different levels of the hierarchy or abstraction happen to be self similar, modeling of any of these layers should cover the other layers with in a scale factor. Any relation defined at the lower levels of the hierarchy of the objects continues to be valid with in a scale factor, as one move along the hierarchies. The inherent properties associated with the self similarity, such as the stability due to associated feedback, remain invariant. The physical parameters such as time however get scaled across the hierarchies.

If the low level hierarchy has to change for some reason, say due to the dynamics of the information system calling for a change in the requirements, the same has to be propagated upwards. Similar scaling of the changes is expected at all levels. It is interesting to see that a small change across the hierarchies bring about an equivalent change with in all the levels of the hierarchy. This is because the feedback signal that gets transferred down the hierarchy would result in the reconfiguration in all the levels appropriately. The converse is also true i.e. any change within a certain hierarchy results in the changes in the information flowing across the hierarchies.

The properties observed with the information are equally applicable for command and control signals, dependencies as well as the commodities over a supply chain. Any inconsistency in the data across the hierarchies destroys the self similar property and the other properties mentioned above. This factor may be used for detecting inconsistencies and assure coherency especially when the data has to be stored hierarchically and mirroring of the data is required.

FUTURE TRENDS

The large size and the huge data generated in the information system calls for the usage of intelligent elements to control various activities along the information supply chain. Any instance of an information system is self contained and comprises of informal and formal informational actions and all knowledge and data processing activities within the organization in question. The organizational system may be thought of as a collection of independent information systems.

Consolidation of Information

With multiple sub systems being monitored by a larger system called organization, there would be contention for resources. In addition, contradicting data could be pumped in. The process may be stream lined by controlling the communication between the organization and the subsystems. Towards this, a technique making use of a feedback signal that can provide the service based information and handle the resources effectively is introduced in the in the section 'intelligent information management'.

The objects in an information system could be related through arithmetic or logical relations. The usage of an intelligent element in the computation of these rules is given in a separate section. I.e. some of the objects may be formed by the arithmetic or logical operations over the other objects.

Data Warehouse

With the size of the organization growing very large in terms of data transactions, the requirement for maintaining huge data bases and records is increasing. A data warehouse or a data mart is designed to support this and cater for a large number of users (Inmon, W.H, 2002). A data warehouse has a couple of unique properties differentiating it from the other storage architectures. In a data warehouse, a separate decision support database is maintained by integrating the data from multiple sources. The data is accessible through on-line navigation while the system is operational. Being fast, it allows distributed access to the information.

The content in a data warehouse is directly accessible for the user in the required format, throwing new opportunities for leveraging the data. The data may be sold like commodity. It allows the decision makers to generate reports from the data at their own machines. All these possibilities reduce the burden on the information system.

CONCLUSION

In this chapter,

- The architecture of information system is provided.
- The flow of signals and information over the supply chain is described.

The timely management of end to end information supply chain has become a challenging task in large and medium information systems with distributed units scattered across the globe

The different issues of the supply chain including the secure and timely movement of the commodities are addressed and a solution has been sought based on a type of feedback from the tail of the supply chain to the head. The feedback includes time shifted version of the extrapolated loss or delay parameter of the commodity as seen by the destination. The feedback signal controls the overall flow in the supply chain.

The problem of resource contention at the intermediate nodes in the supply chain as a result of multiple flows has been defined and the solution in terms of relative quality parameters has been explored.

QUESTIONS

1. What are the components of information system?
2. What are the functions supported by the information system?
3. What are the typical activities taking place in an information system?
4. How do you visualize internet as an information system?
5. How does the data organization affect the performance of an information system?

REFERENCES

Cassidy, A. Guggenberger, K. (1998). *A Practical Guide to Information Systems Process Improvement.*

Cassidy, A. (2005). *A Practical Guide to Information Systems Strategic Planning.* Boca Raton, FL: Saint Lucie Press. Beynon-Davies, P. (2002). *Information Systems: an introduction to informatics in Organizations.* Basingstoke, UK: Palgrave.

Chorafas, D. N. (2001). *Enterprise Architecture and New Generation Information Systems* - 1st edition. Boca Raton, FL: Saint Lucie Press.

Cook, M. A. (1996). *Building enterprise information architectures: reengineering information systems.* Hewlett-Packard professional books. Upper Saddle River, NJ, Prentice Hall.

Green, P. F., & Rosemann, M. (2000). Integrated Process Modelling: An Ontological Evaluation. *Information Systems, 25*(2), 73–87. doi:10.1016/S0306-4379(00)00010-7

Hall, J. (1994). Application Partitioning and Integration with SSADM. *Model Systems, 44*(171), 627–5120.

Hall, J. *Distributed Systems: Application Development. The Information Systems Engineering Library.* Norwich, UK: CCTA.

Hevner, A., March, S., Park, J., & Ram, S. (2004). *Design Science in Information Systems Research.* Forthcoming in MIS Quarterly.

IIS 6.0 Documentation, (2008). Retrieved December 27th 2008 from http://www.microsoft.com/technet/prodtechnol/WindowsServer2003/Library/IIS/848968f3-baa0-46f9-b1e6-ef81dd09b015.mspx?mfr=true

Inmon, W. H. (2002). *Building the data Warehouse* (3rd Ed.). New York: John Wiley & Sons.

Lindsay, J. (2000). *Information Systems – Fundamentals and Issues.* Kingston University, School of Information Systems.

Sloan Career Cornerstone Center. (2008). *Information Systems*. Alfred P. Sloan Foundation.

Soffer, P., Boaz, G., Dori, D., & Wand, Y. (2001). Modelling Off-the-Shelf Information Systems Requirements: An Ontological *Approach. Requirements Engineering, 6,* 183–199. doi:10.1007/PL00010359

Walker, K. B., & Denna, E. L. (1997). Arrivederci, Pacioli? A new accounting system is emerging. *Management Accounting, 1*(July), 22–30.

Wand, Y., & Weber, R. (1995). On the Deep Structure of Information Systems. *Information Systems Journal, 5,* 203–223. doi:10.1111/j.1365-2575.1995.tb00108.x

Warboys, B., Greenwood, R., & Kawalek, P. (2000). Modelling the Co-Evolution of Business Processes and IT Systems. In P. Henderson, (Ed.), *Systems Engineering for Business Process Change*. Berlin: Springer Verlag.

Warboys, B., Kawalek, P., Robertson, I., & Greenwood, R. (1999). *Business Information Systems: a Process Approach*. New York: McGraw-Hill.

Weber, R. (1997). *Ontological Foundations of Information Systems*. Queensland, Australia: Coopers & Lybrand

Weber, R. (2002). Ontological Issues in Accounting Information Systems. In V. Arnold & S. Sutton, (ed.), *Researching Accounting as an Information Systems Discipline,* (pp. 13-33).

Chapter 5
Basic Information Management

ABSTRACT

For the successful administration of the information system, it required to follow a process. The usage of web for information sharing has opened both opportunities and challenges. In this chapter, the different players or agents for information management are detailed. The various factors influencing a successful information system are provided.

INTRODUCTION

In the last chapter, the information system architecture that spans the lifecycle of the information and organized in to an information system is explained. Here, the strategies and need of management of these components loosely coupled along a supply line is discussed.

In the context of the present day activities, information management (Blaise Cronin, 1992) basically deals with design, development and usage of data and knowledge management systems. The fast changes of the business calls for the availability of the information online in ready to use integrated form. Information management (David Aspinall, 2004) also handles the information architecture (IA) that outlines the procedure for the organization of the information. It provides a framework for the usage of the information. Service oriented architecture (SOA) is one such methodology. More details on SOA are provided in the chapter on information storage. The information management deals with the study of collection, usage and storage of information.

Agent based architecture is often used for information management (Jennifer Rowley and John Farrow, 2000). This chapter examines the issues and trends with the usage of agents for information

DOI: 10.4018/978-1-60566-888-8.ch005

management. The problem of quality based data exchange among the agents and the data integration from multiple agents will be addressed here. The concepts of information management provided here would kindle the interest of the future IS managers.

Information management process involves the following activities:

- Identification of the requirements
- Acquisition of information,
- Organization and storage of information
- Development of information products and services
- Distribution of information and
- Consumption of the information.

All these activities are covered in the subsequent sections of the book.

In an organization, the transaction data, i.e. logically related data generated during one transaction, such as the commodities bought under a purchase order, is to be grouped and managed as a single unit. The enterprise resource planning (ERP) architecture is developed based on the transaction data. So, ERP plays an important role in the management of the organizational information (Billy Maynard Andrew White, 2005). This chapter examines information management over the supply chain though no assumption has been made on the nature of the supply chain and organizations in particular.

BACKGROUND

Information management (Gordon, Keith, 2007) spans all the activities involving system and processes in the organization for the creation and consumption of the information. It makes use of a standard process for the acquisition, retrieval (LIU (S) and SVENONIUS (E), 1991), access, translation, conversion, and filtration of the data. However, the implementation technologies are left for the choice of the individual organizations. The activities of information management cover the design, development and usage of the data and knowledge management systems. The exposure and exchange of information with private and public organizations will have impact on the society. Information management is to deals with the same.

The information management in an organization is dictated by various factors including:

- The ecosystem of consumers and producers in which the organization is positioned
- The internal infrastructure of the organization
- The marketing trends
- Roadmaps of the organization.
- Support available for the information management with in the organization.

Components of Information Management

The different components of organizational information management are provided below:

Figure 1. Information management systems

- Infrastructure Task:
  - Choice of the right information source
- Technology Task:
  - Steps in the life cycle of the information
- Management Tasks:
  - Business management
  - Roadmaps
  - Funding the projects
  - Marketing
  - Execution
- The tools and technology of information management span:
  - Procurement management
  - Content management
  - Document management
  - Rights management

To achieve this, the information management calls for collaboration within and outside of the organization, content description spanning metadata and quality of service etc. The various components are related to each other as shown in the figure 1.

Distributed Information

In a distributed environment, the sources of information are placed at physically or logically distinct locations or sites. It is possible to have some of the information sources redundant to introduce redundancy in to the system for fault tolerance. In a distribution system, it is not possible to localize the information and the information is distributed among the objects in the system. The information is represented as stored data in the nodes or as the connectivity of the nodes in the links. The management of distributed information is intended to facilitate the sharing, managing, searching, and presentation of the information that is widely distributed over the supply chain.

The data from distributed information sources in a supply chain is to be integrated to enable the players to communicate with the customers, supplies, and partners down the line. To make it happen, a collaborative and event-driven architecture of supply chain information system (SCIS) is being used. The SCIS framework provides a collaborative, event-driven, object-oriented, and agent-based mechanism for the players of the supply chain to exchange information. It has two components: The information coordinator component (ICC) and agent component (AC).

The ICC is responsible for the information integration management. It manages all the agent components and facilitates the exchange of information by generating event triggers for the same. The description of the agent components is provided in the subsequent sections.

CASE STUDY: MOBILE AGENTS FOR INFORMATION MANAGEMENT

Mobile agents are the intelligent programs (Iida, N. Fujino, T. Nishigaya and T. Iwao, 1998) that propagate themselves over the network to accomplish a fixed task. They are ideal for handling distributed databases over the internet. With the Mobile agents it is easy to handle the systems that get scaled up. Hence they are extremely useful for the automation of web based supply chain management. They also cater for the ease of automation and optimal utilization of the resources over the supply chain. They cover the life cycle of information management. For the same reason, it is taken as the case study.

Compared to the client server architecture, they are more flexible, intelligent, support the automation and ideal for problem solving applications. The automation brings in reduced the cost and time .Hence it is used in applications such as dynamic routing, load balancing, data acquisition from heterogeneous distributed systems and web based supply chain management.

Mobile agents provide the required solution for the information management issues. (Jain, A. K., Aparico IV, M., and Singh, M. P, 1999). Being platform independent, it is possible to port them on to any unit. They work based on the trigger of events asynchronously and may be dispatched over the network anytime without resource reservations or dedicated links. They play a passive role to issue the queries and provide the requisite information with minimum usage of the resources. On the other hand, they are intelligent enough to get involved in complex negotiation process with the other agents.

The agents make use of the computing resources and the network of an organization to achieve a specific goal. (I.B. Crabtree, S.J. Soltysiak and M. Thint, 1998). When the organization has several plants, the resources of each of them are utilized. Thus they are supported by the individual units as well as by the organization as a whole. It calls for the integration of the heterogeneous agents.

Each of the agents is to be self contained as far as possible with less dependencies on the agents from the other units (J.C. Collis, S.J. Soltysiak, D.T. Ndumu and N. Azarmi, 1998) In an organization, there can also be a combination of the fixed as well as the mobile agents to assist the business process. The different agents that take part in the information management largely depend up on the context and application. Here the example of a supply chain is considered. The various agents that help the information management right from the procurement of the commodities up to their utilization are listed. These agents are (Kamil Reddy, Johnson Kinyua, Wayne Goddard, 2003):

- **Database agent:** It enables the other agents to access the database. All agents or applications that are willing to communicate with the database get the help of the database agent. The typical data requirements contain the information about the various players of the supply chain, including the suppliers, material, inventory etc. Typically, database agents are wrapped to the databases, (T. Mohri and Y. Takada, 1998) serving the requests of the other agents. Generally, data will be requested to process the application rather than to serve for the queries.

- **Interface agent:** It provides the interface between the intranet and the internet. Thus, if a mobile agent is outside of a unit, it can communicate with an agent inside, only through the interface unit. This agent ensures interoperability and seamless communication between the agents across the different units of the same organization or across different organizations. In addition, it works as a single point of contact, providing adequate security against intrusions.

- **Dispatcher agent:** Based on the requests and the parameters provided from other agents, it creates and dispatches the buyer and the user agents.

- **Directory agent:** It supplies the network information such as network address for the agents that require the same. It is very important for the web based management of the supply chain to supply the URL of the information and network address of the data source.

- **Finder agent:** Useful for locating other agents.

- **Login agent:** It handles the responsibility of getting the user logged in to the system. Once the user logs in, it provides the right parameters (based on the rendering device) to the dispatcher agent to activate the user agent.

- **QoS agent:** Stringent Quality of service constraints are to be imposed on the agents that exchange data taking part in the integration, which otherwise would end up with improper results (I. Iida, N. Fujino, T. Nishigaya and T. Iwao, 1999).

- **Security agent:** It takes the responsibility of maintaining the security of communication taking place between different agents. It also protects the internal agents from security attacks by filtering the messages in cooperation with the interface agent.

- **Buyer agent:** This mobile agent interacts with the suppliers automatically, gathers the information, negotiates the price and quality and places the order after taking the right decision with the help of other mobile agents. Hence it shares the acquired information as appropriate. For decision and negotiations, it makes use of historical data such as the price in the previous quote, the user input and the preferences.

The agents in an information system communicate with each other by passing the appropriate messages. The end to end communication of these messages forms a supply chain as explained in the previous chapter. Multi-threaded message handling is also supported by the agents. Any information management can make use of a variant of the above example customized to the information system under consideration. The agents form an adhoc network of autonomous system without a centralized controller.

- **User agent:** Provides interactivity between the end user and the system through a powerful graphical user interface (GUI).

Figure 2. Relation among the commonly used mobile agents

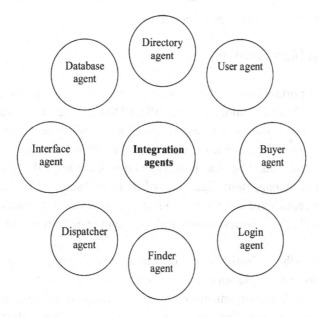

Figure 2 shows the relation among the different mobile agents.

- **Inventory agent:** Visits all the inventories along the supply chain and take a measure of the available stock. Although they work similar to the buyer agents, they are available for the organization and not for the end user.
- **Integrating agent:** Since the agents work independently, they take independent decisions without considering the requirements of other agents. In general, this local optimization does not lead to global optimization and results in the eventual failure of the supply chain. The integration agent collates all the rules for decision making. Each rule may be modeled as an estimator. A single Feedback neural network can be used to combine all of them.

Flow of the Events

In a typical transaction, the sequence of events is as follows: The end user first invokes the application by login through the login agent and the user agent. With a successful login, the dispatch agent wakes up. The find agent searches the presence of the other required agents.

Applications

Typical applications of the agent are:

- Providing response for the queries where a particular group is authorized to get the information
- Get the status of the inventories.
- Negotiation of the best price and quality.

- Analysis of price quotations
- Comparison of offerings from different vendors.

Process of Information Management

Data management is the important part of the information management (Barish, Greg and Dipasquo, Daniel and Knoblock, Craig A. and Minton, Steven, 2000). Data management spans the data as well as the resource management. The resources to be considered here will have direct transactions with the data. Data Resource Management involves the execution architecture, practices and procedures required to manage the lifecycle of the data. The next paragraphs provide a brief description of the important activities of the information management. Each one of them is discussed in depth in the subsequent chapters, providing the concepts involved, the methods being practiced, the issues, technologies and the investment required to handle these issues, trends and the management of the components.

- **Acquisition**: It refers to the collection of the information or data required to drive the Information management, often from multiple sources. The sources may be primary sources of the data, individuals or the databases. The organization generally maintains a database of the sources of different types of data required to maintain the information in the organization. Third party vendors often sell this information, ie the information on where to procure the required information.
- **Organizing and storing:** The data from several sources ids to be collated and a single view of the same is to be rendered across the organization. The grouping of data can happen based on the classification and patterns in the data. The data needs to be classified in to structured and unstructured components. Often, historical data maintained in the archives is required along with the current data calling for the maintenance of the digital archives. The required information needs to be supplied through the queries in a form usable for the applications. Often it is contextual and depends up on the application, attributes, information management etc.
- **Distribution:** The information acquired and maintained will be of no use unless it is shared between the applications and distributed appropriately. To distribute the information over a wider audience, a better retrieval and communication mechanism is required.
- **Application:** The usage of information is application sensitive, providing the right decision based on the context. It calls for a flexible structure for the information. The end users of the information need to have a say in the organization and management of the information and drive the same. As the time progresses, the information in the organization matures to knowledge.

Supply chain has become an integral part of the information management. Supply Chain Management is a proven business strategy that has gained wide acceptance in recent years due to increasing customer demands for quality, cost, delivery, and speed. It binds the supplier, provider, and the customer.

Return on Investment for the Information Management

Information management ensures that the resources in the organization are utilized optimally (Denise Johnson McManus et.al). It provides an opportunity for the organization to adapt to the business. The ecosystem of different players in the ecosystem interacts to see that the creators of the information smoothly transfer the same to the consumers. The transfer happens systematically adhering to a process.

Information management makes use of the organizational learning and the best practices to maintain the knowledge base. The learning provides solution to a variety of issues in the organization.

Information management demands an accurate description of information requirements. The goal of information is to provide the right time information than to provide the real time information.

Human Factors in Information Management

Most of the input and the output devices are designed user centric, providing maximum convenience for the user to interact with the computing system. In all the stages of the information life cycle spanning acquisition, processing, retrieval, and usage, the convenience of the end user are given due weightage. Analysis of the user behavior during the procurement of the commodity or the information over the supply chain is the key for several decisions and all transactions happening over the supply chain. In this book, in each of the chapters, the human angle is considered. The response or feedback from the user, provided explicitly or generated implicitly, is made used in the designs to solve several issues. The detailed discussion on the human factors for handling the information is found in (Daniela K. Busse et.al, 2009).

ISSUES AND SOLUTIONS

One of the challenges for information management is the explosive growth of the information. It generates problems for sorting and proper archiving. Hierarchical storage has been suggested throughout this book. The information may be sorted in to different levels of hierarchy with varying degrees of abstraction. With the inflow of new information, the addendum would fit in to a separate layer in the hierarchy without disturbing the existing structure. It provides a scalable and extensible solution.

There are many non technical issues to be addressed with the information management. First, the process for information management is to be identified. Need of the information requirement is to be understood. The same is to be realized. Next, the organization of the information is to be selected depending up on the business requirements. Fruits of the information management are to be distributed across the organization. A mechanism is to be streamlined to use the knowledge and experience of the individuals to exploit the same for the business needs.

Bibliometrics technique is often used as the input to resolve some of these issues. It is the study of usage and publication pattern of the documents based on the mathematical and statistical tools. The study includes the organization, classification and quantitative evaluation of all the publication and communication patterns, authors of these communication or publications and their impact factor. It indicates the need and usage as well as the strength or weakness of different domains of information with in the organization. It comprises of two categories of analysis: descriptive bibliometrics that deals with the productivity count and evaluative bibliometrics that covers the Literature usage count. It calls for intelligent pattern recognition from the available data.

Network analysis is a powerful technique for information management. It spans the planning, controlling, coordinating and scheduling of the resources for the execution of the projects. Each module of the project is taken and their relations with the other modules are analyzed and represented diagrammatically in the form of a network. The network may be generated through PERT (Program Evaluation and Review Technique) or the CPM (Critical Path Method) and helps in decision making. It is a typical

Figure 3. Decision making in information management.

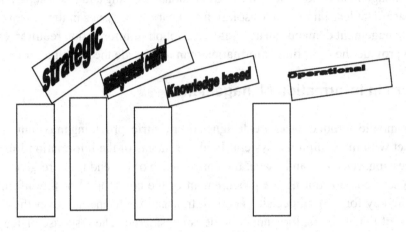

operations research (OR) problem to achieve the goal through minimum cost and resources. Intelligent models based on the optimization techniques may be used to achieve this.

The optimal utilization of resources requires the modeling with an intelligent element. There are multiple levels of decision making for the information management where they are helpful.

1. **Operational:** The process of day to day activities requires the operational decisions to be made at various levels. An intelligent processing element can provide feedback by predicting the deviations from the observed patterns.
2. **Management control**: The resource and performance management calls for usage of the intelligent element for the optimal resource allocation and maximize the resource utility.
3. **Knowledge based**: It stores and maintains the organizational knowledge and learning. The intelligent elements are used to retrieve the knowledge and provide inferences and suggestions based on the requests from the users.
4. **Strategic**: The long term strategies of the organization are always speculative. An intelligent element is required to provide the feedback and extrapolation of the available patterns in the data to make these predictions accurate.

Figure 3 shows the decision making in information management.

Response Time

Though multiple agent based models (T. Iwao, M. Okada, Y. Takada, and M. Amamiya, 1998) can solve most of the issues with the information management (McGee, James V. and Laurence Prusak, 1993), the quality based data exchange among the agents and subsequent data integration from multiple agents will be challenging. The automated agents need the responses from the other agents with in a stipulated time. It calls for imposing stringent constraints on the response time.

A probability of data loss or corruption in the exchange process will be associated with each agent and it changes dynamically with time as the data encounters any queue or dependency in the journey

Figure 4. Agent based data supply chain

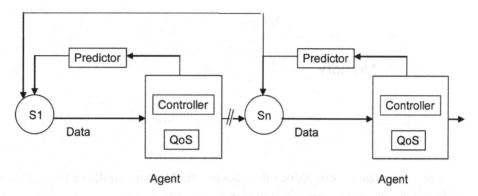

across different agents, specifically when they have to work on the shared resources, they need to fall in the queue.

The probability of data loss may be used as the feedback signal for the source agent. Depending up on its value, at the destination, the agent will predict the trends in this feedback signal 'k' steps in advance and use this information for controlling the size of the data originating from the source agent. The prediction provides ample time for the source agent to handle the situation. The shifted feedback may be used to achieve some quality of service deadlines such as the absolute delay guarantee, fraction of the data lost etc. The usage of shifted signals can reduce the data loss, resource requirement and improve the service quality in terms of overall successful operations in a given time. The trend analysis will be done later. The agent based data supply chain with stringent quality of service (QoS) constraints on the data is shown in figure 4. The agents take the responsibility of maintaining the QoS in the data provided to the end user.

Data Security

The other problem with mobile agents is that they are vulnerable for security threat when exposed to external world. E.g., the applications involving data collections. In addition to providing the wrong data, the host machine can write malicious code in to the agent to spread it across the network. One of the techniques for minimizing the same is to make the agents read only and/or encrypt the data borne by them. Further discussion on the security issues and solutions are available in (Borselius. N, 2002).

Data Structure

The usage of heterogeneous data structures in the agents poses serious challenge for the information management. The issues of asynchronous communication with a Shared memory or message exchange crops up.

The heterogeneous data structures call for merging the information appropriately subjected to a set of rules. A neural network with Bayesian learning may be used for merging or generalizing the set of rules.

The common shared memory results in contention for the access. Hierarchical data organization and the subsequent merging or integration provides a good solution. Figure 5 and figure 6 explain how the

Figure 5. Contention for single memory

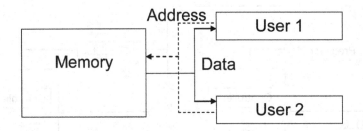

hierarchical memory organization can reduce the contention. Although multiple fetches are required, the contention due to the access of same location may be prevented.

The other problem with the common shared resource is the imposition of a queuing mechanism. An intelligent scheduler may be used to modulate the queue structure depending up on the service class requirements.

The asynchronous communications in general result in waiting, overflow etc. Advance prediction and a subsequent communication of this predicted values throws better insight on the ongoing process and the event timings may be adjusted based on this information. A neural network may be used for prediction and subsequent communication.

In an asynchronous information system, the communication among the agents usually happens without a centralized server. In a way it resembles a self organizing adhoc network. A self-organizing system basically makes decisions using the past experience. Here the feedback from end user plays an important role. It aims to optimize job specific parameters as well as the resource utilization. It provides the additional data of the past experience for decision-making.

FUTURE TRENDS

The large quantum of present day Information Management requires a class of sophisticated tools and techniques such as Artificial intelligence, artificial neural network, signal processing, Knowledge building network etc.

Heterogeneous Information Sources

Management of information requires handling of a large number of independent systems each with its own data convention. Merging and integration of information from these sources is an issue. The concepts forming the basis to automate this task are provided in the next chapters.

Information management in large size comes across direct competition among the elements of an information system. As long as the competition results in an optimized result, it should be encouraged. Optimization algorithms with unsupervised learning may be used to handle this competition methodically in such a way that the globally optimal, minimum entropy solution is arrived at.

Quite often, information systems face with the problem of the inconsistency of information. The inconsistencies may be found out using a pattern classifier. It is tested as follows: Whenever a similar data (input) is applied to the system, the expected output is to be the same. The degree of deviation is

Figure 6. Hierarchical organization of data in the memory

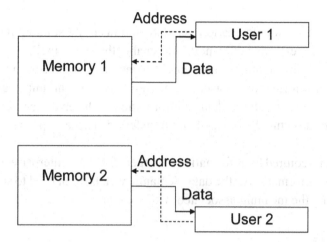

a measure of the inconsistency. More information on the working of pattern classifiers is given in a separate section of this book.

Bigger the organization more will be the issues faced for the information management (MARCHAND (D A), 1998). Although the present technologies have solved most of these issues, they contribute for a new wave of problems as indicated below (James Robertson, 2005):

Management

- Inconsistent and incomplete data, poor quality of the information with duplications.
- No unique view of the information across the organization.
- No clarity in the long term strategies
- No appreciation for the information management and its applications
- Less funds and resources allocated for the information management.
- Lack of motivation and business needs.
- Downtrends in the business.
- No direct mapping with the business to reap the low hanging fruits.

Environment

- Reduced interaction among the information systems.
- Interoperability with the existing systems is an issue.
- Competition for resources among the information systems.
- Heterogeneous information systems in the ecosystem are to be managed.

Staff

- Non consensus and conflicting views in the organization.
- Limited knowledge about the information systems and management for the staff.
- Reluctance for any changes or adoptions.

Ontology

Many applications running in an organization generate and need the storage of large volumes of two dimensional data. It calls for effective data models to enable the query facility over such data.

The use of ontology for information management is increasingly becoming popular. It is also introduced in the context of information measurement. Ontology plays an important role in information management by treating the unstructured data as information with semantics. Knowledge however requires the data to be to be structured, managed and transferred. These steps are crucial for the survival of an enterprise.

Updated information is required for information management in the enterprise. It requires the notifications on any update of the information or the data. Semantic web is often used to support the Information management by providing the meaning associated with the data.

Management Trends

Information management requires change in the handling of the data organization. It happens at various levels.

1. **Source level**: The data collected from the source may be reduced based on the requirement. It saves from the expensive activities of data collection, processing, normalization etc.
2. **Local level**: The collaboration among the peers ate the local level makes it possible to improve the data quality by sharing the information on the best practices, guidelines, standards and tools.
3. **System level**:
    ◦ Only the high quality data needs to go for integration. It calls for the identification of defects and duplications in the data and cleansing of the same before the integration.
    ◦ Usage of intelligent tools for planning and decision making by analyzing the data.

Information Structure

The useful knowledge from unstructured information comprising of text, audio, video, images, etc happens through Unstructured Information Management (UIM). Here the driving software system analyses the information and extracts, organizes and delivers the useful knowledge to the user. For the analysis of the unstructured information, a variety of tools and techniques such as Natural Language Processing (NLP), Information Retrieval (IR), pattern matching, machine learning, neural networks and ontology are made use.

A major part of the book is devoted to the discussion of these topics. Organization of the data in to various degrees of abstraction reflecting the structured and spurious parts throws open new opportunities and challenges for information management.

The rules applied over information or knowledge system in turn may be abstract, as though each being applied over an estimator. The collective nature of the rules may be replaced by a single rule much the same way as the hierarchies of the information or knowledge or knowledge sources. In this context, the equivalent rule acts over the equivalent information or the knowledge.

In a modern organization the data sources are distributed. They may be thought of as representing the different hierarchies of the information. If there is a rule for merging, the databases, then this rule could be used to merge the "rules" used for extracting the information from each of the data sources. Each rule is thought of as an estimator. Merging of the rules among all the hierarchies lead to an ideal estimator. In the subsequent chapters, it has been shown that hierarchical representation of data in to various abstract levels can provide an integrated environment for storage, security and the service quality.

Mobility

Today, the supply chain spans a large proportion of the mobile players who demand and supply the data over the mobile wireless links. It calls for the information management through high speed wireless links with GPRS, 3G and wi-fi technologies. The wireless links have made the information management simple and rapid, although the support for large volumes of data over the wireless channel is challenging. The data spans images, audio, movie clips etc demanding a large bandwidth and processing power. It calls for optimal utilization of the resources, achieved through a mobile agent with differential feedback.

CONCLUSION

In this chapter,

- The paradigm of agent based information management is introduced.
- The various parameters to be considered for information management are discussed.

For the successful information management, lot of transactions with the information such as the sharing, managing, searching and presentation are to be supported. Internet provides a speedy band secure mechanism to achieve the same through the paradigm of the Intelligent Distributed Information Management System (IDIoMS). It provides the tools and techniques for information delivery and management through internet. The mobile agents are also used widely for the information management.

The abstract organization of the information is required for the successful architecture of the information providing new interpretations for the data and assists the evolution of the information system. It helps in the information management as it is modular, simple and economical. The organization of the information in to multiple levels of abstraction may be achieved with the help of a feedback neural network.

QUESTIONS

1. What is information management?
2. What are the activities involved in the information management?
3. How is return on investment achieved with information management?
4. How does the agent help in information management?
5. How does internet help in the supply chain management?

REFERENCES

Aspinall, D. (2004). *An introduction to information management*. London: British

Barish, G., Dipasquo, D., Knoblock, C. A., & Minton, S. (2000). A dataflow approach to agent-based information management. In *Proceedings of the 2000 International Conference of on Artificial Intelligence*.

Borselius, N. (2002). Mobile agent security. *Electronics and Communication*

Busse, D. K., et al. (2009). Fault lines of user experience: the intersection of business and design. In *Proceedings of the 27th international conference extended abstracts on Human factors in computing systems*.

Collis, J. C., Soltysiak, S. J., Ndumu, D. T., & Azarmi, N. (1998). Living with Agents. *BT Technology Journal, 18*(1), 66–67. doi:10.1023/A:1026517703260

Crabtree, I. B., Soltysiak, S. J., & Thint, M. (1998). Adaptive Personal Agents. *Personal Technologies Journal, 2*(3), 141-151.

Cronin, B. (1992). *Information management: from strategies to action* 2. London: Aslib

Engineering Journal, 14(5), 211-218.

Gordon, K. (2007). *Principles of data management: facilitating information sharing*. Swindon, UK: British Computer Society.

Iida, I., Fujino, N., Nishigaya, T., & Iwao, T. (1998). Multi-agent Platform for Seamless

Iida, I., Fujino, N., Nishigaya, T., & Iwao, T. (1999). Multi-agent Platform for Seamless Personal Communications. *Telecom 99.*

Iwao, T., Okada, M., Takada, Y., & Amamiya, M. (1998). Flexible Multi-Agent Collaboration using Pattern Directed Message Collaboration of Field Reactor Model. In *Proc. of the Second Pacific Rim International Workshop on Multi-Agents, PRIMA'99*, (LNAI 1733, pp. 1-15).

Jain, A. K., Aparico, M. IV, & Singh, M. P. (1999). Agents for process coherence in Virtual Enterprises. *Communications of the ACM, 3*, 62–69. doi:10.1145/295685.295702

Johnson McManus, D., et al. *Business Value of Knowledge Management: Return on Investment of Knowledge Retention Projects*. Retrieved May 27th 2009 from http://www.knowledgeharvesting.org/documents/business%20Value%20of%20Knowledge%20Management.pdf

Liu, S. & Svenonius, E. (1991). dors: ddc online retrieval system. *lib res tech serv. 35*, 359-75.

Marchand, D. A. (1998). Information Management in Public Organizations: Defining a new resource management function. *The Bureaucrat, 7*, (1978), 4-10.

Maynard, B., & White, A. (2005). *Enterprise information management requires ERP*. Gartner report. Stamford, CT: Gartner.

McGee, J. V., & Prusak, L. (1993). *Managing Information Strategically*. New York: John Wiley & Sons.

Mohri, T., & Takada, Y. (1998). Virtual Integration of Distributed Database by Multiple Agents. In *Proc. of the First International Conference, DS'98*, (LNAI Vol. 1532, pp. 413-414).

Personal Communications.*Telecom 99 Forum Interactive summit, Int.7, Oct.1999.*

Reddy, K., Kinyua, J., & Goddard, W. (2003). Deploying Mobile agents to solve the distributed buying problem. In R. Akerkar (ed) *Artificial intelligence and its applications.*

Robertson, J. (2005). 10 principles of effective information management. *KM column*, November 1.

Rowley, J. & Farrow, J. (2000). *Organizing knowledge: an introduction to managing access to information.* Standards Institution.

Section 3
Information Acquisition and Processing

Chapter 6
Information Acquisition and Presentation

ABSTRACT

Acquisition of information is the first step in the journey of information along the supply chain. The usage of internet has made it possible to get the information on the fly from a variety of sources at different physical locations which otherwise is impossible. This chapter provides the technology behind the acquisition of information and the usage of signal processing algorithms for the same. Finally, the acquired information is to be rendered to the customer in the best possible form. The different data rendering methods are outlined here.

INTRODUCTION

In the previous chapter, the different steps involved in the management of the information are explained. The lifecycle of the information management starts with the data acquisition. Here, the different steps and techniques involved in the acquisition of the data in the supply chain are discussed.

Data acquisition is the process of meaningful gathering of data from different data sources to be consumed by different players of the supply chain. The raw data available in various forms are acquired and rendered in machine readable form with the help of transducers. The transducer output required translations before being read (John D. Lenk, 1997). This chapter explains the involvement of signal processing activities in the software that drives the input and the output devices.

Visualization of the data demands the appropriate tools for rendering the data appealing and meaningful for the customers. It should provide interactivity with the database as well as control the acquisition of the required data. Under or over acquisition of the data will not be useful for decision making. It will

DOI: 10.4018/978-1-60566-888-8.ch006

Figure 1. Hierarchical representations of data

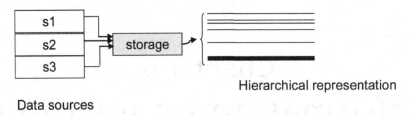

Data sources

Hierarchical representation

have cost implications for acquisition and subsequent handling. The different tools and techniques for the data visualization are provided in John R. Cowell, 1997, Richard Cravens, 1996, Jerry Joyce and Marianne Moon, 1997).

The optimal acquisition of data is coupled with the way it gets processed, stored, communicated and rendered apart from the complexity of the decision process) based on the data) and the market value. Thus, and information value (M. Harrison, 2003) associated with the data is to be considered during the acquisition. However acquisition is not always feasible due to the distributed nature (Pradeep K. Sinha, 1996) of the data sources and the complexity of synchronization among these sources.

In practice, information is acquired from the distributed information sources that are heterogeneous and autonomous. In this chapter the example of RFID is taken to discuss about the issue with the data acquisition. It is expected to provide useful information on RFID and the transducer design, issues and solution in the usage with supply chain etc.

Business Intelligence (BI) is the paradigm used with the distinct components of the distributed and global organizations connected through information supply chain. It is required to provide vital information on business trends required for decision making and to carryout the transactions of the organization. Data warehouses and Data marts are required to support the BI. The data in these storage systems are populated through the ETL (extract, transform, and load) process.

Acquisition of the required data is the first step in the business intelligence process. One technique for the data acquisition is the capture the bulk data and updates the databases periodically. However the enormous transactions in the present organizations can not afford to capture the complete data. Only the incremental changes in the data need to be captured and updated in the database accordingly. The acquired data is organized in to multiple levels of hierarchy as shown in the figure 1. Before storage, the data would be sieved in to multiple levels of hierarchy as shown in figure 2.

BACKGROUND

Data acquisition is the automatic collection of a large volume of raw data and the conversion (Martin S. Roden, 1995) of the same in to useful information. Data acquisition basically involves mustering data from various sources (Barlevy, G., and P. Veronesi, 2000) and converting the raw data in to bits and bytes for storage. On the output side, the rendering operation outputs the information in to a form the user can understand. It makes use of the appropriate input and output devices along with the tools supported by the protocols and software.

In a database management system (DBMS) being used today, event triggers are generated and concatenated to the incremental changes of the captured data and placed in a queue. The queue is also reflected

Figure 2. Data sieve and storage

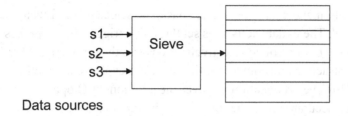

Data sources

Hierarchical representation

in the log that provides the data capture history. Depending up on the network traffic, storage on a third party machine, data acquired from the network involves data compression as well as encoding. It also useful for the ingest of a large volume of data.

Mirroring and synchronization of the stored data is done in order to maintain a single consistent view of the data across the supply chain. In addition, the load on a single database gets shared. In addition, it provides sufficient redundancies to recover from a possible disaster such as data crash, earthquake etc calamities. Mirroring can simultaneously happen over more than one database either in parallel or sequentially from one machine to the other like a systolic pulse. In the first technique, the update happens simultaneously at the cost of increased power and resources. In the second method, there is a less burden on the resources that get shared. However, it leads to data inconsistencies. To implement the parallel updates, the data delivery methods such as uni/multi/splitting/caching are used.

Information acquisition supports several mechanisms:

- **Passive acquisition:** Information is pumped in to the system although it does not explicitly ask for it. The acquisition happens whether the system likes it or not. However, the data is not rejected right at the source. E.g. listening to the radio or watching a random television programs.
- **Passive search:** Here, search for one kind of object ultimately lead to the acquisition of some other information that is interesting for the user.
- **Active search:** Here the user goes behind the required information until it is retrieved. E.g., browsing.
- **Ongoing search:** It is an iterative search for the information required to update the database. It works only on top of an existing database where the old version of the information is already available.

After the data acquisition, timing timestamps are added to the data to maintain the history.

Data fusion can happen over the cleaned data without which the uncertainties in the data propagate down the line. The data from different sources may be organized in the form of databases, flat files, etc. Several operations are performed over this data, including queries of various kinds such as statistical, relational etc. They also support keyword matches. Quite often, they provide the data for some utility that works on this data and provides the result as the response for the user query. Hence, the data from the sources need to be procured effectively.

Data Replication

In the first step of data replication, the data to be trapped has to be selected and frozen. Next, as the data update happens, it gets trapped. The update activity is set through a trigger. In the process of data replication, the trapping of data may be controlled selectively. It ensures the replication of only the relevant data. In general, the process, structure and content for the data to be captured are well defined and documented for subsequent use. However, replication involves the additional I/O operations due to trapping. The captured data may not be accurate down the line due to the rapid changes in the source data.

Data Cleansing

Data Acquisition technology (Tarik Ozkul, Marcel Dekker, 1996) looks in to the process and issues relate to the creation of a single data base from across several data source systems. Data from multiple systems is to be altered and subjected to transformations before taking a single consistent form (Sanjay Gupta and J.P. Gupta, 1995). This process is known as data cleansing. It maintains uniformity in the data from multiple systems. More details on the data cleansing are provided in a separate chapter of this book.

Data Acquisition and Rendering from Mobile Source

If the source of the data is mobile, collecting data will be a bit involved. The acquisition devices are to be portable and hands free. They make use of the existing technologies such as bar code scanning, RFID (Walmart, 2005) and voice recognition for providing quality data. They provide the real-time and accurate data from the operation site and get rid of retyping of the stored data acquired through other means. It reduces transcription errors.

Case Study: RFID

The example of data capture and organization with RFID technology is provided here. It is a matured technique to identify the data source and capture the data automatically helping the business process in tracking (D. Chon, et al, 2004) . However, the captured is time dependent and dynamically changes, making the RFID data management systems to have tough time in handling the queries on tracking and monitoring. So, the technique is useful when data is generated at a limited rate. In a supply chain where the commodity physically moves, it is useful to keep track of the same and provide the up to date information. Any secondary data depending up on the input from RFID should be crisp to get updated and reflect the changes to the users of the data. Good introduction to RFID is available in (Jennifer Maselli, 2004)

Being automated, data collection process from the RFIDs is well suited for the supply chain management. Apart from speeding up the process, the automation helps in product tracking, secure transfer of the products down the supply chain and reduction in the cost. Time stamps are associated with the acquired data. The data may be collected periodically at regular intervals or based on some event. Applications can directly use this data through appropriate data models. For example, the data generated from a trigger can indicate a change in the business process as a result of the change in the location. The automation translates these observations in to the inferences. Figure 3 shows data acquisition with the RFID. Although automation has been achieved over the supply chain, the data collected from the

Figure 3. Data acquisition with RFID

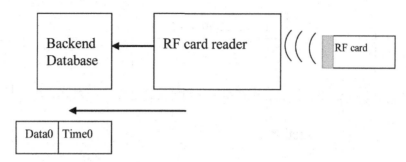

RFID is prone for errors. It comprises of the duplicates data and missing data, calling for a cleansing process before use.

The generated by the RFID is often large calling for a scalable mechanism for the storage. The updates or differential data is to be added on top of the existing data that demands very less data transactions. The RFID data is to be smoothly integrated by the applications. For this to happen, an RFID data has to be in the standard format, resulting in minimum integration cost.

Case Study: User Interface

The user interface provides the mean for communication between the end user and the computing system (F. Halsall, 1996). The interfaces are largely dictated by the type of the communication used.

UI Design

Powerful, yet simple user interfaces are required to support for rendering of the information to the end user. It is as important and complex as the acquisition of the data at the other end of the information supply chain. In some applications and design, the two ends meet. I.e. the user interface controls the data acquisition by setting the right parameters for the data format, interfaces etc. There will be similar interfaces between the modules and functionalities down the line although they do not interact with the end used directly.

Backbone of the information management system is the rendering of the information and support interactivity. The database and the wrapper software are required to handle a two way communication.

A lot of modeling and research has been done for arriving at the optimal user interfaces appealing for the end user. Most of the models consider the end user performance time and the memory transactions. Human eyes are more sensitive to brightness variation to the color variations. The colors used in the user interface are to be pleasant to the eyes. Usage of the same colors would always render the same meaning and the impact. Color may be used to convey the information effectively. For the user who is watching the colors, the magnitude or severity of the event being depicted may be indicated through the degree of change in the color.

The presence and style of the menus, buttons and the icons (Laura Arlov, 1997) have a profound effect on the user. The user interface design and the software used for supply chain management need to consider the activities along the lifecycle of the information management, including the data acquisition, storage, retrieval and management.

Figure 4. Rate controlled data acquisition

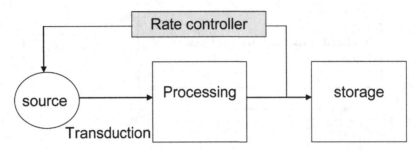

UI for Web Applications

The web based applications support hyperlink and require multiple screens. It should be easy for the user to navigate within and across the screens without a break in the thought process. The User interface for the web based applications is developed using the hypertext markup language (HTML).

The software in the web pages also makes use of PHP to provide the interactivity. It is a scripting language for web interfaces, running on the server side. The PHP code or module can reside in a HTML page. During every load of the page, the PHP code is executed through a PHP processor and communicates with the web server. The server interprets the code and provides the required output through the browser.

The response time of a HTTP client is arbitrarily large when the server is to support a heavy traffic. The stateless architecture of HTTP makes it less sensitive for triggers and result in reduced interactivity. The issue is resolved by using a different GUI client when heavy loads, heavy traffic involving user interactivity are to be supported For example, during in the applications like uploading of a large volume of data, interactive entry of the data etc. Portability of the client GUI across the different platforms (Ken Arnold and James Gosling, 1997, Jesse Liberty, 1997) is challenging.

Acquisition Rate Control

In a sophisticated environment the rate of data acquisition may be controlled by an intelligent element. Adaptive learning may be used for controlling the data acquisition rate in an agent. When the agent implements a 'Markovian' algorithm, the best sequence of traverse of the sources needs to be computed in such a way that the rate of the information acquisition would be maximum. The acquisition rate is coupled to the queries. In a network environment, if the acquisition happens through the network rather than through the transducers directly, the rate of acquisition may be coupled to the service quality, network security etc. A controller is required to assure the data rate and pre fetch the extrapolated data based on the queries.

Contrary to the convention of fast acquisition of the information, often slow or gradual acquisition is suggested for multi layered network. Here the multi-layered networks slowly obtain the requisite information in the course of learning. It allows the network to discover the different features corresponding to the different levels of information. Such a network works as a good classifier. The rate of acquisition of information can be made gradual by providing a deeper historical data as the feedback from the output to the input. Figure 4 shows the usage of a controller to control the rate of data acquisition.

With the huge data coming in, buffer manager has an important role in the data acquisition. A neural network may be used for buffer management.

ISSUES AND SOLUTIONS

Data Fusion

Data arrival at multiple rates is a major problem in the acquisition system calling for multi rate sampling. The problem gets complicated when several such data have to be fused. Usage of time stamps helps in asynchronous fusion. In this case real time data will not be available. Still, the appropriate data will undergo fusion with the help of time stamps.

In case synchronous data transfers are required for data fusion, highly stringent constraints are to be imposed on the service quality of the data such as delay and jitter. Information propagation with these constraints has been addressed in the chapter Information Transmission with quality of service.

Modern technologies have enabled the presence of a large number of sensors to acquire the data fast. It is challenging to merge their output. One of the issues is the optimal acquisition of the information.

A Bayesian estimator may be used for learning by passing the data acquired from the sources. It provides the ideal estimate for the probabilistic data and may be used in cleansing operation. The user feedback and the associated historical data provide adequate knowledge and the ability to learn fast. Figure 5 illustrates the steps involved in data fusion.

Mobility

The modern enterprises increasingly support the mobility of resources resulting in a couple of technical issues as well as the solutions. The mobile enterprises are designed around the paradigm that the resources are accessible and connected throughout. With mobility in-place, the people seeking the resources can work at leisure from any place without pressure and increase the productivity. It also enables the effective sharing of the resources. In supply chains involving mobile resources such as trucking industries, the data sources are bound to be mobile. Sophisticated signal processing algorithms are required for locating and acquiring the data from these data sources.

Adhoc Network

The information sources and the users form an adhoc network making use of a combination of fixed and mobile infrastructure. Bandwidth in such a network is critical as the RF power is involved. Here the

Figure 5. Information fusion.

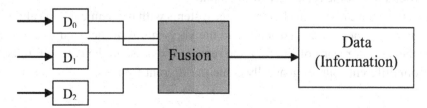

control of buffer significantly influences the effect of data packet or cell loss. A simple Artificial Neural Network (ANN) can be used for resource allocation.

The entire network, being adhoc, gets reconfigured probabilistically. Also, Bayesian learning scheme may be adopted to maximize the mutual information through differential feedback. It provides a way to replace the piecewise learning with global learning. The advantage with such a network is that the QoS is fused with the data acquisition process assuring the data quality down the line. In addition, self organization of the adhoc network requires a kind of past experience that is provided as the feedback input for the neural network based on the user experience.

In future, satellite links may be used to uplink the data. The telecom companies would provide switching service between the satellite or microwave links and the enterprise network.

The other issues with the adhoc network are synchronization and fading. Synchronization of the information transmitter and the receiver is a problem even in a fixed infrastructure network. It is more predominant in a mobile network

The increased mobility in such a network results in frequent handoffs and poses synchronization problems. Precise timing signals are required to assure uninterruptible handover. For the end-user, problems in synchronization lead to low voice & video quality, poor call set-up and drop in the calls. For data services it results in failed data downloads, jerky video, skipped lines in faxes, problems in the utility of software services and loss of location-based services.

Based on the received statistics, the packet loss rates are predicted. This predicted information is used as a feedback to the source. The sources then reduce the transmission rates or signal out busy mode or reduce the activities as applicable. The prediction makes it possible to adjust the transmission rates well in advance and fully utilize the underlying network. The mismatch in synchronization will be reflected as the variation in the prediction step. Hence its impact on the quality of service may be limited by adjusting the prediction step. The prediction can be done with the help of a neural network.

Quality of the Data

The quality of data acquired from the different sources is largely subjective. To make the system to accept this data, majority voting technique may be used with the thresholds set appropriately.

Too much of bad quality data is more dangerous than the lack of data. The acquisition of bad data has to be stalled, which otherwise leads to wastage in storage space, network bandwidth etc. The reliability of the data may be tested quantitatively using an intelligent element. The element, typically a program, would generate different outputs based on the received data. The programs would be as though they are used on the real data. Alternative to the program would be the artificial neural network that would generate appropriate output pattern corresponding to the input pattern. This would provide some flexibility and tolerance in addition to the adaptability to the input out patterns.

The degree of matching between the actual and the expected outputs represent the degree of reliability. The usage of neural network would be attractive especially when the input is noisy and other means find it difficult to test the reliability of the input.

The data acquired from the systems being in use, systems with mechanical parts and vibrating while acquiring the data are vulnerable for errors due to the very nature of the acquisition. It is required to compensate for the data by means of filtering and remove the noise in the data before being used. The data acquired from different sources generally come in different formats.

Power Consumption

Reduction in the consumption of power during the data acquisition is challenging. It is required to be implemented in all sensor networks, specifically in the RF and mobile sensors. The wireless sensors require effective power management as they are generally self powered and deployed away from the power source. It consumes more power for data transmissions than for the computations. This calls for the transfer of the processed data or the results or the compressed data in the place of the captured data. This reduces the transfer of the junk data, a part of which is likely to be discarded subsequently. I.e. more computations are getting shifted to the nodes away from the centralized server.

Further, the optimal decision on processing or transmission may be made on the fly with the help of an intelligent agent based on the amount of computation, transmission power, required service quality, probability of retransmission etc. Retransmission is the biggest problem in these scenarios.

FUTURE TRENDS

Differential Data Capture

The data generated from the sources of information are increasing day by day. To cater for these huge volumes, only incremental or changed data need to be captured and updated in the databases. In order to prevent the overwrite in the data, time stamps may be used along with the data, either in the data stream or as a part of the metadata describing the data stream. The incremental changes in the data are to be updated down the line. Tools and software are available to capture and update only the changes in the data. In case it is not possible to get the time stamps, the data is placed in a first in first out message queue and processed in the same order.

In order to minimize the data transaction and loading of the resources, the Change Data Capture (CDC) is often used for the data integration in the place of the actual data. It comprises of the identification, capture and delivery of the changes happening for the data. The changes taking place in the data source are identified, captured and informed to the applications down the line through data capture agents. These agents are typically implemented as application specific, strongly tied to handle a particular application such as monitoring the stock prices. It is also possible to have generic agents to cater for multiple applications. The agents enter in to the "stock market", observe the price fluctuations, use the triggers and collect the data changes to transfer the same to the intended application.

The array of differential data captured would form different levels of abstraction of the information. Each level of the hierarchy may be thought of as generated by adding incremental information to the previous level. This factor may be considered while deciding the value of the incremental information. In the crude forms, this array of abstract information may be thought of as one of the techniques of the representation of information in various scales of resolution.

For a system, if a new source of information is added and feedback information from the destination to the source is provided, the impact of adding this new source would be uniform throughout. This factor would be useful while determining the commercial implications and advantages of procuring a new data source.

In some applications, it is required to "capture" the data from the secondary sources such as the storage systems or data marts. The data is retrieved with the help of search engines. The chain may continue. Alternatively, a hyperlink to the database or mart may be mentioned if no further processing on the data is required.

Distributed Data Sources

Information is often required to be acquired from distributed sources that are physically located at disjoint locations rather than from a single centralized location. This calls for the efficient algorithms to collect the lowest amount of data from the distributed sources for efficient decision making. If there is a policy or security restriction to acquire the data from the sources, the algorithms have to aid the decision making based on the statistical inference, available summaries and past experience. For example, the increment in the profit of an organization over the previous quarter may be available as the indicator rather than the actual profit. The system is required to retain the historical data and learn through the inferences from the data. A Bayesian network known to learn from the inferences over a small data set can be used here.

The learner interacts with the data repository through queries. If the repository has distributed components, the query is to be split in to sub queries and fired over the individual databases. It calls for a rule based optimization to split the queries appropriately and finally merge the results of the query from different sources. There will be a single answer at the end and the user would be transparent to these activities. A Bayesian network may be used for merging the results from the queries. The rate of data acquisition from these different data sources is determined by the Service quality agreed by the agent that consolidates the query outputs. Depending on the different classes of services, the data acquisition rates from these sources would be determined by the different depth of feedback from the agent.

Web Based Data Acquisition

In order to enable data acquisition from the distributed sources, Network based data acquisition system will be useful in the futuristic data acquisition systems. The database, the data source, the data acquisition client, the data acquisition server over which the management software is running and the graphical user interface are all connected to the network. Programming languages supporting web based applications bind these different players.

Object Oriented Database

A typical program with object oriented design is meant to run over a stand alone machine making use of its processing power and the memory. However, web based data processing required continuous exchange of objects and data over the network. To make it possible, object oriented database management (ODBMS) technology has been used. The technology spans object oriented programming, networking and database management. It provides the option of saving objects in to the secondary memory of the other networked device. Today, language support exists to exchange the code as well as the data over the network. Ie objects residing on different machines can seamlessly exchange data as well as messages over the network.

Data Mirroring

Mirroring of the captured data can happen synchronously or asynchronously.

- **Synchronous mirroring system:** In a synchronous mirroring system, the captured data is written in to the local storage device as well as the remote storage device simultaneously. The write operation is taken to be completed only after both the devices send the acknowledgement for the completion. It is time consuming and keeps some of the devices waiting. If the data is faulty, both the systems save the faulty data. Recovery of the data would be time consuming. These issues are addressed in asynchronous mirroring.
- **Asynchronous mirroring system:** Here the transfer of data on to a remote storage device happens through a local storage device.

In practice, a combination of both of them may be implemented. Rollback mechanism is used for providing fault tolerance. Here, the snapshot of the data states up to a known number of cycles or states would be retained in a separate memory. If a corruption in the data is noticed, it rolls backs to a state when the data was correct and the corrupt data would be replaced by the correct data. Asynchronous mirroring with a rollback of sufficient depth is becoming increasingly popular. The rollback depth may be parameterized and selected by the user. Mirroring should also support the interoperability of the data across multiple devices and vendors.

Code Reader

In the coming days the products with RFID would be widely used in the agricultural products (J. Bohn, 2006); however with one major difference. DNA patters would be used in the place of bar codes and RF power. For example, a pattern reader just has to get a "cell" from an apple to ascertain if it is from Wellington (New Zealand) or Washington. In addition it can detect piracies, duplication and infringements.

In the automobile industry, a centralized onboard management system can handle the opening of the doors, fuel injection, start of the engine etc only when triggered by a secure start code transmitted over the sensors of the key. This start code may be programmable. It substantially reduces the theft of the vehicles.

Tollbooths can read the barcodes fitted on the vehicles automatically when they cross the predetermined points and send the bill to the vehicle owners. It enables a seamless traffic flow and overcomes the long stranded time near the tool gates. It also minimizes the human interventions. The same concept is getting extended to parking lots.

Barcodes are on the way to replace the postal stamps of today. With this, it would be possible to trace the whereabouts of the envelopes bearing the stamps. It helps in sorting and routing. It substantially reduces the required workforce and at the same time makes the process fast. The same concept is being extended for sorting baggage in the airports.

The RF cards and barcodes would replace the expensive telemetric equipments especially in the study of animal behavior in the wild. It minimizes the inconvenience to the animals and provides details as the animal passes near the pre installed data collecting points.

CONCLUSION

In this chapter,

- The data acquisition techniques are explored.
- The data rendering techniques for the end user are discussed.

Optimal acquisition of information has become a challenge with high volume of data from multiple sources is flowing in to the organization. Over information often results in the same consequences of the wrong or insufficient information. The right time information would be preferred in the industries rather than the real time information. This chapter advocates the usage of structured data organization to address the issues in data acquisition and presentation.

QUESTIONS

1. What are the different ways of acquiring the digital data?
2. What is the need of mirroring the data?
3. What are the different ways of mirroring the data?
4. How does the RFID help in the supply chain management?
5. How does the design of user interface influence the web based supply chain management?

REFERENCES

Arlov, L. (1997). *GUI Design for Dummies.* Boston: IDG Books.

Arnold, K., & Gosling, J. (1997). *The Java Programming Language.* Reading, MA: Addison-Wesley.

Barlevy, G., & Veronesi, P. (2000). Information acquisition in Financial Markets. *The Review of Economic Studies, 67*, 79–90. doi:10.1111/1467-937X.00122

Chon, D., et al. (2004). *Using RFID for Accurate Positioning.* International Symposium On GNSS, Sydney, Australia, December 6-8, 2004.

Cowell, J. R. (1997). *Essential Visual Basic 5.0 Fast.* Berlin: Springer Verlag.

Cravens, R. (1996). *The Essential Windows NT Book.* Roseville, CA: Prima Publishing.

Fieldbus Foundation. (1996). *Technical Overview: Foundation Fieldbus.* Coulouris, G., Dollimore, J. & Kindberg T. (1994). *Distributed SystemsÑConcepts and Design,* (2nd Ed.). Reading MA: Addison-Wesley.

Gupta, S., & Gupta, J. P. (1995). *PC Interfacing for Data Acquisition and Process Control.* ISA.

Halsall, F. (1996). *Data Communications, Computer Networks and Open Systems* (4th Ed.). Reading, MA: Addison-Wesley.

Harrison, M. (2003). *EPC Information Service - Data Model and Queries*. Technical report, Auto-ID Center.

ISA. (1995). *Dictionary of Measurement and Control: Guidelines for Quality, Safety, and Productivity*, (3rd Ed). Bohn, J. (2006), *Prototypical Implementation of Location-Aware Services Based on Super-Distributed RFID Tags*, 9th International Conference on Architecture of Computing Syst.–System Aspects in Organic Computing (ARCS 2006), March 2006

Joyce, J., & Moon, M. (1997). *Microsoft Windows NT Workstation 4.0: At a Glance*. Redmond, WA: Microsoft Press.

Lekas, S. (1997). *Signal Conditioning & PC-Based Data Acquisition Handbook: A Reference on Analog & Digital Signal Conditioning for PC-Based Data Acquisition*. Cleveland, OH: IOTech, Inc.

Lenk, J. D. (1997). *Simplified Design of Data Converter.* Oxford, UK: Butterworth-Heinemann.

Liberty, J. (1997). *Teach Yourself C++ in 21 Days*. Toronto, Canada: Sams Publishing.

Maselli, J. (2004). Startup seeks organic RFID chip. *RFID Journal*, March 29.

Omega Press LLC (1997*)*. *Omega¨ Universal Guide to Data Acquisition and Computer Interface.*

Omega Press LLC (1997*)*. *Analog and Digital Communication Systems.*

Ozkul, T. & Dekker, M. (1996). *Data Acquisition and Process Control Using Personal Computers.*

Roden, M. S. (1995). *Analog and Digital Signal Processing,* Omega Press LLC (1997*)*. The Data Acquisition Systems Handbook. *New Horizons in Data Acquisition and Computer Interfaces.*

Walmart (2005). *Supplier Information: Radio Frequency Identification Usage*. Retrieved 2005, from http://www.walmartstores.com

Chapter 7
Information Cleansing and Processing

ABSTRACT

The data gathered from the sources are often noisy Poor quality of data results in business losses that keep increasing down the supply chain. The end customer finds it absolutely useless and misguiding. So, cleansing of data is to be performed immediately and automatically after the data acquisition. This chapter provides the different techniques for data cleansing and processing to achieve the same.

INTRODUCTION

In the previous chapter, the different techniques for the acquisition of the data from various sources are discussed. The data from these heterogeneous sources and from the different points in the supply chain require formatting before use. Here, the data cleansing and processing techniques over the acquired data are explained.

Information processing refers to transforming the raw data (L. Truong, T. Fahringer, Schahram Dustdar, 2005) in to a form useful for the end user. As the name suggests it is a process that spans everything happening over the information. Depending up on the application, information may be centralized, distributed, processed in sequence or in parallel. The raw data collected from the information source consists of both informative and fuzzy parts. Appropriate processing is required to bring out more information per unit data. In this chapter, information feedback technique is applied to identify the unstructured part of the data and maximize the information content of the same. The example of GRID computing is considered to explore the feedback based solutions. It is expected to be useful for the design of data marts providing tips for reducing the time overhead for data cleansing.

DOI: 10.4018/978-1-60566-888-8.ch007

Information processing enhances the data quality. The preprocessing carried out over the data includes removal of the noise, populating the missing data fields etc. The removal of noise requires accurate modeling of the noise. The missing data in the sampled set may be computed through interpolation or time series prediction. Regression technique is often used to find out the relation in the dataset.

In a modern organization, the information from various distributed sources has to be consolidated. Also, conversely, the data from a server is to be rendered to multiple users. All these transactions require high quality data, based on which important business decisions are taken. Corrupt data, in general, leads to inappropriate decisions.

The ETL model of data handling, which involves the extraction, transform and loading of the data, requires the clean Data at each step. In general, the acquired data will not be clean and directly usable (H. Gall, R. Klösch, and R. Mittermeir, 1996). It requires processing without which the junk data can propagate down the line and create more trouble later. In addition, the consumer of the data often requires the same in a totally different form, calling for the transformation on the data. Both these issues are addressed in this chapter. A good introduction to scientific data cleansing and transformation is available in (L. Singh, G. Nelson, J. Mann, A. Coakes, E. Krzyszczyk, and E. Herman, 2006).

As a first step of data cleansing, the data is profiled and rules for cleansing are built to automate the process. The automation makes the cleansing process fast and error free. The clean data is taken by the information supply chain for further processing. The cleansed and processed data should be acceptable for all elements over the supply chain.

In a small organization, data processing and management is not an issue. However, with the increase in the business and with proliferation to multiple sites, the organizations find it difficult to process the data in spite of automation. The availability of high speed tools, hardware and displays has helped to address this issue.

The link between information processing and learning is very strong. In the process of learning the individuals get exposed to new information and attribute meaning for the same.

BACKGROUND

Data processing involves data cleaning (Maletic, J., & Marcus A., 2000) as well as restructuring carried out using transformations. The Information processing involves removal of redundancies from the data. It comprises of the data fusion and integration. Finally, the processed data would be stored as data mart or data warehouse.

It is wise to clean the data available at the source database before transferring the same to the data warehouse. It is required primarily because the defective data propagates upwards affecting all the decision making processes and ultimately leads to catastrophe. When it is not possible to correct the defective data before storage, a confidence interval or reliability is to be set for the data quality so as to indicate it is not 100% perfect. The losses include spoiled reputation apart from the rework and slippage. It corrupts even the correct data and renders it useless which otherwise has no problem.

Business intelligence applications require the clean data in large volumes for analysis and decision making through OLAP, data mining etc. The different players along the supply chain look for this data. The data warehouse provides the perfect solution. Hence, the data warehouse has to maintain clean data. The raw data acquired from multiple sources has to undergo this process before the ETL process begins.

Figure 1. Compression before cleansing

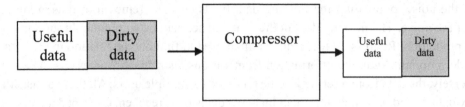

Rule Based Cleansing

Any processing on the information includes profiling of the data and transformation over the same. The raw data will turn in to useful information only when it is processed in to a form acceptable for the end user. The data acquired from the sensors, documents from the web or otherwise would be compressed if required to be stored in larger volumes. Different standards are available for compressing the information. Data compression is a complex process involving advanced signal processing. It is required to share the resources such as bandwidth and memory effectively. In general, compression of the data after cleansing would be meaningful. The figures 1 and 2 illustrate the process.

Data Quality

A high quality data is required for the success of the business. The bad or poor quality data propagates and results in errors and inaccuracies down the line. This data, often shared with the customers, results in the reduced credibility for the organization. It affects the business and brand values of all the products from the organization, including the good ones. Considering all these factors, cost of quality is taken as zero; meaning any investment for enhancing the data quality does not go as a waste.

Statistics shows about 20% of the data in a typical organization suffers with inadequate quality. The poor quality originates due to minor issues such as the typos, missing entries, incompatible formats etc often arising due to non adherence to common standards. The pronounced effect of bad quality in the data is the interoperability issue. The data cleansing is to address all these issues by removing the errors and inconsistencies. High quality data is to be self contained, meaningful, an ambiguous, accurate and come from an authentic source.

Data Audit

Usually, the acquired from the source contains some junk or useless data as seen by its user or application. This data has to be discarded before use, which otherwise results in propagation of the errors down

Figure 2. Compression after cleansing

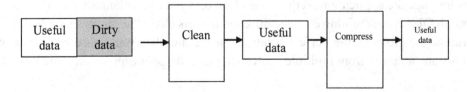

the line (Bansal, N., Chawla, S., & Gupta, A., 2000). To prevent this, the identification and categorization of the errors is required. This is called data audit. The audit is done based on the architecture of the legacy system containing different degrees of the erroneous data. Mathematical models are used for the prediction of the impact for different kinds of the test cases composed of different degrees of the junk data. The data audit provides information on the error types, their severity etc. based on the severity, appropriate cleansing techniques are invoked. Some of the non critical errors may be ignored without impacting the functionality and the business. The erroneous data is to be extracted out and verified before cleansing.

Automated Data Cleansing

This technique is used over large data with multiple error types. Depending up on the error type, most of the errors would get corrected. However human intervention is required to correct the leftover errors. The cleansing happens as a batch process. The cleansing programs correct most of the logical errors in the data structure. In order to make sure that the automatic data cleansing process has been accomplished successfully and the data has not been corrupted during the batch processing, the same operation is run over the data again. Adequate care taken to prevent the production system getting the incorrect changes made to the data accidentally. This is because the same data cleansing software will be running over different data sources and the cleaned data will be stored in the common memory. Hence the memory needs to be staggered appropriately.

Generally, automated cleansing process is used over large data sets which otherwise is very difficult to handle manually. In some cases, (the same set of) complex chains of rules are to be applied for cleansing of the data. Programs work often faster, better and cheaper than the human beings to handle them. However, the accuracy and reliability of either of the methods is subjective. Moreover, the programs used for cleansing are portable, can be executed in parallel and reusable. It is not one time job and required to run multiple times, as long as the legacy system that needs the data in the prescribed format exists. Often it calls for transformations over the raw data before it is accepted.

Data Analysis

The raw data collected in the organization may not make sense as it is. To convert it in to useful information or knowledge, aggregation, processing and fusion of the data is required.

Analysis of the data often involves finding the mathematical relation with in the data or between the data and a set of parameters. Vendor supplied software often does it, working together with the data acquisition software. Generally the same vendor supports both the software.

There are two mechanisms for the data analysis:

1. **Concurrent processing**: Here, the data analysis can happen over the real time data as it is being streamed.
2. **Post processing:** Here the analysis takes place over the stored data.

For data analysis and rendering the results of the analysis, the analyzed data needs to be plotted in time domain (as it is) or along the transformation domain. Handling of these results or waveforms over the screen such as drag, drop or zoom is supported by the rendering software.

Figure 3. Transformations on a time domain signal

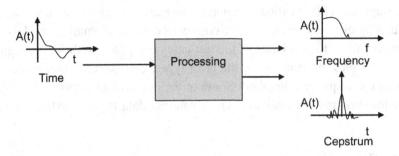

The random noise associated with the data may be eliminated or minimized by averaging the data (Weiss, G.M. and Hirsh, H, 1998).

The data sampled is often stored in the compressed form to minimize the storage space over the disk, tape etc. Often, data storage happens based on some event. Eg, when the value of the sampled data is more then or less than a pre specified value, it is only then the value will be stored.

In an organization, the rate of usage of information is relatively slow compared to the rate at which it is created or processed. Hence, the organization looks for new avenues to consume the data and translate it in to knowledge. The conversion of the raw data to in to knowledge happens as a supply chain in the pipeline. The sequential processing of the information makes it unusable for most of the time and results in resource contention when put in to use. These extremes need to be addressed with the availability of clean and ready to use data at any point of time shortening the sequential process.

Data Manipulation

The data manipulation requires various mathematical and graphical tools. The tools support a lot of mathematical, statistical, trigonometric and logical functions. They operate over a data set or on a single data point. The data may be projected in graphical or tabular format.

Curve Fitting: Curve fitting is extensively used for generating the calibration curves of the devices, process control optimization etc. The curves are first plotted for the data provides and based on the shape, appropriate mathematical expressions are derived. Once curve fitting is done, appropriate models may be selected to fit with.

Peak Fitting: It refers to the identification and separation of the peaks in the data. It is quite challenging and calls for the powerful techniques of non linear signal processing. The input data needs to be as clean as possible with the noise removed through the de-convolution techniques. The noise filters such as Weiner filter are often used to maximize the Signal to noise ratio in the region of interest of the spectrum. The spectral peaks are characterized by amplitude, central frequency, width of the peak and the area. These factors are made use for the resolution of the peaks. Statistical parameters such as moments are used to characterize the peaks.

In some complex applications, up to 100 peaks need to be separated. Although they overlap in the spectral domain, with some pre processing or post processing, it is possible to resolve them. The commonly used transformations on a time domain signal such as the magnitude spectrum (Absolute vale of Fourier transform) and complex cepstrum are shown in figure 3.

Figure 4. Rate Based Data Transfer

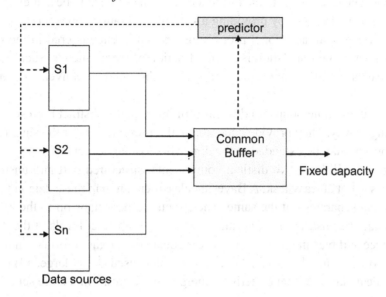

Data analysis software is extensively used for statistical analysis of the data, including the time series prediction, variance estimation, bias estimation, data fusion etc.

Heterogeneous Sources

The major problem in Enterprise information integration is handling the data from multiple sources each rendering the data independently. The transformation would be complicated further if they are heterogeneous sources of data.

The data acquired from different data sources generally come in different formats that call for cleaning before use. The common data format across the enterprise may be used.

The data integration from multiple sources is often challenging. A learning algorithm may be effectively used for data fusion. The weighted sum of a set of information or data provides the useful data with reduced entropy and enhanced information

When multiple sources are transferring data on to the same or common buffer, there will be a contention for the resources. Moreover, there are scenarios where the data from the same resource shall not be predominant and the relative ratio has to be maintained. The data from a nonlinear predictor such as artificial neural network can be used as an effective scheduler to control the data rates from the different sources. For better results, it makes use of a predicted feedback signal as shown in figure 4. More details are provided in the chapter on Information Transmission with quality of service

Hierarchical Representation

In the representation of data in to multiple levels of abstractions, when the data from the sources or different abstract levels need to be made closer to a reference, it is required to convolve the same with an abstraction function such as Gaussian or exponential pulse of arbitrary scale. The resulting data would be having a different abstract level closer to the reference data. The same may be achieved by providing a feedback with more historical data or by providing a kind of long range dependency to the data

Sampling rate conversion is an additional processing frequently encountered in the processing of audio/video and speech data. The translation is often a fraction or a non integer. Such translations are brought out with filter banks. Multirate signal processing algorithms may be conveniently used to implement the filter banks.

If the multiresolution in the time or spatial domain is of interest, the abstract representation of databases may be used straightaway. They provide a hierarchical representation for the signal similar to the wavelets. The same concept may be extended to the dimensions of any order.

The data from a source will have two distinct components- structured part and unstructured part. Separation of these parts is not an easy task. A Bayesian classifier can map these data in to the different abstract levels of data and separates out the same. The structured part maps on to the core part of the data without feedback and the unstructured part maps to the set of abstract levels of the data.

Estimation of variance and bias in the error or noise associated with the information or data is often challenging especially when the number of classifiers or estimators used is very large. A Bayesian estimator may be used as an ideal classifier that effectively merges the result from a large set of classifiers.

Case Study

Information Processing with GRID computing

Along the supply chain, due to the presence of a huge data, it is too complex to maintain and operate the information. The complexity increases exponentially with the addition of new players as they have to interact with the data from all the existing players as well as the historical data. To effectively handle the complexity, new technologies that are scalable in the same way are required. GRID computing is one such paradigm for information processing in large scale (Smith, Roger, 2005).

GRID computing provides a mechanism for information processing from across the different distributed data sources in the supply chain. The powerful resources are shared effectively by means of collaboration. The resources include processing power, data, software, storage etc. Hence, good network connectivity is required to enable the same. The collective availability of massive resources make it possible to realize the applications that demand large resources and impossible to be executed on stand alone systems. E.g. Simulation of explosions, weather data forecasting etc.

The Grid plays an important role in information processing. It is composed of tiny computing units capable of processing information and communicating among themselves. The components of a Grid include:

A. **The processing components.** It consists of the hardware unit up on which the grid-aware software as well as the Grid management software will be running. The hardware can be a PC, a dedicated embedded processor, server etc.
B. **The communion components.** It includes wired connectivity such as Ethernet wireless connectivity such as wifi that binds the members of the Grid.

The software running over the Grid, composed of Grid management and enterprise software, is to consider the Grid architecture and the resources such as memory, processing power, I/O bandwidth available over the Grid. The programs are to be optimal with reduced calls, minimum number of APIs etc to utilize the resources effectively.

Command Processing

Command processing is the backbone of GRID computing. In general, it is too complex due to a large size decision making. Hence, the GRID programs target at reduction in the number of decisions to be made. The program structure is to support the same.

The software has to be designed as a sequence of commands executed by the command processors as shown in figure 5. The resulting software executes and may create new commands executed by other command processors as a tree. A feedback is supplied to the originating command up on the execution of each command. The focus will be on creating the closed logic for a specific command. The feedback on the execution of the command in the feedback path and the dispatch of the command in the forward path resemble a feedback neural network. All the properties of such a model including the abstraction across hierarchies, long range dependencies etc are applicable here. The model may be used to dispatch commands optimally and share the resources effectively. The concept may be fused in to the GRID program. The GRID adaptively learns to dispatch the commands at the right time and for the right processor so that the queuing and contention would be minimized.

GRID Command is like a function comprising a list of command name and the argument. The command will be executed over the data indicated by the argument. Command feedback is also a list of name and argument pair. Example: The command can "xml" and the associated value or argument for this command can be a data fie over which it operates or it can be the entire "xml" package, which it can use for configuration.

The command processors get attached to the operating system threads during the run time and Depending up on the availability of the command processors and the number of threads being generated for the execution, there can be several command processors and thread pairs active at a time. Each command processor executes one thread at a time. A command processor can process one or more GRID commands. The constraints of operating system such as memory, number of active threads etc has to be considered in the parallelism. If the operating system does not support threads, a bulk of work or job would be dispatched to a command processor.

Figure 5. Command processor architecture

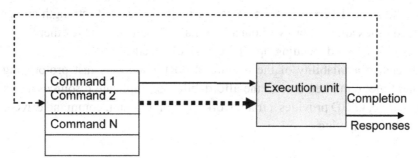

GRID Model

The grid resembles an adhoc network with multiple resources as well as the requests joining and leaving randomly in between. The Individual processing units can join or leave resulting in the GRID dynamically in real time. The GRIDS can also be dynamically connected or disconnected with other GRIDs in the real time by switching on or off the underlying network connectivity. The design has to consider the fact thet the local resources tot the organization has to be available on the priority basis even if the resources from the GRID are not accessible. In effect, the model proposes the distributed computing.

Another model that goes well with the activities in the GRID is the dynamic supply chain model. Here the demand for the resources as well as their availability changes dynamically with the entry or exit of the resources as well their users. Size of the supply chain increases or diminishes accordingly.

GRID Commands

First, the requirements of the information processing system are to be converted in to a set of commands and the associated data up on which they are expected to run. Some of the typical commands are getCustomerRecord, validateXML, formatOutput. Next, these commands are to be converted in to a program. The enterprise information processing system takes the responsibility of getting the program executed. The load balancing and performance of GRID requires the command processors to be scalable and loaded or unloaded dynamically. The GRID processors are often used by the information processing systems for co-processing, accomplishing a specific dispatched task. The command processors can communicate data and command among themselves. The commands may be intercepted, replicated, altered or re-routed.

GRID Activities

The different activities with GRID computing spans file transfers, configuration for connection, disconnection or broadcast etc. This is accomplished through various commands of operating system, GRID management and processing.

Benefits of GRID Computing

Grid computing provides a mechanism for effectively sharing the resources over the network and supports a kind of distributed computing. The idle time of the resources may be reduced by sharing the same with others who need the same. Every organization can virtually increase its strength and capabilities multifold and support complex applications without additional investment. On the other hand, it reduces the investment over the resources, depending up on the business needs.

Because of the extensive availability of the resources, GRID supports fast prototyping, reduced development cycle and time to market. Due to the affordability of duplicate resources and processing power for a roll back in time, GRID provides a framework for fault tolerant, command driven, self healing, real time and scalable computing.

ISSUES AND SOLUTIONS

Data Cleansing

Cleansing with XML

XML provides a layered approach for the cleansing (Peter Fankhauser and Thomas Klement, 2003) of data at various stages of life cycle of the information including cleansing, enrichment and combination of the data. It supports indexing and storage of bulk data and processing of an arbitrary schema less data. To start with, the acquired data is converted in to XML format and stored. This conversion is lossless. As the XML support is universally available and platform independent, this data can be later converted to any format and used by any platform. It reduces the development effort by avoiding the data transformations back and forth. Also, the maintenance of (raw) databases would be easy. Any change desired may be carried out at one place and one time over this data, that would be understood by diverse programs and platforms in the subsequent stages.

Representation of data in to multiple levels of abstraction may be mapped on to the XML hierarchical form and subsequent transformation. The model may be learnt to clean the running data in the data stream and push the noise in the data over the higher levels of abstraction. It supports the existing standards for XML processing in a scalable way and thus, provides a future-proof solution for the creation of complex data cleansing processes. Subsequent cleansing tasks like format conversions, detection and elimination of the duplicates or referential integrity checks may be supported by an intelligent element.

Data Processing

An organization generates huge volumes of data for processing (Kroenke, D. M. 2005). Conventional programming languages find it too complex to perform operations such as join, group, multiple scan and processing over this data. It requires a specific index structures to simplify. It calls for the development of new languages and the associated tool chain for modeling, development, validation and testing. The alternate approach is to process the data in to the required form before storing. This data is to be accepted by the underlying software or the platform. It requires the interoperability of the data, software and the hardware. The software accepting such a data need support real-time execution, scalability, fault-tolerance, platform independent, fault tolerant, easy to maintain and simple to create.

Example: Fast Fourier Transform (FFT)

Fast four transform is a mathematical marvel used to translate a time domain signal in to frequency domain with minimal computation and memory requirements (S. G. Johnson and M. Frigo, 2007). The signals that are closely spaced and indistinguishable in time domain get well resolved in the frequency domain. The transfer function of a system is computed by dividing the spectrum (including magnitude and phase) of the output signal from the spectrum of the input signal and then taking the inverse transform. Computation of accurate spectrum is however challenging. With exponential weights, a neural network may be used for online and crisp computation of the spectrum of the signal. The accuracy may be improved with the historical or previous data samples given due weightage. It reduces the window effect by providing a smooth transition for the samples beyond the window of the choice.

Example: Curve Fitting

Curve fitting is the extensively used mathematical operation that has sneaked in to several user applications. However, quite often, it is transparent to the end user. Depending up on the size of the dataset and the resolution of the display, rigorous computation involving interpolation and extrapolation are required. Interpolation of linear functions is easy compared to the polynomial functions. Least square error, cubic spline technique are often used for the polynomial approximation of the function. The variance and correlation of the approximated data obtained from the curve fitting with the actual data set provide a measure of the degree of accuracy of the technique (and the degree of the polynomial required to meet the pre specified accuracy). The degree of accuracy is governed by the nature of the application. In addition to providing the missing values, curve fitting can get rid of the storage required to keep long tabular columns. The data points may be generated in real time corresponding to dent resolutions of rendering.

If the data happens to be nonlinear and not possible to capture the data with a polynomial, regression (Richard A. Berk, 2004) technique or neural network may be used to learn the curve and start predicting the future values. It is significant especially in Finance time series prediction where the curves are highly nonlinear.

FUTURE TRENDS

Data Processing Framework

Programming Language

Since diverse activities such as dynamic memory allocation, handling recursions, data types (casting), index tables, lists, schemas, algorithm implementations, retrieval packetization, multitasking (Parallelism) etc are repeatedly performed over a large databases in an organization, it desirable to have a common language to support the same. The information processing language (IPL) provides these desirable features. The language has built in intelligence required to support machine learning and Artificial intelligence programs.

MPEG-21

MPEG-21 standard addresses the issue of information processing (Chris Poppe, Frederik De Keukelaere Saar De Zutter Rik Van de Walle, 2006). It provides a mechanism (like "classes" of object oriented programs) to bind the data and the code to process it that are being held separately. It is left to the implementation to run the code over the data and get the "processed" output.

CONCLUSION

In this chapter,

- The need and techniques for the data cleansing and processing are discussed.
- The mathematical tools required for the transformation and handling of the data are provided

Internet provides a rich source of information with data accumulated from across the world. However, this data often consists of virus/worms that can sneak in to the private data of the individuals and create enormous damage. The raw data needs to be cleaned and undergo a series of transformations before being used as useful information. Here the transformations based on the signal processing tools and techniques are introduced. The data organization techniques, that have been introduced in the first chapter are repeatedly made use for information processing activities.

QUESTIONS

1. How does the data gets cleansed at different stages in the information lifecycle?
2. What are the applications of GRID computing?
3. What are the steps to be taken to improve the quality of the data automatically?
4. What are the different mathematical tools used to process the data and depict the results?
5. How do the signal processing algorithms help in the cleansing of the acquired data?

REFERENCES

Bansal, N., Chawla, S., & Gupta, A. (2000). *Error correction in noisy datasets using graph mincuts*, Project Report.

Berk, R. A. (2004). *Regression Analysis: A Constructive Critique*. Newberry Park, CA: Sage Publications.

Gall, H., Klösch, R., & Mittermeir, R. (1996). Application patterns in re-engineering: identifying and using reusable concepts. In *5th International Conference on Information Processing and Management of Uncertainty in Knowledge-Based Systems (IPMU '96)*, (pp. 1099-106), Granada, Spain.

Johnson, S. G., & Frigo, M. (2007). A modified split-radix FFT with fewer arithmetic Operations. *IEEE Transactions on Signal Processing, 55*(1), 111–119. doi:10.1109/TSP.2006.882087

Kroenke, D. M. (2005). *Database Processing: Fundamentals, Design, and Implementation*. Upper Saddle River, NJ: Pearson Prentice Hall.

Poppe, C., De Keukelaere, F., De Zutter, S., & Van de Walle, R. (2006). *Advanced Multimedia Systems Using MPEG-21 Digital Item Processing*. Eighth IEEE International Symposium on Multimedia, (pp.785-786).

Singh, L., Nelson, G., Mann, J., Coakes, A., Krzyszczyk, E., & Herman, E. (2006), Data cleansing and transformation of observational scientific data. *Proceedings of the ACM SIGMOD Workshop on Information Quality in Information Systems (IQIS)*. Chicago, Illinois: ACM.

Smith, R. (2005). Grid Computing: A Brief Technology Analysis. *CTO Network Library.*

Truong, L., Fahringer, T., & Dustdar, S. (2005). *Dynamic Instrumentation*. Maletic, J., & Marcus, A., (2000). *Data cleansing: Beyond integrity analysis*. In proceedings of the Conference on Information Quality (IQ2000). Fankhauser, P. & Klement, T. (2003). XML for Data Warehousing Chances and Challenges. In *Data Warehousing and Knowledge Discovery* (LNCS).

Weiss, G. M., & Hirsh, H. (1998). The problem with noise and small disjuncts. In *Proc. of 15th International Conference on Machine Learning,* San Francisco, CA, (pp.574-578).

Chapter 8
Information Compression

ABSTRACT

If a large data transactions are to happen in the supply chain over the web, the resources would be strained and lead to choking of the network apart from the increased transfer costs. To use the available resources over the internet effectively, the data is often compressed before transfer. This chapter provides the different methods and levels of data compression. A separate section is devoted for multimedia data compression where a certain losses in the data is tolerable during compression due to the limitations of human perception.

INTRODUCTION

In the previous chapter, the data processing and cleansing techniques are explained. In spite of removal of junk and duplicate data during the cleansing, the large volumes of data originating over the supply chain requires a huge memory for storage and large bandwidth for the transfer. The consumption of these expensive resources may be reduced by exploiting the redundancies in the data. Here, the different techniques for the compression of the data are discussed.

Compression of information is important requirement to maintain the information systems. In this chapter, various scenarios and methods of information compression are examined. The techniques cover data from multimedia sources and the files. The techniques are expected to be useful for system design involving optimal design of the memory, data transactions, multimedia data compression, data retrieval and transportation etc. It is important to compress the data, because of the cost associated with the storage space and bandwidth. A compression or coding algorithm assigns codes of variable length to

DOI: 10.4018/978-1-60566-888-8.ch008

symbols, or groups of symbols depending up on the probability distribution of the data. Typical source compression algorithms are Huffman coding and Shannon-Fano coding. The relative frequency of occurrence of the symbols in the compressed data is linked to probability distribution of the data. I.e. more frequently found strings are assigned with shorter symbols and vice versa. The recent treatment of the topic is available at (David Salomon, 2002).

When the metadata alone is stored in the fast memory, it will be of little use as the major chunk of the actual data still has to be retrieved from the disk. Today, in addition to the disk space, the access time of data is becoming a bottleneck. When the files are stored in compressed form, it reduces the storage space as well as the band requited to transfer the same over the communication channel. However, decompression of the compressed files takes some time and adds to the latency. This is small compared to the time taken to transfer the uncompressed file. In practice, small files are stored in the main memory while the larger ones reside on the secondary storage such as tape and disk. If the files are stored in compressed form, more number of frequently used files can reside on the main memory reducing the latency significantly. A good treatment of the topic is found in (Peter Wayner, 1999) and (David Salomon, 1997)

BACKGROUND

The compression of data is closely linked to the architecture of storage of the data. The advantage of keeping the data in compressed form is that, even if the network is slow and the infrastructure is no so good, there will be little impact on the retrieval of the data. The files system JFFS2 is optimized to support the compression of data and the metadata in the flash memory. However, it does not speak about the mix (A. Kawaguchi, S. Nishioka, and H. Motoda, 1995) of the flash and the disk storage (T. H. Cormen, C. E. Leiserson, R. L. Rivest, and C. Stein, 2001). When the flash memory available to store the data is slow, it is advantageous to compress even the small data objects as it reduces the latency.

Cache Compression

In the compression cache architecture proposed by Douglis, there will be an intermediate layer of virtual memory between the physical memory and the secondary memory. It provides the requisite docking space for the compressed pages. The implementation provides a reasonable improvement in the performance (T. Cortes, Y. Becerra, and R. Cervera, 2000). However, the performance may be improved further for the compressed page cache on Linux (S. F. Kaplan, 1999, R. S. de Castro, 2003).

Metadata Compression

In practice, a number of compression mechanisms are used for handling the metadata. It comprises of known techniques such as Shannon-Fano, Huffman coding with a pre-computed tree, gamma compression and similar prefix encodings. They provide different degrees of compression as well as the computational complexities. In Linux system, block or stream-based compression mechanisms are used.

Figure 1. Information redundancy

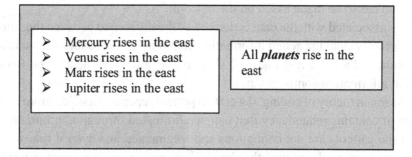

File Compression

For file compression a different set of algorithms are used. Unlike Metadata which is more regular and structured, no such assumptions can be made for the data stored in the files. In general, for a machine, a file stored on a machine, is a random sequence of the bytes (D. Roselli, J. Lorch, and T. Anderson, 2000). However, a kind of similarity may be expected for the data stored in files of the same type e.g. Audio files. Some times the file metadata indicates the file types (M. Kallahalla, E. Riedel, R. Swaminathan, Q. Wang, and K. Fu. Plutus, 2003). When no information is available on the file type, a generic block or stream compression algorithm may be used. Some of the practically used generic compression algorithms are dictionary-based compressors, bZip2 etc. The latter is widely used (J. Seward, 2005) with a block-sorting algorithm.

Redundancies

In a data string, the entropy associated with one symbol in the string is

$$H = -\sum p_i \log p_i \tag{1}$$

where p_i is the probability of occurrence of the ith symbol in the set of all available symbols. The entropy is measured in the units of bits/symbol with the logarithm taken to base 2.

When all the members of the set are equally likely to occur or equi-probable, then the information conveyed by any of them is the maximum. For example, if an unbiased coin is tossed, probability of

Figure 2. Information redundancy

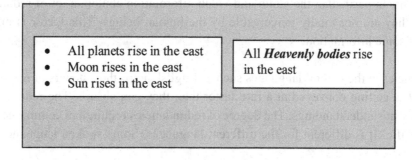

getting a head or a tail is 0.5. When the head turns up, it carries maximum information or meaning especially if a decision has to be made based on the outcome.

The redundancy associated with the data is defined as the difference between the (theoretical) maximum possible information and the actual information contained in the string. Redundancy in the string reduces its randomness. Figure 1 and Figure 2 show redundancies in the strings. Redundancy in the strings is related to information compression.

According to Shannon theory of coding, if a certain pattern repeats in a string more than other patterns of same size, then it contains redundancy that can be eliminated through appropriate coding scheme. It is valid even if the patterns are not contiguous and fragmented and even if the substring or pattern is composed of a single symbol. On the other hand, if all patterns of same size in a string repeat with the same frequency, then it carries maximum entropy or chaos; occurrence of a pattern of given length can not be predicted easily and there will be no redundancy of information in the string. The increased repetition of one of the patterns provides a bias for the prediction of its occurrence relative to the other patterns of the same size. However, redundancy is often retained in the message string for error correction (E. Reidel, M. Kallahalla, and R. Swaminathan, 2002), so that even if a repeating pattern is lost at one (or more) occurrence, it may be recovered.

The degree of compressibility of information associated with the data is described in algorithmic information theory (AIT). More the compressibility more is the redundancy associated with the data. Given a string, if it can be generated by a program shorter than itself, then the string contains redundancy and not totally informative or random. On the other hand, if no such program exists, the string is non compressible and totally informative. The degree of compressibility is the ratio of the length of the program that can generate the string to the length of the string.

Information Compression

The goal of information compression is to e the redundancies associated with the data. Depending up on what is treated as redundancy and how much of redundancies can be taken out, there are two (M. Klimesh, 2000) compression schemes.

1. **Lossless compression**: Here the redundant information associated with the data is removed. The useful information is totally preserved so that it is possible for the receiver to recover the original information completely. There will be however, a reduced degree of compression.
2. **Lossy compression**: Here the redundant information is removed from the data along with some useful information which is affordable to be lost with little impact. As a result of removal of a little useful information, it is not possible to recover the original information completely. However, it is not desirable when such a scheme is opted! It results in increased compression as well as reduced computations. In particular, the audio and video information contain a lot of redundancies in the sense that they are not totally perceivable by the human beings. This factor is made use in the removal of some information.

The redundancies in the natural languages such as English helps the listeners or readers to grasp the information that is getting conveyed at a rate faster than they can absorb. The redundancies provide correction for any misunderstandings. The degree of redundancies required in communication is person and context specific! It is different for the different languages. Some spoken languages support up to

Figure 3. Compression of data hierarchy

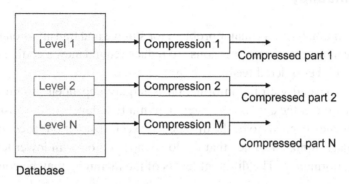

50% redundancy, meaning half of whatever is written or spoken is redundant. However it is not useless. Redundancies are exploited in the natural language processing. Given a word in the language, its meaning depends up on the context of usage qualified by the noun, verb, adjective or adverb. The degree of redundancy is also determined by these qualifiers. The redundancy in the sentence is determined by the redundancies of the composing words as well s the absolute redundancy of the sentence based on the same set of qualifiers.

The process of normalization that is widely used in the design of relational databases is basically a process of removing redundancy associated with the tables and columns in the databases.

Coding Schemes

Depending on the redundancies associated with the data, there are three coding schemes:

1. **Static coders**: Here the same code table is used for all, the symbols of the data. It is a one time effort to generate the code table. The code table is generated based on the relative frequency of occurrence of the samples in the data. Since the table is generated only once, it is known in advance even for the user of the data and not required to bundle or transfer the entire table with every stream or file of the data. One of the issues with this method is that the table is data sensitive. The relative frequencies are 'hard' tied to the sample set. The compression will not be efficient for a different data set.

2. **Semi-adaptive coders:** Here, the entire input stream is read first. The code table is built afterwards. Coding is done later. It is a two pass approach making it relatively slow. However, it provides a better compression at the expense of computational and algorithmic complexities and resources.

3. **Dynamic coders:** these are the adaptive coders where the building of the code table and the data compression or decompression happens simultaneously. It is not required to maintain and transfer the code table separately. The input stream is read only once reducing the IO operations. The compression is optimized for the data and depends up on the local changes. However, the underlying complex algorithms and complexity of the computation make it run slowly.

Information Redundancy

Redundancy in the information poses a major problem for storage and transmission resulting in wastage of the resources for the unnecessary transmissions. To reduce redundancy, a coding scheme making use of neural network with higher ordered feedback might be used.

The Redundancy associated with the information is largely dependent up on the organization or structure in the information. If the data is organized in to multiple levels of the abstraction to represent the information, redundancy happens to be the distance between abstractions used to represent the compressed code and the data. It may be noted that the lower abstraction with lower level in the hierarchy carries the maximum information. The different levels of the hierarchy may be compressed separately as shown in Figure 3.

Most of the compression algorithms used in practice make of the fact that the frequently repeating patterns contributes to the redundancy in the data. Thus, the redundancies may be removed from the data by reducing the repetition of these patterns.

Example: Run Length Coding

Here, a sub substring or a pattern repeats in the data string. The repeating symbol is retained only once along with a mechanism that tells how it repeats. For example, consider 62 '0's followed by the symbol '1'. Instead of writing 62 zeros, it may be recorded in short form as 1(62). Knowing this convention, the receiver easily appends 62 '0's after '1'. It calls for the transmission of both '1' and 62, assuming that the convention is known.

In effect, a pattern search algorithm is used to identify the patterns in the data stream which helps in reducing the redundancy by appropriately mapping the code to the abstraction of the data in the hierarchical organization. The usage of a feedback algorithm for this kind of arithmetic code is explained in a separate section of this book.

Clustering and Classification for Compression

In a set of patterns that are similar but not the same, the common part that is identical in all of them may be recorded as the schema and the parts that are different in each of them may be recorded as correction or compensation for the schema. The schema here will be recurrent and often fragmented to be consistent with the set of patterns. A neural network may be used to find out the hidden patterns.

Human perception of information involves classification and clustering. This is done to assign a single attribute for a group of objects and thereby achieve a way of information compression. The objects are clustered in to classes. A neural network can be used as a good classifier. The usage of a Bayesian neural network as a classifier is given in a separate chapter.

The class of objects may be grouped together to form a bigger class. There can be an overlap among multiple classes or groups. Each class will have unique attributes and description. The overlapping classes share the common attributes.

Clustering of the similar objects in to the common group helps in the compression of the information. For example, all the common features of the group that is shared by all the members may be stated only once instead of repeating the same as many times as the size of the group. The common description of the group provides its schema. The member specific description for the group may be specified by providing the minor corrections for the schema as applicable for the individual members of the group. Thus clustering or grouping helps in storing the information in a compressed form. The clusters may be clustered together to form a bigger cluster and in the same way, the description of this cluster results in further compression. However, this hierarchical grouping results in the abstraction of the description providing less and less compression with each iteration. It is more readily usable for the compression and association of the metadata tags.

To achieve better compression and better interface with the built in compression system present in the human beings, the same methodology may be followed.

Parsing

In a conventional computer program, syntax analysis of the program is done by parsing or "string matching". A string of natural language, on the other hand, makes use of pattern matching in the text. The text being analyzed is compared with each element in the grammar to find a degree of match or a relation in the text. It invokes the rules of the grammar of the language, unification of the patterns and search operations. A neural network can be used for the matching process involved.

To know the best match, the parsing or pattern matching algorithms make use of a redundancy based metric associated with the parser or the grammar.

ISSUES AND SOLUTION

Run Length Code Tables

One of the drawbacks with the Huffman codes in file compression is the presence of low-frequency values. The tree required to generate prefix codes turns out to be quite deep, adding to complexity and code length. In order to reduce the depth of the code tree, the frequencies below a certain value are ignored. In the average sense it has very little significance as their contribution for perception is minimal. In addition, their occurrence is also less frequent (low frequency). It reduces the size of the maximum length code. Overall, the length of the file being compressed gets reduced.

Redundancy Computation

The first step in the encoding process of any compression scheme is to find out the redundancies and remove the same. However, finding the redundancies is a challenging task. Since redundancies are associated with recurrence of some patterns in the data, removal of the same calls for pattern matching in different domains. In a self similar signal or data, the patterns match in log domain corresponding to different time scales. The patterns can be contiguous or scattered across the data string. The usage of neural networks for pattern matching is provided in a separate chapter.

The redundancy associated with the string is given by:

$$R = \sum_{i=1}^{n} (f_i - 1) * s_i \tag{2}$$

where f_i is the frequency of occurrence of the ith pattern of size s bits in a set of n patterns. Hence, large patterns or more frequently occurring patterns in the string make it more redundant and ideal candidate for compression.

Complexity of Searching

Searching of the possible patterns in a data string to get large number of big frequent patterns (and later replace them by the shortest strings and achieve compression) is a non linear optimization problem that may be solved using a neural network. In a string with N sub strings or symbols, the number of possible patterns P is

$$P = 2^N - 1 \tag{3}$$

The number of possible pair wise comparisons C of these patterns is

$$C = P(P - 1) / 2 \tag{4}$$

This turns out to be a very large value for large N. The number of pattern matching will be of the order of 2^{N2}. It turns out to be costly and difficult to afford. A call has to be taken if it is worth going for this type of comparison and compression ot leave the data as it is.

In order to reduce the search space, different techniques are used in practice. The search space can be restricted based on the data being searched using a Context adaptive Binary Arithmetic coding scheme. Video compression schemes such as H.264 support the same. Restrictions, can also be on the number of possible comparisons, the number of chunks, size of chunks, the mode of comparison (e.g., strings of same size need to be compared) etc. The past experience of searching (and learning), restriction on the maximum redundancy etc are the other parameters that make the search practical.

FUTURE TRENDS

Compression Techniques

In compression technologies, there is a large number of possible areas that can still be explored (A. Kiely, R. Manduchi, M. Klimesh, 2000). One such thing is the efficient encoding of consolidated strings, which otherwise take large number of bits if encoded individually. For file compression, in the place of using a single type of compressor as in figure 4 for every field in an inode, it is often possible to have efficient compression with a hybrid compressor as shown in figure 5. Here appropriate compressor is used for each field. Smart selection of the compressor is possible with the knowledge of the type of the file being compressed.

Multimedia Data Compression

Motion estimation is a vital module in motion picture processing techniques such as MPEG both in terms of complexity and compression (A. Kiely, S. Dolinar, M. Klimesh, A. Matache, 2000). Deviating

Figure 4. File compression with single compressor algorithm

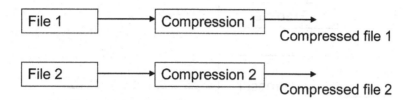

Figure 5. File compression with hybrid compressor algorithm

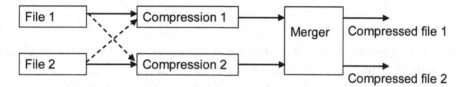

from the conventional methods that find a best match for the macro blocks in the current frame using the macro blocks of the previous frame, the operation may be carried out in frequency domain to ensure maximum compression.

The Discrete cosine transform of the block to be transmitted is ensured to have maximum number of zeros. Up on reordering the coefficients for variable length encoding, the resulting long chain of zeros increases the compression. It leads to improvement in both compression and Signal to noise ratio values.

Video signal processing in real time require intelligent elements to capture the features and trends in the non linear, time varying data and take appropriate decisions. The blocks associated with video processing such as dynamic Scene change, adaptive search range, filtering, object extraction, Classification, Pattern recognition etc call for online decisions. Neural networks are used to capture the non linear features and help in decision making.

A general purpose neural network can be used to perform any signal processing function like DCT, Motion estimation, filtering etc required in the video CODEC. The properties such as prediction, unique to a neural network can be exploited to generate highly compressed stream at the encoder end and high quality image at the decoder end. Presence of a small block of neurons (Artificial Neural Networks) on the video encoder or decoder chip can improve the performance

In image and video processing, adaptive variations in the quantization step size are often required to account for the agreed bit rate. However, increase in the Quantization steps results in information loss.

As an alternative for changing the quantization steps, the problem may be addressed in a different way. The quantized output may be subjected to convolution with a Gaussian pulse at the encoder end to result in an abstract signal. Such a signal has been found to be taking minimum bits for representation. At the decoder, it is further deconvolved with an appropriate Gaussian pulse to get back the original signal.

De-Convolution with Gaussian pulse reduces information loss and makes the signal abstract. With this, it is possible to achieve increased compression for the same SNR. Human perception of the information makes the quantization possible and results in audio/video compression.

Figure 6. Predictor based compressor

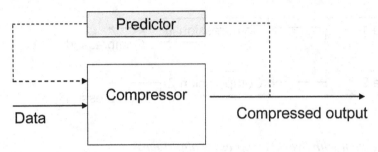

A neural network with feedback directly takes care of this factor. It provides due weightage for the feedback signals in the decision making process. A feedback based data compressor is shown in figure 6. Here neural network is used as the predictor to control the rate of compression.

The audio signal exhibits similar model. A linear prediction model goes well with it. Any difference in the predicted and the observed speech may be coded with less number of bits.

In the moving pictures, there will be a very little change in the information across the frames. This is because a typical rendering device has to display 24 to 30 frames second.

The predicted picture differs from the actual frame very slightly so that the difference requires less bits to transfer.

To model speech signals, homomorphic filtering may be used. Here the speech is synthesized by exciting the model either by an impulse train or with the random noise resulting in the naturalistic speech. The difference may be compressed separately.

Bioinformatics: Genome Data Compression

Data compression is being put in to unknown applications such as bio informatics. Here the sequence DNA over the genomes may be compressed and stored. To compress this apparently random data, a good understanding of the generation of the sequence is required. Compression is possible if the redundancies may be identified or if there exists a method to encode the string of data with a shorter string.

Alternative approach is the usage of models. Model based compressions are becoming popular especially when a certain structure is found in the data. In the example of DNA strands, it has been found out that the structure exhibits self similarity. I.e. the sequence may be generated with a self similar model. This finding greatly simplifies the issue of compression of the strand. A model with appropriate parameters can generate the sequence on the fly. Only the parameters of the model need to be stored. However, the modeling is still under progress.

Language Support for Compression

Object oriented programming provides a mechanism for the way the information gets compressed and processed. The information associated with a class is passed on to the derived class with abstraction to form a hierarchy of objects. There is a provision to sample a variable up to a certain level in the hierarchy, beyond which it is not accessible. The same variable may be 'protected' from getting corrupted at various levels of the hierarchy. The 'protected' variables at different levels of hierarchy cater to a variety of users interested in different levels of information.

CONCLUSION

In this chapter,

- The commonly used compression algorithms are described
- The relevance of data organization to achieve maximum compression is explained.

The limited resources available for data communication often require the data to be compressed before transmission over the network. The additional advantage is that the compressed data takes less storage space.

The fact the there will be some redundancies in the generation and usage of the data has been made use for achieving compression. The tools and techniques of information theory provide the requisite compression. These techniques can be conveniently implemented over a signal processor.

QUESTIONS

1. How does the signal processing help in data compression?
2. What is the need of the compressed data over a supply chain?
3. What is the yardstick for the choice of the compression technologies?
4. How and why, controlled redundancies are introduced in to the data?
5. What are the techniques used for the multimedia compression?

REFERENCES

Cormen, T. H., Leiserson, C. E., Rivest, R. L., & Stein, C. (2001). *Introduction to Algorithms, Second Edition*. Cambridge, MA: MIT Press.

Cortes, T., Becerra, Y. & Cervera, R. (2000). Swap compression: Resurrecting old ideas. *Software. Practice and Experience (SPE), 30*(5), 567.587.

de Castro, R. S. (2003). *Compressed caching: Linux virtual memory*. Retrieved 2003 from http://linux-compressed.sourceforge.net/

Gailly, J.-L., & Adler, M. (2005). *zlib 1.1.4*. Retrieved from http://www.gzip.org/

Kallahalla, M., Riedel, E., Swaminathan, R., Wang, Q., & Fu. Plutus, K. (2003). scalable secure file sharing on untrusted storage. In *Proceedings of the 2003 Conference on File and Storage Technologies (FAST)*, San Francisco, CA, March, USENIX.

Kaplan, S. F. (1999). *Compressed Caching and Modern Virtual Memory Simulation.* PhD thesis, University of Texas at Austin, Austin, TX.

Kawaguchi, A., Nishioka, S., & Motoda, H. (1995). A flash-memory based file system. In *Proceedings of the Winter USENIX Technical Conference,* (pp. 155.164), New Orleans, LA, Jan. 1995. USENIX.

Kiely, A., Dolinar, S., Klimesh, M., & Matache, A. (2000) "Error Containment in Compressed Data Using Sync Markers," *Proc. 2000 IEEE International Symposium on Information Theory,* (p. 428), Sorrento, Italy.

Kiely, A., Manduchi, R., & Klimesh, M. (2000). Maximizing Science Return: Data compression and Onboard Science Processing. *TMOD Technology and Science Program News,* 12.

Klimesh, M. (2000). *Optimal Subtractive Dither for Near-Lossless Compression, Proc. 2000 IEEE Data compression Conference (DCC '2000),* (pp. 223-232), Snowbird, Utah.

Oberhumer, M. F. (2005). *LZO data compression library 1.0.8.* Retrieved from http://www.oberhumer. com/opensource/lzo/

Reidel, E., Kallahalla, M., & Swaminathan, R. (2002). A framework for evaluating storage system security. In *Proceedings of the 2002 Conference on File and Storage Technologies (FAST),* Monterey, CA

Roselli, D., Lorch, J., & Anderson, T. (2000). A comparison of file system workloads. In *Proceedings of the 2000 USENIX Annual Technical Conference,* (pp. 41-54).

Salomon, D. (2002). *Handbook of massive data sets* (pp 245 - 309). Norwell, MA: Kluwer Academic Publishers.

Seward, J. (2005). *bzip2 1.0.2.* Retrieved from http://sources.redhat.com/bzip2/

Ts'o, T. (2005). *libext2fs.* Retrieved 2005 from http://e2fsprogs.sourceforge.net/

Wayner, P. (1999). *Compression Algorithms for Real Programmers.* San Francisco: Morgan Kaufmann.

Chapter 9
Meta Data Representation

ABSTRACT

In the ocean of information that gets transferred over the supply chain, it is difficult to get what is required for the customer. Toward this end, a description of the information is necessary. This chapter explains how metadata describes the information. In addition, it provides the framework for service description and message exchange in web services. Hierarchical representation of data abstractions to cater for the services is introduced.

INTRODUCTION

In the previous chapter, the different techniques of generating the quality data consuming less storage space are provided. The data is still large and requires universally accepted description or tagging before it is ready for use. Here, the usage of Metadata in general and XML in particular for the description of the data is provided.

Metadata (David C. Hay, 2006, Erik Duval, et al, 2002, Martha Baca, 2005) is the descriptive data used to record the characteristics or attributes of the information (Amy Brand, Frank Daly and Barbara Meyers, 2003). It helps in the identification, discovery, organization, retrieval and management of the information being described.

The content acquired from the source or data mart will be useful only if the description of the information is available in the form of metadata. It also helps in content search operations. On the other hand, without a metadata description associated with a file, its visibility and use would be limited. Hence all files containing audio, video, image, software etc will have metadata associated with them.

DOI: 10.4018/978-1-60566-888-8.ch009

The metadata description depends up on the language chosen for the description. A good description should be able to help to retrieve the specific information or object from the file under some criteria (David Marco, 2000). If a file contains a list of items, the metadata should also describe the relationship between these items, if any and retrieval of any of them should help in retrieving others based on some criteria.

The metadata provides data about the data stored in the form of tables, programs etc. The metadata often contains the complete description about the data, including the source of the data, creation, modifications done, location, access technologies, keywords, limitations etc.

Along the supply chain, the databases get changed dynamically. As the database gets updated with changes, metadata also follows the same. Sophisticated, user centric languages such as XML are used to support the metadata. The metadata contains information about the source, context of the data generated, the time of data creation and updation. With the inclusion of the context, the data gets converted in to useful information. The metadata is useful in describing the data quality (Michael H. Brackett, 2000) and used in all applications that make use of the data. The metadata provides useful information about the data abstractions along the supply chain.

In this chapter, various issues associated with the Metadata description language, integration and fusion of the associated data are brought out. The hierarchical representation of data is related with metadata. The example of XML metadata is considered as it is extensively used. This chapter is expected to be useful for describing data architecture, integration, handling queries in search engines, data and rights description etc.

BACKGROUND

The data from different sources available in heterogeneous format calls for modularity in the metadata description. The users can make use of the existing schemas rather than defining something new from the scratch.

The support for interoperability allows the data from different schemas for the seamless syntax and semantic integration. This helps in re usability of the module in different applications.

Case Study: HTML

HTML based metadata is popularly associated with the content and services associated with the web. Although it is simple, it fails to provide the description in a structured fashion.

Case Study: XML Markup

It supports the structured data although used in a small scale. Like XML, it is modular and extensible and interoperable.

Case Study: RDF

The Resource Description Framework (RDF) provides the description of the content on the web. It supports the semantic description of the content and the services and referenced in W3C standard. RDF describes the reuse and exchange of the vocabularies. It is often used as a wrapper on the XML description for the same task. The applications around RDF are still being tried out.

Case Study: XML

XML is a modeling language to provide the description of the components of information systems. Based on this description, the components of the information system reconfigure themselves and get connected. Thus a single XML description is enough to capture the possible reconfigurations instead of modeling each of them separately.

XML is required for storing (Clifford A. Lynch, 2001), retrieving, and managing information. It can model the information in XML to simulate the use cases of the information system. XML provides the required syntax to represent the information and resembles the system behavior.

XML has become the information-structuring tool. It supports the storage, retrieval and management of the information. It supports the queries by expressing in XPath or XQuery patterns. XML is used where the systems reconfigure rapidly.

XML Based Security Tokens

XML supports the security tokens through the formats Security Assertion Markup Language (SAML) and the eXtensible rights Markup Language (XrML). The XrML also covers the digital rights supporting the interoperability.

The <wsse: BinarySecurityToken> object provides a mechanism to associate the security tokens. However, it is not directly usable with XML. However the <wsse: Security> header is extensible for defining the security tokens.

Metadata for Content Management

The metadata should support a reasonable automation so the both machines and human beings can use the same seamlessly. With Metadata it is possible to retrieve the content automatically. Metadata provides an abstract view of the documents. With metadata, it is easy to find out the duplications in the data and the documents.

Metadata description of the information, used for the retrieval, helps in fast search. It is used in authoring tools during content creation or in the browsing tool during retrieval or both and present in intranet or the Internet. Metadata used for the retrieval shares much in common with the metadata defined for reuse. However, it is required to be more extensive to support real time transactions.

Metadata supports heterogeneous systems with different hardware and software platforms, data structures and interfaces. It allows the exchange of data with minimal loss or distortions while providing the data of the right abstraction. In addition to the information, Metadata allows the seamless exchange of services and the resources across the network.

Schema

Metadata schemes or schemas provide the metadata description of a set of attributes of the data such as the name and the semantics of the objects. It helps in the identification of the content through the attributes such as the main title. The schema makes use of a set of descriptors to form the vocabulary.

Metadata for File Search

In generally the Metadata is not mixed up with the data. It is stored in separate files or directories or inodes. It is composed of various descriptors such as text, image, attributes, time stamps, bits etc. The metadata contents often help in the search of the files. The organization and description of the metadata have a say over the retrieval of the data.

Web Services

In addition to data description, Meta data is required to support web services across the supply chain. A Web service can basically expose a set of services that can be accessed over the network by passing the messages through a metadata. Service-Oriented Architecture (SOA) and Event-Driven Architecture (EDA) are the two different paradigms for the web services that address the complex integration challenges.

Case Study: SOAP

The Simple Object Access Protocol (SOAP) provides a mechanism for the web services to access one another by interacting with each other to complete a specific task or service. It is based on XML using which the applications can invoke the methods on remote objects through the internet and widely used and supported by the World Wide Web consortium. Since XML provides the data description independent of the platform, seamless exchange of the data is possible across the system, resolving the interoperability issues. Although web services are metadata drive, it is more of business description of the services than the technical description of the content.

The web based service architecture SOA consists of the three main components as shown in figure 1.

1. **Service providers** advertise their services over the Web. The applications being offered as Web services are described using the standard templates of the Web services description language (WSDL). Service provider gets the help of the broker to publish the services.
2. **Service requestors** are the consumers or end users who first contact the service broker to learn about the services. With the advice of the broker, the appropriate service of the service provider would be invoked.
3. **Service brokers** introduce the service providers to the appropriate service requestors and vice versa. Thus they maintain the information of the requested as well as the offered services.

Figure 1. Supply chain model for SOA

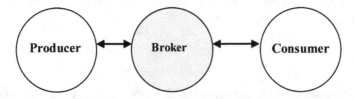

Figure 2. Event driven architecture for query

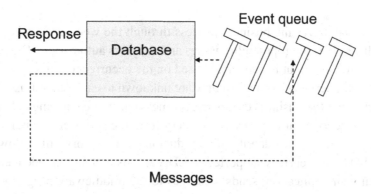

Interoperability is a major issue in the communication of the three players mentioned above. The goal of SOA is to bind these interacting objects. This can happen through a platform independent language. . The objects interact through the protocol SOAP. It assures the scalability, granularity and interoperability among these objects.

SOAP provides a secure mechanism for the inter object communication the <wsse: Security> header provides a mechanism for conveying the security information with a Simple Object Access Protocol (SOAP) message. The header is extensible to support the different types of security information.

The application of hierarchical representation of data is used for the implementation of SOA. It enables the web services to operate on different abstract level that can re-evaluate, modify or dynamically handle the data types on demand.

An important activity required in the organization is the support for services for the business processes and the users. It happens through service oriented architecture (SOA). The services are to be available independent of the underlying hardware or the platform. I.e. it drives the interoperable services. To make it happen, the information representation has to be interoperable. More information on SOA is available from (Jon Udell, 2005)

Along a supply chain, there is a variant in the semantic description of the data and the format of business object representation. The support for interoperability may be achieved through the XML schema or the Common Information Model (CIM) to realize the SOA. The scope of CIM is generally limited to a domain to ensure a focused SOA and application integration.

Information Management

Information management is extensively used in the implementation of the SOA, specifically to handle the life cycle of the information spanning information representation, analysis, integration and maintenance from across different sources in different formats. The data sources may be structured or unstructured. However, they are integrated to provide a single view. The structured data is composed of the XML description of the information while the unstructured data is composed of documents, textual description like web pages etc.

Case Study: EDA

Another architecture that drives the business process through the web services is the event-driven architecture (EDA). It resolves interoperability issues and supports automation. The EDA based query is shown in figure 2. Here the output is generated based on the occurrence of the event.

EDA can integrate the services even when they are unknown to each other. It is used when the applications are required to call the business events trigger messages to be exchanged between the different services. For a browse service, an event can be a query from the end user or a purchase order over the supply chain when the price or the quantity of a product in the inventory falls below a thresh hold.

Contrary to the SOA, the services supported in EDA are distinct and independent. First, the source of the event, typically an application, sends messages to the middleware program. The messages are matched with the subscription. An event source sends messages to middleware software that notifies the trigger to the relevant services depending up on the subscription for the services. The messages can be simultaneously delivered to multiple destinations using the publish-and-subscribe approach.

In lines with the SOA, an event driven architecture requires a strong Metadata architecture. It is required to specify the events and the event processing rules. The paradigm is still being tested.

The events form a queue of commands for execution. In order to utilize the resources optimally and assure the agreed quality of service, a smart scheduler needs to be used to arbiter and shuffle the events. In addition it has to integrate the two independent protocols SOAP and EDA.

Semantic Web

Semantic web supports a seamless exchange of data and information between the individuals and organizations by supporting the integration of the enterprise integration aand information management. It is implemented through the Resource Description Framework (RDF). The RDF integrates a set of applications including audio, photos, software etc with the help of the underlying XML to exchange the syntax. A good discussion on semantic web is available in (Tim Berners-Lee, James Hendler and Ora Lassila, 2001).

Although video indexing is possible with the Dublin Core (DC) or the RDF, schemas for the video description are still being worked out. The schemas provide the editing tools for the video. Schemas are also required for the other multimedia data description such as Description Definition Language (DDL) of the MPEG-7.

The metadata for video representation (Baca, Murtha ed, 2000, Caplan, Priscilla, 2000, Caplan, Priscilla, 2003) can make use of the object-oriented definitions of the semantic concepts of RDF, expressed with XML schema.

The Metadata model provides the representation and usage of the information. It provides a unique mechanism for conveying the high level or abstract knowledge of the business.

Hierarchical Organization

The language XML was originally designed for interchange standard of data. It is capable of modeling all the components of information systems (Ralph Kimball, 1998). With XML it is possible to model the information systems in parts specific to the business under consideration (Adrienne Tannenbaum, 2002). It provides the requisite features for specific information modeling. It is proposed here that the

Figure 3. Hierarchical representation of data and Metadata

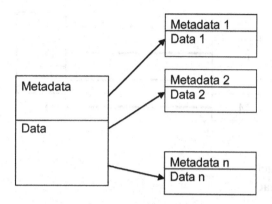

data may be arranged in the form of hierarchy with varying degrees of abstraction. With the hierarchical description of the data in place, the description of the model features would be:

- **Extensibility:** This feature permits the record to contain different data fields. The different data types corresponding to different levels of abstraction may be specified in the same record to distinguish different flows. In the hierarchical data representation, each level would have the associated metadata as shown in figure 3
- **Scalability:** A new type of data may be easily added during the run time. For example, depending up on the network conditions or query performance in terms of the time required for the query response, an appropriate unknown abstract level may be generated for the data and sent to the broker. These activities require built-in intelligence.
- **Flexibility:** The flexibility in the model allows the data to have an arbitrary hierarchical architecture independent of the other data.

Hierarchical Data Storage

XML meta language makes use of tags, attributes data elements and hierarchy to describe the data..In XML these elements are stitched together. It results in data hierarchies. The hierarchies provide a mechanism for the ordered arrangement of the components of XML information. In the hierarchy, logically related information are placed at various levels depending up on the abstraction. The hierarchy is also an indicative of the relation among the objects. The data attains meaning only if the complete content along with the tag or attributes is presented. The hierarchical storage mechanism explained in the part, Information storage can be conveniently captured with XML. Figure 4 gives hierarchical metadata organization

Data Abstractions

The hierarchical representation of the data results in various levels of the abstractions.

- PrincipalPatternAbstract
- RightPatternAbstract

Figure 4. Metadata organization binding with data.

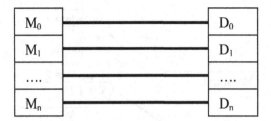

- ResourcePatternAbstract
- ConditionPatternAbstract.

The XML elements to describe the new patterns in the data may be specified by defining a new class derived from the XmlPatternAbstract. It provides an alternative for defining the patterns using the existing objects.

The new class may be derived from one of these classes depending up on the new application and the context. The rights description variant of XML, the XrML provides a rich set of constructs to define the new objects to cover the rights, content distribution etc.

In a quality-based data integration or SOA scenario, the data rate, quality or equivalently the data abstraction needs to be changed adaptively based on the feedback information from the broker sensed through the network load, query statistics etc.

ISSUES AND SOLUTIONS

Interoperability

The digital documents often come across interoperability issues due to the XML architecture and the availability of very few storage standards for implementation. With the usage of the conventional database architecture and the search engines for storing the XML documents and their retrieval respectively, the lack of interoperability can produce irrelevant output for the queries and take a large search time. There are two approaches to improve the performance: using a XML friendly database architecture or XML friendly query language so that any browser can understand.

The hierarchical representation of information goes well with XML description- both in terms of the architecture and the query. The lengthy query time may be attributed to the fact that the XML description is stored in parts on the server of the database and it takes time to collate them as a response to the query. Hence, the solution is to store the Metadata as a single document, as a single object, large object field or by mapping the schema of the XML document to the database rows or to change the database organization to reflect a kind of hierarchy.

Interoperability of Data

On the web based supply chain, the data comes from a variety of sources and information models with distinct syntax and formats. It results in interoperability issue between the applications the exchange this data. Although XML model has resolved this issue to a great extent, the problem still persists due to the different choices of the optional syntaxes supported in different implementations.

In order to facilitate the interoperability, it is possible to have a direct translation from one schema of the XML to the other schema using the language XSL transformation (XSLT). However, the complex translation or the transformation is to be described by the human expert. The problem here is that a mapping between two XML representations needs to be specified by a human expert. The additional issue is the, when the original description or the schemas changes, it invalidates all the translations and calls for a lot of rework.

To get rid of this, alternative intermediate models of description may be used. Here, rather than specifying the translation, the human expert has to work backwards and find out the conceptual model from the XML schemas and record how the original schema maps with these models. This will simplify the specification of the deviations in the conceptual models.

One of the solutions for these issues is to go for layered architecture where the primitives of the model are organized in to three distinct layers:

- Syntax layer
- Object layer and
- Semantic layer.

The abstract layers of this kind of information representation may be mapped on to the hierarchical data organization highlighted in the previous chapter and implemented by providing a type of feedback across the layers of the hierarchy. A fusion of data in metadata space results in equivalent fusion in data space as shown in figure 5.

XML Model

The description of the model with XML is context sensitive and data sensitive. Often the model is erroneous due to insufficient and inappropriate context description. Hence adequate tags are required to be provided. However, the redundancies in the tags are to be removed. Otherwise, it results in the poor hierarchy of description.

Figure 5. Fusion of data.

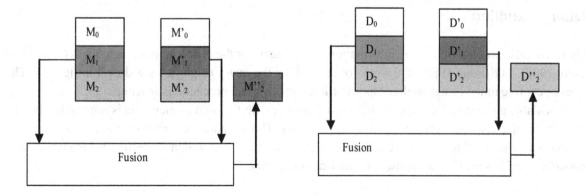

In a good model, the attributes and the data are to be totally separate. Attribute is not the data but provides the Metadata description. It provides the correct interpretation of the data. Sufficient attributes are to be assigned with the data to enable classification and subsequent clustering. Contrarily, if the metadata is contained in the data field, it is not very easily accessible and takes more time for the search operation.

A good information description model needs to consider these factors for a smooth operation and deployment although the implementation is a bit more time consuming. The generic and more intelligent models can assure robustness and reusability of the same.

Information Quality

Maintenance and assurance of the information quality is an important component of information management (Guy V Tozer, 1999). An intelligent algorithm would be required to be implemented across multiple databases to support quality-based query and assure quality results. Consider the example where the data source s_1 is queried with a rule r_1 that in turn queries source s_2 with rule r_2 to get the required search result. The same result may be obtained by querying the source s_2 straightaway with a rule r'_2. An intelligent agent used along with the search engine can learn the chain of rules adaptively and replace a set of queries with a single one.

FUTURE TRENDS

Metadata Hierarchy

The model of information and the transactions over the same are described in a language. The language, in turn, is modeled with the meta-language. That meta-language will be provided a description in the meta-meta-language, and so on. This results in the formation of a open ended meta-level hierarchy, which begins with the original model and its description. As one proceeds upwards in the hierarchy, the content and the description becomes more and more abstract. Still, the bias or fixed part of information in all these levels of the hierarchy remains the same. I.e. each abstract level of the information description provides the same fixed amount of information over the database on top of the variable information specific to the level in the hierarchy. This property may be used to ascertain the market value of each level of the hierarchy.

Query Handling

Hierarchical representation of the information is necessary for the efficient query responses (Norm Friesen, 2002). The usage of a neural work for controlling the query responses are shown in figure 6. The query gets fine tuned based on the response till the appropriate precision is reached.

A scalable and extensible representation of the same with the help of metadata is required to handle this. Typically, new user services get added frequently. The metadata description is required to support an extensible set of objects specific to information services. The system architecture is also required to consider service specific mechanisms to provide scalability.

Figure 6. Neural network based query response.

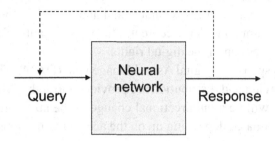

Data Pattern

The patterns associated with the data are to be identified for the effective description of the data. The data classification, indexing, grouping and retrieval happen based on the description of these patterns. XML provides a rich set of constructs to support the same. The description stems up from the inferences. Here a neural network may be used as a look up table as well as arriving at the inferences. Usage of signal processing techniques in arriving at the recognition of natural patterns is given in the section on intelligent information processing.

Data Integration

While converting data to information, lot of intelligence is involved bringing in the context information and effective integration of the data. The agreed quality of service of the data dictates the mode of integration. I.e. the service parameters are linked with the weightages to be assigned to the different heterogeneous sources of the data during integration. The weighted integration of the data requires effective data fusion. E.g. a multi resolution data fusion technique is based on wavelets. The different resolutions of the data are scaled appropriately and fused to get a unique integrated view of the data. The integration in data domain will have similar impact on the associated Metadata. While decimating the information in to a context-coupled data, the hidden intelligence or knowledge may be extracted. This is exactly what the organizations need.

Web Services

A combination of both SOA & EDA technologies, called enterprise service bus (ESB) may be used for better results of the web service. The optimal use results in maximizing the returns on the investment and effective business solution. They maximize the reuse of the services and resources, providing the flexibility in usage.

Digital Content Security

Metadata is increasingly used for the description and enforcement of the content security (Rachel Heery and Manjula Patel, 2000). It covers the document management, the description of data security and its subsequent distribution. A variant of XML, called XrML may be used for associating the consumption rights to the content. It is extensively used with the e- publications, multi media content such as movies, games software etc. The access rights are defined in a platform independent way so that the devices enforcing and monitoring the rights can easily understand and use this information. It clearly specifies what the end user can and can not do with the content. The other variants of this Meta language include MPEG REL, used for the expression of the digital rights.

The content security also spans the Digital Asset Management (DAM). The description of protocols, grouping, maintaining, archiving and distribution are provided through a Meta language.

All along the path, there will be a unidirectional change in the abstraction. In the data retrieval or queries, the path may be terminated depending up on the access permissions.

Hierarchical Content Distribution

In a multi-level content distribution scenario, an owner of a service provides access (issues licenses that are used to access the services) to a predefined class of customers or distributors. These customers/distributors in turn have the authority to provide access to their own predefined class of customers. The same authorization mechanism can be used and propagated from one level to the other. The data hierarchies can be mapped on to these levels to facilitate the flow of required amount of information. XrML provides the necessary abstractions of the hierarchies.

Pattern Matching

A variant of XML called XrML is used for the pattern matching application where the rights and conditions to use the data or resources are specified. The data pattern matching techniques using signal processing algorithms have been explained in a separate chapter in the book. The feature of XrML is that, one right is to be granted over one resource under one condition. When the data is hierarchically represented, pattern matching will be more effective for handling of the queries. The following XrML structures support this:

- **XmlPatternAbstract**: This is the parent construct from which all the patterns of XrML are derive.
- **XmlExpression**: It provides a mechanism or interface for all patterns defined in language outside of XrML 2.0 can directly be used. It provides interoperability among the different versions of the description. The particular expression language being used is denoted by the attribute **lang**. It is a URI with the default value http://www.w3.org/TR/1999/REC-xpath-19991116, indicating that there it is an XPath expression.

Document Binding

Documents are generally clustered and do not exist in isolation. The clusters of documents or multiple versions of related documents are generated in a work flow or over a supply chain. For example, each follow up of a certain activity resulting in a document. The quarterly budgets of an organization, progress reports of a project, maintenance records of a plant etc give rise to clusters of related documents. The documents are later retrieved in a specific order, often together. They need to be archived together for a better maintenance practice and ease of retrieval. The binding is however virtual. The same document can also belong to more than one group depending up on the cluster defined. XML provides mechanism to bind these documents.

Data Security

Security parameters are blended with the Metadata description associated with the data. XACML supports rules that are used to describe different overlapping policies. The different policies or rules may be merged using a Bayesian network. This merging may be characterized and captured through XACML. Conversely, the overlapping policies achieved through XACML represent the feedback of information or the merging of the policies. The XCML may be implemented with a broker-based model that uses a service-oriented architecture (SOA).

CONCLUSION

In this chapter,

- Metadata description and associated issues are discussed.
- Relevance of the Metadata for the service description is provided.

The effective management of the information over a web based supply chain requires assigning appropriate meaning for the data sources so that the required information may be retrieved at will. The attributes of data are described using Metadata. The metadata description of the data is linked to ability of the search engines to provide quality results.

QUESTIONS

1. What is the difference between EDA and SOA?
2. How does the metadata help in the supply chain management?
3. What is the role of Metadata in the realization of the web services?
4. How does the Metadata capture the abstractions in the data?
5. How does Metadata help to achieve the data integration?

REFERENCES

Baca, M. (Ed.). (2000). *Introduction to Metadata: Pathways to Digital Information*, (version 2). Getty Information Institute. Retrieved from http://www.getty.edu/research/conducting_research/ standards/ intrometadata/index.html

Baca, M. (2005). *Introduction to Metadata: Pathways to Digital Information*. Retrieved from http://www.getty.edu/research/ conducting research/standards/Intrometadata/index.html

Berners-Lee, T., Hendler, J., & Lassila, O. (2001). The Semantic Web, A new form of Web content that is meaningful to computers will unleash a revolution of new possibilities. *Scientific American*, (May): 2001.

Brackett, M. H. (2000). *Data Resource Quality*. Reading, MA: Addison-Wesley

Brad Eden Library Technology Reports (2002). Metadata and Its Application. Retrieved from http://jodi.ecs.soton.ac.uk/Articles/v02/i02/Lagoze/

Brand, A., Daly, F., & Meyers, B. (2003). *Metadata Demystified: A Guide for Publishers*. NISO Press & The Sheridan Press. Retrieved from http://www.niso.org/standards/ resources/ Metadata_Demystified.pdf.

Caplan, P. (2000). *International metadata initiatives: lessons in bibliographic control*. Conference on Bibliographic Control in the New Millennium, Library of Congress, November 2000

Caplan, P. (2003). *Metadata fundamentals for all librarians*. Chicago: American Library Association.

Duval, E., et al. (2002). *Metadata Principles and Practicalities*.

Friesen, N. (2002). *Semantic interoperability and communities of practice*. (CanCore, February 1).

Hay, D. C. (2006). *Data Model Patterns: A Metadata Map*. San Francisco: Morgan Kaufman.

Heery, R., & Patel, M. (2000). Application profiles: mixing and matching Metadata schemas. *Ariadne*, *25*(September).

Hunter, J., & Lagoze, C. (2001). Combining RDF and XML schemas to enhance interoperability between metadata application profiles. In *Proceedings of the Tenth International World Wide Web Conference*, Hong Kong (May).

Kimball, R. (1998). *The Data Warehouse Lifecycle Toolkit*. Mahwah, NJ: Wiley.

Lynch, C. A. (2001). *Metadata Harvesting and the Open Archives Initiative*. Retrieved from http://www.arl.org/newsltr/217/mhp.html

Marco, D. (2000), *Building and Managing the Meta Data Repository: A Full Lifecycle Guide*. Mahwah, NJ: Wiley.

National Archives of Australia (1999). Record keeping Metadata Standard for Commonwealth Agencies (Version 1.0). Retrieved 2005 from http://www.naa.gov.au/recordkeeping/control/rkms/summary.htm

Tannenbaum, A. (2002). *Metadata Solutions: Using Metamodels, repositories, XML, and Enterprise Portals to Generate Information on Demand*. Reading, MA: Addison-Wesley

Tozer, G. V. (1999). *Metadata Management for Information Control and Business Success*. Boston: Artech House.

Udell, J. (2005). Building SOA Your Way. Every enterprise needs to find its own balance between complete, scalable architecture and simply building a service-oriented architecture that works. *InfoWorld*, (September): 12.

Wilson, T. (1998). *Information management: A new focus.* Paper 56 - TRAIN - 2 - E. 53rd IFLA Council and General Conference, Brighton, UK, 16-21 Aug 1987.

Section 4
Information Storage

Chapter 10
Information Integration

ABSTRACT

In an information supply chain, data gets pumped over the web from several distinct sources in various forms calling for efforts towards data integration. The integration happens at various levels by means of different algorithms. This chapter provides a framework for the interoperability of the data from different sources. The use case of integration in data warehouses is provided.

INTRODUCTION

In the previous chapters, the data acquisition and processing steps of the information lifecycle are discussed. The information originating from various points in the supply chain are in different format making it difficult for an application to integrate and consume the same. Here the different aspects of the data integration in a supply chain are discussed.

In this chapter the service based architecture for data storage is addressed. The service parameters are fused in to the data storage mechanism. The ever-increasing business size of the organizations has led to the deployment of multiple functional units at different geographical locations. It calls for the continuous exchange of signals among these units before the data gets fused and used.

Data integration happening at the right time is preferred over the one happening at the real time. Especially in the business such as retail, the data needs to be integrated several times a day to provide accurate information. This puts stringent bounds on the delays. The data collected across the multiple sources could lead to inconsistencies unless it is cleaned before use. The quality of the resulting data after merging the data from different sources would be subjective.

DOI: 10.4018/978-1-60566-888-8.ch010

Figure 1. Architecture of ETL in modern organization

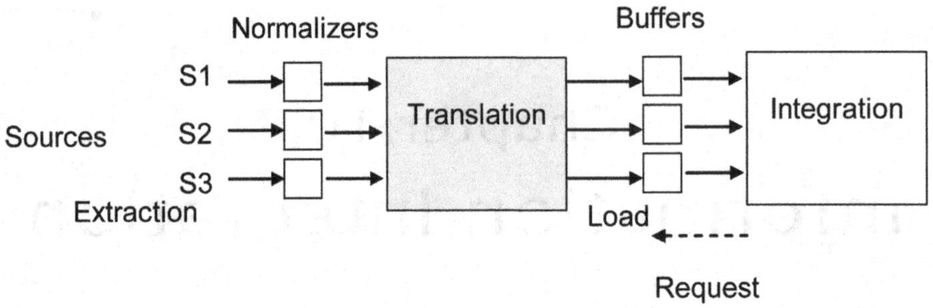

The integration process of data largely depends up on the underlying storage mechanism. The storage techniques in turn depend up on the data acquisition and processing methods resulting in a dependant chain. The methods used for the retrieval of information also have a say on the data integration techniques. In this chapter, hierarchical representation of the information is discussed. The databases are organized as a collection of hierarchies each with a different level of abstraction. Physically there will be a single view of the data. However the different levels of abstraction may be achieved by linking the appropriate data.

In adding to providing a common platform of the data for understanding, data integration is required for the automation of the business transactions and processes among the organizations. It calls for interoperability of the data and collaborative workflow across the organizations. The metadata model described in the previous chapter provides a framework for the data representation and the associated workflow engine for the effective integration of the business process and the applications.

BACKGROUND

In a distributed environment, with multiple users having access to the database for updating the data, inconsistencies crop up posing a challenge for the database management system. It calls for restricted access for the data update in the EII products. In general, the database is to be maintained read only. To make it happen smoothly, the metadata of the different data sources is to be integrated and a centralized metadata based retrieval mechanism should be in place.

Case Study: Integration of Data over a Supply Chain

The data getting generated along a supply chain gets stored in a data warehouse accessible for the different elements of the supply chain. A data warehouse performs the conventional extract, transform and load (ETL) operations over the data (O'Leary, Daniel, 2000). The enterprise information integration (EII) technology and the tools can be used to support the integration of the data. ETL can sit as a part in EII, enhancing the different abstract levels of the data over which EII operates. The architecture of ETL in a modern organization is shown in figure 1

Figure 2. Collation of data in different formats.

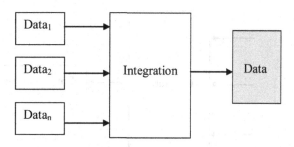

Application Integration

In order to achieve integration at the application level, a supply chain makes use of plug and play architecture. For example, over a supply chain, there will be a planning functionality, a procurement functionality to procure materials and the sales related functionality for order taking and order fulfillment. These different applications need to be integrated for the smooth functioning of the supply chain. The paradigm of application integration (Gable, Julie, 2002) is explained in (Acharya, Ravi, 2003) and (Correia, Joanne, 2002). Planning has to send quality data to the procurement for procuring components. Then the information should flow to the supplier of the commodity, who in turn needs to know how much to produce. This information comes from the sales data and trends. Hence information integration forms the backbone for the success of any supply chain and to take the decisions effectively.

Web services technology has opened a variety of possibilities. The technology is independent of the platforms and supports seem less communication among the different applications. This technology is attractive specifically where it is possible to control the application through the network connectivity. However, to exploit this technology completely, web services technology still has to be matured to provide the required throughput and to support the process.

Data integration

The data from different sources comes in various forms and fields. Before integration, it is required to put them in the same form so that they can mix with each other (Ives, Z, Florescu, D, Friedman, M, Levy, A, Weld, D, 1999) and the applications using them can get a single view of the data. Hence, after the data acquisition, it has to be processed and subjected to normalization, translation etc and stored in a common format keeping in mind the future integration with the data from a different source. The storage mechanism in turn is related to the data integration and retrieval as explained in the future chapters. The usage of intelligent elements (Dorian Pyle, 1999) for data processing is explained in a separate section of this book. Figure 2 shows the collation of data from different sources.

The data warehouses can serve as the secondary sources of the data. Conversely, the data acquired from the different data sources can serve as the data warehouse or as primary source of data depending up on their organization, importance and online requirements (Knoblock, 1998). The path of the data transfers between the data warehouse and the data source is provided in the metadata. The data integration products are designed to maintain the data quality to meet the requirements of the business process.

An organization requires both current and historical data values as well as the predicted values for making sound decisions and trend analysis. Data integration is required to consume this data available

Figure 3. Resulting probability of data after integration.

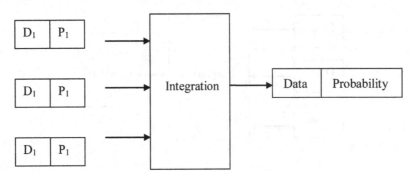

in different formats and originating from different sources. This secondary information source consists of data warehouses, data marts, and operational data stores.

The data integration may be carried out through the vendor provided software or through the in-house development (Alistair Grant, et.al, 2008). The in-house solution would be more customized, optimal and cost effective. However, it may lack technical maturity due to its uniqueness or first of its kind nature. It is difficult to customize to the changes in the business. The vendor supplied integration is, however, more generic, adaptive and often comes with a warranty. It integrates smoothly with the other tool supplied by then vendor all along the supply chain, starting from the acquisition software. Such integration generally does not happen with the in-house tools.

The first step in the data integration is to capture the data from the distributed data sources. The heterogeneous nature of this data results in implementation issues. If this data is to be normalized to several scales and stored in relational database tables, the size of the memory required will be too large.

As the organizations increasingly turn in to mobile with its resources supporting distribution of the data across multiple locations, data needs to be captured from hundreds of independent sources. Data may also originate from the parties outside to the organization, posing security issues. Real time Integration of this mobile data with different quality and different degrees of security threat is challenging.

When the data to be integrated is probabilistic in nature, it continues to be of the same type even after integration. The associated conditional probabilities may be derived from Bayes' theorem. The probability of resulting data is a single number computed as shown in figure 3. A confidence interval would be defined for the resulting integrated data.

The fusion of information from different sources reduces the total uncertainty associated with the fused data. The common information content among them gets counted only once. In addition, the unstructured component of one of the sources may overlap with the structured component reducing the uncertainties. More the common part more would be the advantage. In the extreme case, the differential feedback may be thought of as additional sources that undergo fusion. The advantage of such a fusion has been observed in the first chapter. Thus, more the number of data sources, more would be the abstractness of the resulting data.

Storage Integration

As a part of the Data integration, the data acquired from the different sources is to be consolidated with the available historical data and stored in the data warehouse. This integrated data should be taken as the new operational data when the applications access the data warehouse and ask for the data. The storage integration covers the consolidation of the active data with the historical data and at the same time retaining both for potential applications in the future.

Like the sources of data, data storage is increasingly getting distributed in architecture. It is spread out across multiple data centers as remote storages. As a part of maintaining secure storage, tools such as replication, remote disk and remote tape are being used increasing the vulnerability of the data for attacks during the process. So, even the vender provided storage devices are to be examined as their security processes and the policies can be different. Storage management also spans security issues of the data. Often, multiple standalone storage arrays are maintained. This requires multiple passwords, access points, and identification of new areas prone for the security threats that need to be considered while designing the storage security.

Integration Levels

Over the supply chain, Integration will happen at various levels:

- **The service integration:** It encompasses all the portals under one umbrella and provides a single access point to the user that in turn links the other required portals internally.
- **The business process integration:** It collates various processes being followed in the organization and provides one common view. It happens through an automated supply chain. More on business perspective of enterprise integration is discussed in (Aranow, Eric, 2001).
- **Workflow integration:** Like a supply chain, workflow is the pipeline over which the data flows while getting processed. It works similar to the business process integration. Scientific and enterprise data would have the well-defined lengthy workflows.
- **The application integration:** It includes the aggregation of logically similar applications that communicate with each other. It involves data transformations and message queues.
- **Information integration:** Here the complementary data are physically or logically brought together.

The other integrations include (Kernochan Wayne, 2003) control and connectivity integration.

Network Support for Integration

The integration process requires a large volume of data transfers from multiple sources over the network. The firewall facilitates the data integration by preventing the entry of the unauthorized data in to the network and the efficient allocation of the bandwidth and resources for the transfer of the data.

A firewall looks at every packet passing through it, both in to and outside of the organization and checks for certain conditions. The packets are allowed to cross the wall provided they pass the security condition. Thus it protects the resources from the intrusion. The firewall implements the protocols of the network layer. Often, intelligent algorithms are used to learn the condition to pass the packets, unforeseen circumstances etc.

Often the users can access the network through the proxy servers. The user commands or requests first reach the proxy machine although they are meant for the server in the same network. The proxy collects the data for the user from the server machine. Often, the proxy masks the user identity and changes the

Figure 4. Integration of hierarchical data.

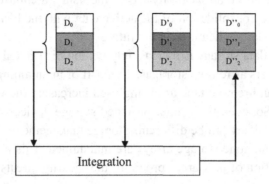

user commands or the data in between, much like a firewall.

Networks form the gate for the intruders. Hence, the network services, devices and the settings are to be password protected. Protection is also required for the network and the storage devices.

Hierarchical Representation

The data that is represented in hierarchical form has to undergo fusion at the appropriate levels of the hierarchy or the abstraction. I.e. at each level of the hierarchy the information associated with the resulting integrated data (Xin Sun, Derong Shen, Zhenhua Wang, Yue Kou, Tiezheng Nie, Ge Yu, 2008) would have an abstraction that is the weighted average of the information at the same level of the hierarchy of the different databases that undergo fusion. Thus the integrated data would also form a hierarchical structure as shown in figure 4. Again, along another dimension, the integrated data happens to be the weighted sum of these abstractions. In the integrated data, information associated with any level of the abstraction can be derived from the mean value by adding the incremental information associated with the deviation of data from the mean value.

The integration would be meaningful and effective if the abstractions of the data are shaped as desired. The shaping of abstractions happens through the measurement of information content of each level in the hierarchy. If each level in the hierarchy has to carry the information that is too different from the mean value, a larger variance has to be imparted in the integrated data.

The agreed service parameters are defined and described with respect to this mean value parameter. Each of the abstract levels in the hierarchy will have different response times. It is dictated by the quantum of the information associated with that hierarchy. If it is too far and too abstract, the information content will be less. Such a data would require a smaller time for transfer. The desired query response over the integrated database has to match with the response times of the integration. The service parameters or QoS for query are judged based on this response curve of the integration that provides the unified view of the databases.

At a given level of the hierarchy, the response time of any of the databases may be obtained from the mean value by considering the deviation of the corresponding database from the mean value. I.e. the response times form a hierarchy similar to the data hierarchy. On the orthogonal dimension, the convolution of the mean value with an abstraction or spreading function such as Gaussian pulse provides the response time of the corresponding hierarchy in the integrated data. The spreading is such a way that by applying the same function over the integrated data, it should be possible to get the corresponding data in the hierarchy of abstraction.

The abstract levels often need to be fused based on a set of rules. A Bayesian network may be conveniently used to simplify and learn the rules. In the web service scenario, if some databases undergo changes, the same has to be reflected everywhere. It calls for data synchronism. In such cases, delay involved in the integration or the response time described above would turn catastrophic as tariffs are involved in the web service transactions. Hence, the integration has to happen with right time data. Time stamps may be used to assure the availability of the right time data

ISSUES AND SOLUTIONS

Data fusion in an organization happens with a set of rules. However, following each rule for enhancing the information quality in the data is time consuming. With Bayesian decisions it is possible to merge these rules in to a single one and address rather than apply several rules individually over the data. It provides a mechanism for merging them in to a single rule saving the time significantly. There are different tools and techniques for the fusion of the data. It includes Enterprise information integration (EII) and ETL

In the presence of multiple streams, corruption in any of the data sources or streams affects all other streams and hence the fused data derived from them. This is true especially when the data is acquired from the sources with guaranteed quality of service and the data from different sources have to share the common resources such as buffers.

Data integration over a stream of data is practically very difficult. The running stream of data does not permit a common stationary database where the integrated data has to be stored. The weather conditions at different regions of the world provide a good example. The integration strategies are to be redefined to capture the average fused value over time windows of appropriate resolutions.

Data Interoperability

The data emanating from different sources often come in different forms creating interoperability issues (Lewis, Grace and Wrage, Lutz, 2005). It requires appropriate interface models and definitions to make the integration smooth. Often translators or converters are used to put the data in the common acceptable format. The tools remove platform dependency for the data. In the example of figure 5 the weather forecast data depends up on the previous weather forecast data, the traffic in the street and the number of ants per square kilometer in and around that area! It is interesting to note that each of the inputs have different units and come in different formats.

Syntax Analysis

For a semi-structured data, Metadata such as XML provides the description of the data through an effectively structure of the metadata to code and display the data. However, it can provide syntax integration and does not highlight the semantics of the data.

The problem may be attacked in three ways: Firstly, the semantics associated with the data may be described with ontology languages. It works in lines with XML for the syntax. Secondly, a translator may be used. Finally, the data may be represented in multiple formats in lines with the multiple resolutions

Figure 5. Data integration in a simple weather forecast system

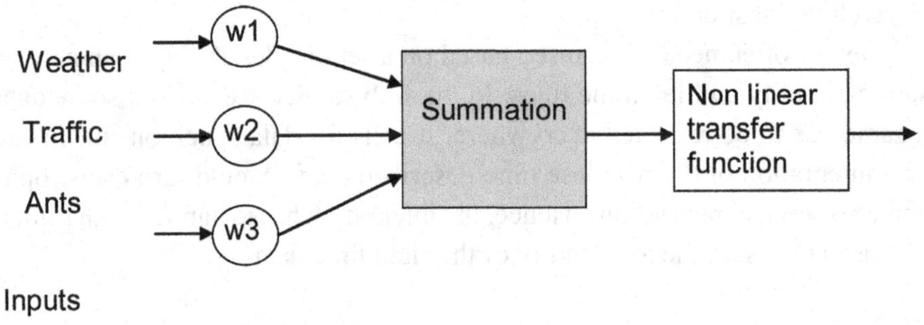

Weather → w1

Traffic → w2   → Summation → Non linear transfer function →

Ants → w3

Inputs

and the appropriately matching data may be chosen for integration. This method works similar to the second one except that the translations are done in advance saving the computation time. A combination of all these methods may be used with hierarchical representation of data, wherein the hierarchies represent the syntax and semantics in different formats. The multi resolution property provides both syntax and semantics features for the data represented in hierarchical form.

Data Arrival Time

A major issue with the data integration is the arrival timings of the data. The data to be integrated or used together may not arrive together by default. In such scenarios, data needs to be buffered for the later use calling for a huge memory requirement. A feasible solution is to store the data in compressed form so that it occupies less space and expand the same at the required point of time. The architecture of such a system is shown in figure 6. The method involves the overheads of latencies in compression, decompression in addition to the processing power.

Hierarchical arrangement of data can provide a better solution for the problem. The integration can start before the availability of the complete data in hand. The different abstract levels can undergo integration as and when they arrive. With the arrival of the last abstract level data, the integration process gets over. It works especially when the integration has to happen online. The data retrieval mechanism is closely related to the data organization and integration. That in turn is related to the web services that often require the real-time updating of the data.

Figure 6. Data transfer with compressed data

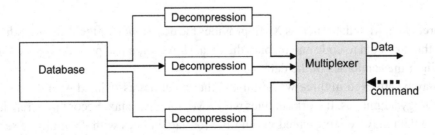

Data Abstraction

After integration, the data loses its identity. The integrated data would be the weighted average of the individual databases of the same level of hierarchy. As a result of averaging, the data turns abstract. The different databases can have some common shared information. In such cased the corresponding data has to be updated synchronously all along. Otherwise it leads to confusion and chaos. Alternatively, the data needs to be synchronous only at the time of usage by the end user. It provides sufficient time for up gradation. However the integration tools have to ensure the same.

Data Quality

Maintaining data quality in enterprises during the data integration and communication has turned in to a major challenge today than ever before. Cost of poor data quality is often unbearable to the organizations costing them revenue losses and inability to achieve the desired results in spite of expensive investments. A predictor is required for the analysis of failure as a result of poor quality.

The merging feature of a Bayesian neural network may be used to predict the impact of the bad or faulty data across the organization. The data originating from various departments such as marketing, finance result in organizational or department level consolidation of the data. The resulting data may be faulty or having fault components due to the contribution from the lower levels in the data description. Merging and subsequent usage of the data from the different sources results in a new defect density or failure probability for the resulting data:

a* probability of failure or faulty data in finance +b* probability of failure or faulty data in marketing+…=m* probability of failure or faulty data at the organizational level

Here a, b, m etc are arbitrary constants. The Metadata describing the fused data has to consider this defect density for the fused data.

Data Description

The data originating from hundreds of independent sources need to be bound to the corresponding descriptors appropriately. XML can provide the requisite binding feature between the data and its description. The descriptions are developed independently and later hyper linked. The description starts as a XML document during the data entry and later gets converted in to HTML page using XSLT5. Depending up on the requirement, the document may be distributed to a specified distribution list, stored in a local database or placed on the ODBC compliant relational database. Based on the contents of the document, conditional distribution of the same is to be supported. . This feature is realizable with the help of XML.

Since the XML description documents are user defined, it is possible to generate them with the help of any editing tool. The process is simple and user driven making it fast, efficient and cost effective. Since the XML schema is in ASCII format and devoid of any Meta characters, it is portable and easy to distribute.

Another level in the data integration is the integration of the metadata (Young-Kwang Nam and Guilian Wang, 2002). The metadata that gets altered with the hierarchical representation of the data needs to undergo integration or fusion appropriately to represent the integrated data. Hence, the techniques applicable for the integration of the data as described above are equally applicable for the Metadata. I.e. metadata is organized as hierarchy of abstractions.

The integration of data will have an impact on the integration of the corresponding metadata. It is done with the help of schema mapping and schema matching tools. The schema mapping tools are used to provide the required information for the translation of the data. In addition, they provide the relationship among the schemas.

In order to make the dynamic hierarchical representation of the data feasible, a glue layer has to be introduced in to the storage software wrapping around the metadata. Such a layer also helps in the query for data providing the required information based on the keywords or semantics.

Document Storage

For the ease of retrieval, the documents are to be stored in the form of files and directories with a known structure of the hierarchy exposed the same fr the navigation when the applications call the same. The documents are indexed to assist full search. To speed up the retrieval process, metadata may be added to the directories containing the document. Alternatively, documents may be classified based on similar characteristics and grouped together.

To prepare for the data integration, the documents may be manually copied in to the relevant folders. However, if any updating happens for the document in any of the folders, it has to be reflected in the copies of the document in the other folders. Hence the automated version control software, where the document is physically placed in on place and its different versions are accessible through many folders is required to support it. It is possible to connect the different documents smoothly.

XML description of a document helps to fetch the required documents for integration (Bean, James, 2003). Once the required document is obtained for the requesting application, the XSLT transforms the same to HTML, that is displayed subsequently.

In several applications, the data required to be integrated flows unevenly along the two different directions between the server and the client. Also, one of them is to be updated frequently. It results in under utilization of resources and bandwidth along one direction and a stretch of the same along the opposite direction. Ultimately, it leads to denial of services along one direction. Consider the example of the stock market data. The user very rarely needs to send the data to the server, typically for a change in stock vendor or for setting the thresholds. On the other hands, the server has to send all the fluctuations in the stock prices, that too for all the clients who have subscribed. The client machine keep requesting for the data increasing the congestion over the server.

There exist a number of solutions to this problem. Firewalls, proxy servers or traffic shapers may be used to control the bandwidth. As a result of traffic shaping, the bandwidth allocated for the input traffic would be reduced. The differentiation between the different streaming media such as video conferencing, training, music is very difficult as the data packets look alike from outside. However, the Firewalls and proxies can continuously monitor and recognize them. Alternatively, a rule based traffic shaping can solve this issue.

The security parameters are associated with the different abstract levels of the data organization. While integrating the data in a large organization, especially when the movement of the data is involved across different business units of the organization, it is required that the different data need to have different security parameters and a consistent ratio of these parameters needs to be maintained. E.g. the data of salary and the income tax of an employee should be at the similar security level. The information feedback can maintain the relative parameter constant. The feedback including the data rate, loss rate, integration quality, threat to the security etc as seen by the end user of the information may be provided to the source. This would further enable the data sources to adjust the abstraction levels and the associated security parameters.

FUTURE TRENDS

The business integration happens at four different levels-data, application, business process and user interaction. The integration is feasible with the help of different tools available from the vendors (Shenyong Zhang, Yun Peng, Xiaopu Wang, 2008). The concept of abstraction is applicable for all of them. The inter process communication among the various business processes call for a service quality constraint to be met. This makes the graph of the evolution of the business three dimensional.

Interactions

The user interaction integration is required for the personalized and secure access to rest of the integrations. This happens by providing user permissions to different levels of abstractions of the data process. This integrated business environment necessitates the usage and adherence of SOA. It ensures that the data transactions are agreed up on by both the parties.

There will be interaction among these units. The interaction can be made to adhere to the service guarantees. This leads to three way integration. It happens by providing a view or link to the data as the data propagates from one database to another and from one process to another. With merging, it is possible to maintain the fixed ratio of the quality of information. Quality of the resulting data to any of the data remains the same.

Data Centralization

In scenarios where most of the data originating from the distributed sources are consumed locally, integration of this data with the other sources may not be required. These local databases may be connected through a schema to form a global database. The data is actually not integrated although a global view of the data is available.

The global database provides the response to the queries on the data from any of the sources. The global database is generally virtual and is represented by a schema to avoid the duplications in the data.

In a modern organization, centralization i.e. getting the data at one place has become difficult to achieve. However with the centralization of the data, it cannot be shared freely among the departments, putting constraints on the usage of the resources. So it is better to maintain the data at the place where it originates. This is also called data federation. In practice, a mix of centralization and federation is used for better results.

Data Distribution

Web services may be used to connect the distributed data from several sources. Grid computations also support the distributed data work and exchange the messages as well as the final results for storage. Security of data in distributed environment is a threat as there are many players making the whole architecture vulnerable for attacks. Smart and intelligent data mining tools are being used in the integration process. The usage of data mining tools would be helpful in the online processing, semantic database queries etc.

Response Time

In order to support the different applications driven by the human beings or the machines, right data is to be provided. The data often requires the integrated or composite data from many data sources. It calls for the integration of the data from these data sources, often on the fly. The software driving the integration of the data needs to meet the timing constraints on the response time. If it is not with in the acceptable limit, the purpose of integration fails. Thus, it is religiously considered in the design of an integration tool. Modern integration tools have to be designed keeping the response time in mind. The tool needs to be optimized if the response time is poor.

The response time of some of the databases may be too large. For the other databases, it is small making them fast. After integration, the response time of the resulting data would be the weighted average of the response times of the individual databases. This value has to be taken as the mean delay. In order to make sure that the integration happens smoothly in spite of the databases with different timing response characteristics, the variance of the delays about this mean value is to be small. I.e. the impact of changes in one of the databases on the overall delay of integration is to be minimal. Another measurable parameter for the success of integration is the mean deviation. The mean deviation has to be small to ensure the right time data in the enterprise. Those data sources having a large positive mean deviation are to be speeded up proportional to the deviation by upgrading the link. It will have a say over the investment over the infrastructure. Support for the different web services largely depends up on this value.

Data Semantics

In the modern organization, data comes in various forms carrying different meaning depending on the context. The information consists of 2 parts- syntax and semantics. The syntax fusion happens as explained above. The semantic integration depends up on the context. A trained element is required to understand the context, weigh the data components and integrate.

In multimedia data involving audio, video and the picture, the integration has to happen in the feature space as well. Mpeg-7 provides the required tools and techniques for the integration.

Vendor Support

In general, the software used for data integration over a supply chain is application specific and depends up on the database organization. The architecture is required to be developed from the scratch. However, in some cases, the existing tools and techniques may be readily used or fine-tuned. Finally it is the responsibility of the tools supporting the integration and the other associated software to ensure the availability of the right data at the right time over the supply chain.

With the help of associated forecasting engines it would be possible to simulate and predict the future business flows and the corresponding changes inn the integration levels to support the same. It provides sufficient time to change the business process to maximize the benefit.

With the help of vendor supported APIs the applications at the remote users can import schemas during the integration of the data. The APIs include the provision to enter the data and distribute the same. Some of the applications involve the local storage as well and carried out off line. It solves the problem of lengthy transaction requirements.

CONCLUSION

In this chapter,

- The hierarchical representation of the data in to various levels of abstractions is proposed.
- The solution for data integration issues is explored based on this representation.

Accurate and meaningful data is a must for the right decision-making. The business intelligence tools as such will be of little help if the data they are working with is not accurate. Organizations are to maintain both Operational and analytical systems for a successful deployment (Derome Jon, 2003).

Some applications such as the forecasting, trend analysis large volumes of data from multiple sources with timestamps are required. The current data would be marked as operational data and accessed frequently. Data integration brings together the operational data from multiple sources. The data integration solutions in an organization may be developed in-house or procured. If the software is procured, the expertise of the vendors may be utilized apart from using the staff for a better work. However, it provides access to the sensitive information of the organization for the third parties.

In addition the available data integration products usually provide Metadata interoperability among themselves. Irrespective of the source and means of data acquisition, the data integration ensures uniformity in data warehouses, data marts and the data stores and help to make consistent business decisions. Successful data integration is required for the success of the supply chain.

The data after integration consists of the information from all the underlying databases much like a swarm. The individual databases lose their identity. The resulting value or the abstraction happens to be the weighted sum of the abstractions of the individual data sources.

QUESTIONS

1. Why, data integration along a supply chain is a tough task?
2. What are the typical issues faced in data integration?
3. What are the different levels of integration happening over a supply chain?
4. How does the internet help for the data integration?
5. How do the abstractions and the response time affect the data integration process?

REFERENCES

Acharya, Ravi (2003). EAI: A Business Perspective. *EAI Journal*, April 2003.

Aranow, E. (2001). Enterprise Integration: Business' New Frontier, Distributed Enterprise Architecture Advisory Service. *Cutter Consortium, 4*(12).

Bean, J., (2003*). XML for data architectures. Designing for reuse and integration.*

Correia, J. (2002). *Gartner Enterprise Application Integration and Web Services Summit presentation*, Fall.

Derome, J. (2003). *2003 Integration Expense Survey*. Boston: Yankee Group.

Gable, J. (2002). Enterprise application integration. *Information Management Journal*.

Grant, A., Antonioletti, M., Hume, A. C., Krause, A., Dobrzelecki, B., et al. (2008). *Middleware for Data Integration: Selected Applications.* Fourth IEEE International Conference on eScience.

Ives, Z., Florescu, D., Friedman, M., Levy, A., Weld, D., (1999). *An Adaptive Query Execution Engine for Data Integration. SIGMOD-99.*

Kernochan, W. (2003), *Enterprise Information Integration: The New Way to Leverage e-Information.* Boston, MA: Aberdeen Group.

Knoblock, C. A., Minton, S., Ambite, J.L., Ashish, N., Modi, J., Muslea, I., et al (1998). *Modeling Web Sources for Information Integration. AAAI-1998.*

Lewis, G., & Wrage, L. (2005). *Approaches to Constructive Interoperability* (CMU/SEI-2004-TR-020 ESC-TR-2004-020). Pittsburgh, PA: Software Engineering Institute, Carnegie Mellon University.

Nam, Y.-K., & Wang, G. (2002). A Metadata Integration Assistant Generator for Heterogeneous Distributed Databases. In *Proceedings of 16th Conference on Ontologies, DataBases, and Applications of Semantics for Large Scale Information Systems*, (LNCS Vol 2519, pp. 1332-1344). Berlin: Springer.

O'Leary, D. (2000). Enterprise resource planning systems: systems, life cycles, electronic commerce and risk.

Pyle, D. (1999). *Data Preparation for Data Mining*. San Francisco: Morgan Kaufman Publishers.

Sun, X., Shen, D., Wang, Z., Kou, Y., Nie, T., & Yu, G. (2008). *LAD: Layered Adaptive Data Integration Architecture,* The 9th International Conference for Young Computer Scientists, (pp. 897-902).

Zhang, S., Peng, Y., & Wang, X. (2008). *An Efficient Method for Probabilistic Knowledge Integration.* 20th IEEE International Conference on Tools with Artificial Intelligence.

Chapter 11
Information Storage

ABSTRACT

The success of information transfer from the suppliers depends largely up on the organization of the data to cater for different categories of the users. It calls for quick, competitive and cost effective solutions. To meet the same, hierarchical data representation is introduced in this chapter. The example of Data warehouse is considered to explain the concept.

INTRODUCTION

The last chapter provides the different techniques for the integration of the data. Once the data is available in the common format, it would be stored in the memory for the future consumption. Here, the different storage techniques are discussed.

Right storage device has to be provided for the right content depending up on the application, frequency of access, retrieval method, content security, underlying data transfer mechanism etc. The devices are expected to support Multi channel access simultaneously, calling for data caching and fast access, queuing and buffering policies.

Data warehousing systems consolidate the data from a large number of distributed data sources and store the integrated data for efficient data analysis and mining. The various techniques of data storage, including the data abstraction in a data warehouse, are addressed in this chapter. The case study of a data warehouse is taken to examine the issues with the storage and solutions have been proposed.

For efficient decision making data is to be accessible for all the players of an organization. This requires the data captured from various data sources to be stored in homogeneous and consistent form

DOI: 10.4018/978-1-60566-888-8.ch011

at a centralized location. It requires a separate centralized database that caters to various independent applications. There are two technologies for handling the data:

- **OLTP:** It is the Transaction oriented, online transaction processing system
- **OLAP:** It is the Analysis processing or online analytical processing (S. Chaudhuri and U. Dayal, 1997).

These two systems are repeatedly and interchangeably used in the organization. The process to store the heterogeneous data in a homogeneous form involves three stages:

- **Data Acquisition:** It is required to get the data from various data sources stored in their respective databases.
- **Data cleansing:** It involves the purification process of the data to make t homogeneous.
- **Loading:** Finally there is a loading process to put the data in the storage system.

BACKGROUND

Access to the right data would be required for effective decision making. The data is generally spread across the organization or over the supply chain, each being maintained in a different format. The data storage system has to collate the heterogeneous data. It calls for the data processing for storage and subsequent retrieval and rendering. Computationally intensive algorithms are to be executed to support the depiction of complex reports.

Case Study: Data Warehouse

Data warehouse (DW) is a common practice of storing the data from multiple, distributed and hetero-geneous sources of data. A good introduction to Data warehousing is provided in (W.H. Inmon and C. Kelley, 1993). Instead of collecting and integrating the data from the sources on demand during the query time, data warehousing systems collects the data in advance, cleanse and integrate the data. The data warehouse masks the actual data sources from the end users. So there is a less burden on these resources. When the source data changes, the same has to be reflected in the data warehouse to keep it updated. The ready to use integrated information is stored at a centralized data repository. With the data available on the warehouse in usable form, the end users can directly interact with the data warehouse and mine the data for analysis and subsequent use. The data warehouse caters for different users. Correspondingly, the relevant data, each requiring different access technologies is to be made available.

Structure of the Warehouse Data

The stored data consists of two components: the structured part where there is some pattern in the data and the unstructured part where the data is totally uncorrelated and random. It caters for the needs of decision making in business based on the historical data, trend analysis based on predictions etc.

Figure 1. Database generation in Data warehouse

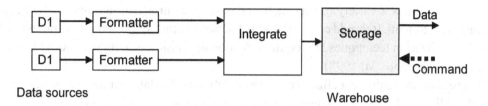

The stored data can come in many forms from the heterogeneous sources, including the documents, queries, reports etc and finally rendered in user friendly manner. The issue of heterogeneity is resolved by associating a standard schema, independent of the platform.

Objectives

A data warehouse is used to addresses a wide range of data storage problems. It manifests in a variety of forms like the data marts and the operational data stores containing the current view of the data instead of the historical values. Each implementation is used depending up on the application. By consolidating, standardizing and integrating the data contained in multiple forms, it should be possible to arrive at the single view of the data for the consumption.

A data warehouse supports large and multiple data formats, coexisting with the operational system present. It integrates the data from different sources that are present in multiple types as well as the legacy data. This helps in creating single view of the information across the organization. Data prediction and trend analysis are the other value add services provided.

The operational data store (ODS) aims to get a general view of the customer in addition to support the integration of the information from multiple sources. It supports data integration for certification from compliance bodies like CMM.

Architecture

The activities involved in the database generation in a typical warehouse (Matthew West and Julian Fowler, 1999) is shown in figure 1.

Data warehouse is a data storage system with its own database for maintaining the business information. It helps in Decision making in the organization by providing accurate information on the production, purchase, sales and distribution and marketing departments. For this, the individual business information as well as the data of the entire business group is required by all these individual components of the business, increasing the demand for the data.

In order to maintain the coherency of the data captured from different sources of the data, a single view of the data is to be maintained across the organization and the same is to be provided for all the applications.

Data warehouse provides access to a variety of vital information for the business at a single point. For this to happen, Information must be combined homogenously and consistently and stored at a central point from which it can be retrieved. A separate database is maintained in a data warehouse and helps in getting the required services in a stand alone application. The requirement analysis of a modern database is provided in (Maddalena Garzetti, Paolo Giorgini, Stefano Rizzi, 2005)

Data warehouse provides a variety of reports to the customers in a semi-automated form, mostly driven by the interactive menu. It should cater for users of different kind. To present the attractive reports, multimedia and visualization techniques are required. A good discussion on data warehouse is available in (Adamson, C., & Venerable. M, 1998).

An architecture supporting the cost effective implementation of the data warehouse makes use of the straightforward loading of the heterogeneous data and integration in to an OLTP system.

Features of the Data Warehouse

The characteristic features of a data warehouse (Inmon, W.H., Imhoff, C., and Battas, G 1999, Inmon, 2002) make the design process and strategies to be different from the ones for OLTP Systems. For example, in the data warehouse design, redundancy in data is assumed to exist to improve the timing performance of the complex queries. It does not create the issues with the data update as it is not done on-line and performed through controlled loads as a batch process. In addition, a data warehouse design must consider not only its own requirements, but also the features and the requirements of the source databases.

Although data warehouse provides a rich source of historical data, quite often, there is less demand for the same in the industries. The end user of the business has limited interest in all the transactions that have taken place. Only recent reports will be of some interest. It would be useful for decision making. A tapering threshold is to be set for the importance of the historical data in the warehouse. It will be relevant in the fast changing market. This perspective of the data will have a profound impact on the investments over the data warehouse and does not justify the return on the investment. The implementation of a good Data warehouse is provided in (Kimball, R., & Caserta J, 2004)

The data warehouse supports data of multiple formats stored in different levels of abstraction. As a result, the architecture is scalable capable of storing terabytes of data, extensible and provides data at multiple resolutions. The data warehouse provides sufficient information on the trends in the data, market opportunities etc.

There can be distributed data warehouse wherein the architecture supports direct storage of data from the distributed data sources in to the data warehouse. There is a centralized database that facilitates the data integration and provides the requisite data to the end user. The data warehouse supports a string of queries from the user, processed sequentially. A metadata repository helps in the content search and retrieval of the data. The usage of metadata in Data warehouses is provided in (Vetterli, T., Vaduva, A., & Staudt, M, 2000).

Storage Network

Storage area network (SAN) is a high-speed network connecting the different sources of the data along the supply chain, often through the service providers. It is composed of the data catering to the user applications and the back up data running over the high speed communication channel. In addition to the storage, SAN supports the data transactions such as mirroring, migration, retrieval etc. The SAN generally does not carry application software and is confined to the servers. Another advantage with the storage area network is that the data can be mirrored from geographically different locations. It provides additional security for the data. Today, the existing technology allows the usage of a single centralized

Figure 2. Data selection from hierarchical clusters

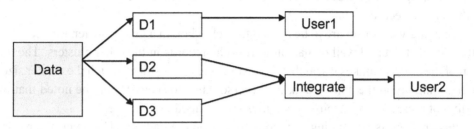

server for control, chosen from any of the servers in the loop. The ideas from swarm computing may be used to ensure the decentralization of some of the features. Instead of separate archival mechanisms and storage devices for each user in the distributed system, usage of a single centralized server in a Storage area network has reduced the cost of archival.

Data Clustering

The pattern of clustering of the data has a say on the data integration. Based on the organization of the data in to the clusters, there are two mechanisms of data clusters.

1. Hierarchical cluster
2. Non hierarchical (flat) cluster

In hierarchical cluster, as the name suggests, the data is organized in to clusters forming a hierarchy of abstraction, relevance, quality or security. The hierarchy spans from small to big. It provides different denominations of information. As a result, different number of clusters may be chosen to cater for a variety of customers as shown in the figure 2.

It opens up an interesting optimization problem on the number of clusters to be formed out of the data. On the extreme, the number of clusters can be as large as the number of records present in the database. However, such a clustering conveys no information to the user. Depending up on the number of records and the underlying application, the number of clusters should be as few as possible. As such there is no rigid rule for clustering. The similarity in the data pattern is the underlying rule of thumb.

Figure 3. Cluster of clusters

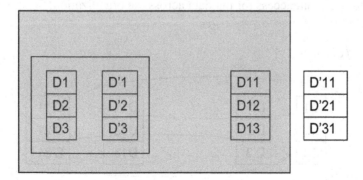

The goal of clustering is to improve the presentation apart from better readability and reduced search efforts for the similar records.

The records of a given cluster are to be related to each other. In a given cluster, the records should be such that they are distinct and well demarcated from the records in the other clusters. The hierarchical organization of the clusters makes it scalable and extensible as a result of which the cluster size can grow or shrink depending up on the application, user (personalization) etc. It may be noted that the records are physically not merged. Only their index tables are grouped in to clusters.

In a flat cluster, there is a grouping of records based on the patterns. However, the records are not organized hierarchically making it difficult to scale up.

Hierarchy of Clusters

The cluster of data hierarchy is modeled as a tree wherein the small clusters are grouped together leading to a bigger cluster of higher levels. The process continues like the streams forming rivers and rivers merging to form oceans. This clustering mechanism provides an opportunity for the user to group the relevant information based on the context. Again, a cluster with a single element will be overloaded with summarized data and does not paraphrase specific meaningful information. Figure 3 shows the cluster of clusters, forming a hierarchy. The algorithms that generate the clusters can also form the hierarchies.

In flat clustering, the number of clusters is predetermined. As a result, scaling is very difficult. However, in a hierarchical cluster, it is possible to expand or shrink the cluster by moving up or down in the hierarchy as appropriate. There are two ways of creating the hierarchy:

1. **Top down:** In this approach, one starts with a single record and start dividing the same in to required number of fragments. In general, a cluster gets divided in to two fragments at a time.
2. **Bottom up:** Here, initially, there will be as many clusters as the number of records that later merge to a few disjoint meaningful clusters. In general, two clusters are merged at a time

The data organization in the form of multiple levels of abstraction can form optimal clusters by mapping these levels to the different abstractions of the cluster. Another advantage in hierarchical representation is that, multiple, simultaneous or parallel data access is possible. Figure 4 shows the hierarchy of clusters. An arbitrary example is taken where in data at the same level of hierarchy are grouped.

The design of a data warehouse has to consider the following points:

*   Organization of the data structures and how it gets rendered to the user of the data.
*   Single view and one point access for the data across the organization.

Figure 4. Hierarchy of clusters

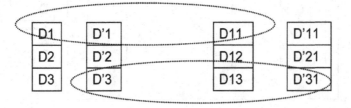

- Provide access to the data at various levels of abstraction and catering the details at different resolutions.
- Scalable architecture required to cater to a wide user group.
- Fast mechanisms for the retrieval of the information.

Graded Memory

A new storage methodology for video and picture images may be explored. Here an artificial neural network is used as a memory. It works in conjunction with the wavelets. During the operation, when the address is applied, the network first gives out some coarse output. The finer details may be synthesized based on the coarse output. The network now starts outputting more and more accurate values with lapse of time, as more and more wavelet coefficients are included. Figure 5 provides the schematic representation of the graded memory.

This multi resolution property has been used in graded memory where the image quality in a stored image increases with lapse of time if one can afford to wait for sufficiently long time. Compact storage and online generation of the multi resolution components are the essence of this concept.

ISSUES AND SOLUTIONS

There are different storage formats such as a query language. Conversion from one form to other to maintaining synchronism and coherency of data is a time consuming task. The web publishing tools extensively make use of the query language for storage format to make them more scalable and accessible to the web. The translation brings about change in the hierarchy of the data base organization calling for the merging or splitting of some of the hierarchical levels. Accordingly the service quality parameters associated with each level would undergo changes. The translator has to look in to these aspects.

It throws out different possibilities for the abstractions.

1. A certain abstraction at one of the databases happens to be the weighted average of a few abstraction levels of another other database (or weighted average of the same abstraction level of different databases).

Figure 5. Graded memory.

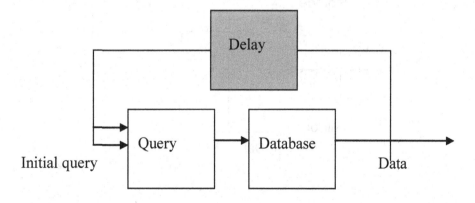

2. A certain abstraction at one of the databases happen to be the interpolation of a pair of abstraction levels of another database
3. A certain abstraction at of another other database happen to be the extrapolation or predicted version of a few abstraction levels of another data base
4. It could be the translated version

Data Integration

A broker may be used for data integration taking all the responsibilities and mask the end user from the issues of integration. In includes format conversions, data transfers etc. Synchronization of the data with the different levels of abstractions at the broker, throws open a set of problems as well as the architectures. When the level of abstraction is the same across the data to be integrated, the only parameter that dictates the integration is the time. In multiple abstraction scenarios, the integrated data should have the information as the union of the information content in the different data. The resulting data will have an abstract level that is finest among all the data sets.

The execution of ETL process involves a series of data integration tasks. Although the individual tasks perform well, their integration is still challenging. The problem is further compounded if different programmers with their own programming style or language are involved in the individual data integration. To minimize the impact, it is required to have a common and agreed interface defined and a specific coding guidelines followed across.

Data Mirroring

Hierarchical data organization goes well with the concept of mirroring. When the database is duplicated, the broker that supplies the data to the end user can get the requisite but non-overlapping data from both the sites. This would reduce the overall query time as the load on the database servers gets shared. The architecture of data mirroring is as shown in figure 6. Some of the user queries would be supported by the mirrored site. Natural choice of query is the division of abstraction levels accessed from the mirrored servers. The different abstract levels are then fused at the broker before rendering the total solution of the query to the end user.

Figure 6. Mirroring of databases

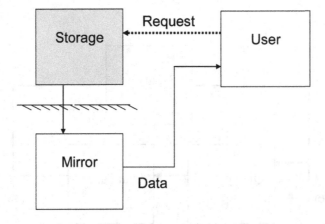

The partition of query and fusion of abstract levels calls for the intelligent database organization and specifications of the appropriate mirrored sites. However synchronization is still a risk leading to the fusion of inappropriate data.

Independent Sources

An organization having branches at multiple locations encounter the problem of consistency of the process and the definitions apart from the data inconsistencies. The same divisions or functional units such as payroll, inventory control, purchasing are maintained at different locations. However, they maintain their own databases in a customized format for their consumption. Each of these functional units with in the local site operates independently with little or no coherency although they often require the common data. Being independent data sources, they maintain their own data definitions. For example, for the marketing department, customer means the organization with whom purchasing has been done. For the payroll department, customers are the employees of the site.

Each system can have its own set of acronym lists. For example, in an organization, the codes for the North, East, South, and West sales regions may be stored as "1, 2, 3, 4" in one system and then as "N, E, S, W" in the other. The Units of measure can also be different among the systems with the weight represented as pounds in one system and kilograms in the other or with monetary figures represented as dollars in one and Euros in the other. In a multinational organization, a system in the United States might represent the date of June 12, 2009 as 06/12/2009 while the same system in the United Kingdom might be required to store this date as 12/06/2004.

Due to the independent nature of the data sources, quite often, it is not possible to get the data adhering to the common (and desired) enterprise standards. However, before the data is loaded in to the data warehouse, the data may be transformed to the common form in compliance with the standard. The common standard format of the data is to be frozen by the organization before populating the data warehouse. It is difficult to change the format every now and then. As seen by the end user, the data stored in the warehouse would have common format and indistinguishable although their sources put them in different formats.

Commercial Data Integration

Commercially available integration software is required to be interoperable with the third party software (Tian Mi, Robert Aseltine, Sanguthevar Rajasekaran, 2008) solution. The interoperability of the data is often tested before integration (Kernochan Wayne, 2003). Often APIs are developed as the interface to handle different third party software. They handle the required translations or transforms over the data before integration. As a result, most of the code may be reused across different vendors. These wrappers may be selected on the fly depending up on the vendor software, making it cost effective.

Metadata Integration

Data integration logically involves the integration of the corresponding metadata. The commercially available integration tools generally support the same. In order to support the interoperability, Object Management Group Common Data Warehouse Meta model (OMG–CWM) is used for the metadata integration. Thus, the different vendor tools used for the integration are to support the metadata integration seamlessly. Also, the data will be interoperable across the tools of the same vendor. A Bayesian network with the feedback information can easily support the integration of the heterogeneous data

Data Consistency

Maintaining consistency in the warehouse data is challenging especially if the data is getting acquired from multiple sources. Refreshment of the data in a warehouse consists of propagating the updates on the source data to correspondingly reflect them in the stored and its derivatives in the warehouse. When to refresh the data and how to refresh the data are the two issues to be resolved before the refresh.

Usually, the data in a warehouse is refreshed periodically; for example, daily or weekly. Depending up on the application, if some queries require the current data such as up to the minute stock quotes, it is necessary to propagate every update. Based on the requirements of the user and the traffic, the administrator of the warehouse selects the data refreshing policy. It is generally different for different sources. A Bayesian network with information feedback may be used for controlling the resources during refreshing. More details of the feedback for data transfer with agreed quality of service are provided in the last part of the book.

Data Refreshment Techniques

The nature of data sources as well as the capabilities of the data servers dictates the choice of refreshment technologies. Refreshment of a large file turns out to be expensive. Often, the technique of incremental refreshment is used for updating.

The data refreshment process is a time and resource consuming operation in the maintenance of a database. A huge volume of data needs to be transported, processed and stored with in a very short span of time, demanding a large power consumption and resource utilization. Refreshment of such data needs to be incremental and staggered for the optimal utilization of the resources. It calls for the prioritization of the data to be refreshed, the frequency and order of refreshment as well as the duration for the refreshment. The prioritization has to consider these and various other factors such as the life and priority of the data, and requires an intelligent algorithm to implement the same. In order to share the resources effectively, the updates are applied to the previously stored data through a data propagation mechanism. The refreshment happens over the updated data only.

In the data refreshment process, time scheduling is a concern. The time of starting, the order of execution and the particular steps to be followed are to be worked out in advance. An intelligent scheduler may be used to if multiple sources are to be refreshed.

After data refreshment, the aggregate view of the data is to be maintained. Answering the queries over the aggregated data requires the implementation of sophisticated algorithms.

FUTURE TRENDS

Data Compression

The storage networks today transfer the entire multimedia data for archiving, mirroring etc. As the data in future takes multimedia format, it is quite possible to stream the data across the high-speed storage area network in compressed form and locally generate the data at the mirrored sites. It reduces the network load and bandwidth effectively and easily meets the QoS constraints such as delay and jitter. It is affordable to maintain the decoders at the mirrored sites as it happens to be one time investment rather than streaming more data continuously. New compression standards may be required for synchronizing the multimedia data across the mirrored sites and streaming only the incremental changes.

Data Quality

Maintenance of the data quality and interoperability (Price, R. and Shanks, G, 2004) are important issues of any implementation of the data integration. Available data integration solutions are frequently integrated with the data quality and data profiling (Kahn, B., Strong, D., Wang, R, 2002) capabilities. In some cases, the data integration vendor will be a OEM and who makes use of the third party data cleansing software. The organization making use of such software has to evaluate the performance and compatibility before deployment.

The quality of data would be given more importance. The topic is discussed at length in (Vassiliadis. P., Bouzeghoub. M., Quix. C, 1999). Usage of poor quality of data would incur losses in long term due to rework, loss of credibility and inappropriate decisions. With hierarchical data organization, the quality would be fused deep in to the data.

Quality of the Data Required for the Data Warehouse

Since the data warehouses are predominantly used for decision making, the high level summarized and integrated data will be more useful than the fine grain detailed data from individual records. As a result of integration of data from several sources, the quality of the data tends to deteriorate unless the individual sources adhere to the quality norms. In addition to the absolute quality of the individual records, what would get provided to the end user is also important. The large size of data warehouses, of the order of terabytes, puts constraints on the search time of the requisite records that in turn translate to quality of the data provided to the end user in agreed time. To support multi dimensional data as in OLAP, special data organization and implementation technologies are required to reduce the access time.

A neural network with information feedback from the end user produces the outputs that are functions of the weighted averages of the long time history of the data. Adequate weightage may be provided to the historical data that forms the feedback information. Being Bayesian in nature, these neural networks may be used for merging the data from different databases effectively. The usage of such a neural network to process queries has been provided in part four of the book.

While an operational database stores current data, a typical Decision Support System requires historical data for predictions and trend analysis. In such systems, in order to take the right decision, data from multiple sources in different formats, often from the sources external to the organization needs to be consolidated. These sources provide the data with varying quality making it difficult to maintain the agreed quality in the consolidated data. The usage of a neural network for handling heterogeneous data sources is provided in the chapter on Information Transmission with quality of service.

Centralized Data Warehouse and Distributed Data Warehouse

In centralized data warehouse, all the data required for one group or division or Business unit are placed in a single physical location and accessed by a variety of end users. This architecture is recommended when there is a frequent data transaction by a large number of end users in different formats and denominations. A single view of updated, integrated and readable data would be available for the different users of the group.

Since the data is stored at one centralized place, the server is to be powerful and support a heavy traffic. The accessibility or browsing of data would be a potential issue, to be handled by the appropriate architecture. So, in practice, a Multi dimensional database server with advanced data base management software running would be used.

In a distributed data warehouse, the fragments of the data are distributed across different physical locations sitting on multiple servers. This is useful when different units of a large organization function independently enjoying the delegated power. They find the limited need of the global data that may be accessed by a centralized data warehouse on need basis. For all operational purposes, the local data is good enough for decision making. Since various players tend to the same data, distributed data warehouse carries redundant data. However, the browsers do not face the issues seen in a centralized data warehouse.

A mix of both these types may be used in an organization. The centralized data ware house can contain the abstract version of information (or gist of the relevant data) that becomes more elaborate at the lower levels in the hierarchy with the local distributed data warehouses. By mirroring the databases, it would be possible to reduce the burden on a single server and improve the browser performance.

CONCLUSION

In this chapter,

- The data organization and the related issues in a data warehouse are discussed to provide links and useful tips.
- The architecture of the data warehouse being practiced today is provided

Over the next few years, the growth of data warehousing is going to be enormous with new products and technologies coming out frequently. In order to get the benefit of this growth, it is important that the data warehouse planners and the developers have a clear idea of what they are looking for.

QUESTIONS

1. How does the hierarchical representation of the data help in the supply chain management?
2. What are the factors to be considered for the choice of the storage technology?
3. What is the role of data warehouse in the supply chain management?
4. What are the strategies to be followed for the Metadata integration?
5. How do the available storage technologies affect the data compression technologies?

REFERENCES

Adamson, C., & Venerable, M. (1998). *Data warehouse design solutions*. Chichester, UK: John Wiley & Sons.

Chaudhuri, S., & Dayal, U. (1997). An overview of data warehousing and OLAP technology. *SIGMOD Record, 26*(1), 65–74. Mi, T., Aseltine, R., Rajasekaran, S. (2008). Data Integration on Multiple Data Sets. In *IEEE International Conference on Bioinformatics and Biomedicine*, (pp. 443-446).

Garzetti, M. Giorgini, P. Rizzi, S.(2005). Goal-Oriented Requirement Analysis for Data Warehouse Design. *8th International Workshop on Data Warehouseing and OLAP (DOLAP 2005)*.

Inmon, W. H. (2002). *Building the data warehouse* (3rd Ed.). New York: John Wiley & Sons.

Inmon, W. H., Imhoff, C., & Battas, G. (1999). *Building The Operational Data Store* (2nd Ed.). New York: John Wiley.

Inmon, W. H., & Kelley, C. (1993). *Rdb/VMS: Developing the Data Warehouse*. Boston: QED Publishing Group.

Kahn, B., Strong, D., & Wang, R. (2002). Information Quality Benchmarks: Product and Service Performance. *Communications of the ACM*, 184–192.

Kernochan, W. (2003). *Enterprise Information Integration: The New Way to Leverage e-Information*. Boston: Aberdeen Group.

Kimball, R., & Caserta, J. (2004). *The data warehouse ETL toolkit*. New York: John Wiley & Sons.

Price, R., & Shanks, G. (2004). A Semiotic Information Quality Framework. In *Proc. IFIP International Conference on Decision Support Systems (DSS2004): Decision Support in an Uncertain and Complex World*, Prato, Italy.

Vassiliadis, P., Bouzeghoub, M., & Quix, C. (1999). Towards quality-oriented data warehouse usage and evolution. In M. Jarke & A. Oberweis (Eds.), *International Conference CAiSE* (LNCS 1626, pp. 164-179). Berlin: Springer-Verlag. Vetterli, T., Vaduva, A., & Staudt, M. (2000). Metadata standards for data warehousing: Open information model vs. common warehouse metadata. *SIGMOD Record, 29*(3), 68-75.

West, M., & Fowler, J. (1999). *Developing High Quality Data Models*. The European Process Industries STEP Technical Liaison Executive (EPISTLE).

Chapter 12
Information Archiving

ABSTRACT

In order to keep the information accessible for the customers over the supply chain, the data in demand is to be archived and rendered with attraction. One of the major issues with the data archives is the access time. The same is addressed in this chapter with new archival methodologies.

INTRODUCTION

The previous chapter describes the different ways of storing the data to cater for various applications along the supply chain. This is required to be maintained in the archive if it is to be retained for referencing by a large number of users simultaneously over a long period of time. Here, the different techniques and practices used for the data archiving are discussed.

The archiving system provides storage, archive and restore functionalities to the applications. These functionalities are extensively used to transfer the data from the storage media to the server and vice versa. In addition, information also gets transported across the archives for various reasons such as mirroring, conditional access etc.

Archiving is a bit different from back up though they share many properties in common. In this chapter effective achieving methods exploiting the different data storage models and business models are highlighted. The data organization required for an archive bears a lot of similarities with the one in the conventional storage system. The archive consists of digital libraries, enterprise data, digital cinema, songs and similar contents available for a large group of people over the intranet or the web. The example and case study of digital libraries are considered throughout this chapter. Here, the achieves are

DOI: 10.4018/978-1-60566-888-8.ch012

interchangeably used with the libraries (Murthy. T A V and et.al, 2005) to the extent that it provides the requisite data for the future references. The different methods of archiving digital data, digital libraries, the storage media and the associated issue with their usage are discussed in detail.

BACKGROUND

Standardization of Archives

In order to support seem less interoperability, the International Standardization Organization (ISO) has defined a mechanism for the long time archival of the data, acquired specifically from terrestrial environment & space. The model is based on the Open Archival Information System (OAIS) reference model.

For document ingest or administration, the standard called Producer-Archive Interface Methodology Abstract Standard was developed. It was further enriched by the standard on data Ingest, Identification, and Certification in Archives, the Archival Workshop on Ingest, Identification, and Certification Standards (AWIICS).

The standard is open and available for implementation free of cost, getting rid of the expensive licenses. As a result, the standard has to be independent of the format used for the representation of the information. The standard provides detailed description for the implementation of the hardware and software components as well as maintenance of the same through the information acquisition, preservation and distribution.

To assist document retrieval, the objects in a digital library are described using XML. The metadata encoding and transmission standard (METS) schema provides the XML description for encoding descriptive, administrative and structural metadata.

Archive Model

In the archive model, two types of information are associated with a document- the content description information and the archival description information. It supports the binding of the data with the metadata or information. In archival system, the fundamental units of transaction are the objects. An object is a set of files (R. Allen Wyke, 1999) over which operations such as store, restore, archive and copy may be performed.

Components of the Archive

The typical Archive is composed of the following software components:

1. **Archive manager:** It is required to control and manage all the archive operations including archive, restore, copy, delete and retrieve.
2. **Archive actors:** they are required to copy of the data between servers (Mathew Strebe, Charles Perkins, 1998) serving as the data source or destination for the objects getting archived or retrieved.
3. **Archive API:** It is called by the applications interacting with the archive to control the same.

Figure 1. Components of Digital archive.

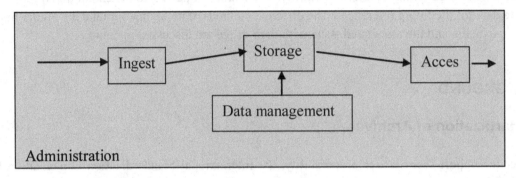

4. **Archive Control GUI:** It is required to monitor and interact with the archive (Evangelos Petroutsos, 1998).
5. **Message transfers:** It spans the requests and responses getting exchanged between the archive Control GUI (Mike Gundearloy, 2000) and the archive Manager

Functional Units of Archive

The OAIS standard model comprises of the following entities in the digital archive.

1. **Ingest:** This is the input unit of the archive capable of accepting the documents and helps in archive management.
2. **Access**: This is the output unit of the archive providing the required document up on request. It maintains the information on the availability of a document, its storage location etc.
3. **Archival storage:** This unit handles the physical storage part, maintenance of the documents and helps in the retrieval of the documents.
4. **Data management**: This unit is responsible for all transactions involving the data and house keeping such as accessing the metadata, identification of the required and maintenance of the archive administrative data.
5. **Administration:** This unit handles the management of the archival information system.

The components of an archive are shown in figure 1.

All the documents in the archive are not accessed and used regularly. A selected few of them are requested very often. An Audit report data shows that 66% of the primary capacity of the data had not been accessed for more than 1 year. Under such circumstances, it would be beneficial for the organizations to shift this data out of the active zone and free the memory.

Case Study: Digital Archive and Libraries

The huge demand and supply of the digital content has opened the way for digital libraries. The main attractions are portability, accessibility and affordability of the digital content. With the analog content and its players becoming obsolete and less attractive, digital archiving mechanisms have turned in to the right choice. The digital content includes pictures, video, audio, tables etc. It renders even the printed versions of the books less useful relative to the digital version of the same content. The digital version such as document or portable document format supports search facility through the keywords that is not possible through the hard copies although the index helps to some extent. However, copy and paste of the content is unique to digital copies saving the time enormously. One typical example is the e-mail data. By moving the same in to archive memory, statistics shows that a company saved $ 600 million.

Still a lot of information and rerecords from the government organizations is archived in the analog form and required rapid digitization. However, they also would like to retain the traditional structure of retaining the documents more for the security reasons. The digital archives are used in libraries, knowledge base organizations, business and information supply chain etc. the cycles in the supply chain involve acquisition, organization, accessibility, preservation etc

The digital archives are extensively used by Information and Library Network (INFLIBNET) to support the instructional work (Witten Ian. H and Bainbridge David, 2003). It enables a large student community to access the digital library simultaneously. It also caters for the general public who seek information in a particular domain. The Objectives of DLAA are provided in listing 1.

Compared to the conventional print and analog medium of data archive, the digital archiving of data has become very popular with the availability of a huge volume of data and document. The special effects and video associated with the text will be far more effective than the text. In addition, the digital media may be shared among unlimited number of readers without additional investment. The environmental friendly digital libraries have started replacing the conventional libraries that demand paper in large quantities. The advantage of the digital library over the conventional archiving system is provided in listing 2.

Listing 1. Objectives of digital libraries and archives:

1. Provide access to the computerized information system through the intranet as well as the Internet.
2. Management of the learning resources.
3. Provide solutions for the problems in copyright, content security, subscription and licensing.
4. Maintenance of the learning resources composed of audio, video and print material.

Listing 2. Advantages of digital archiving over the conventional archiving:

*   Easy to access the resources through the internet or intranet for the consumption at anytime. The same may be copied in to a local machine and used in leisure (Er. S.K. Soni, 1997).
*   Supports the simultaneous access of the content by many people. Compared to the traditional libraries, it is a giant step in the content distribution.
*   Online trading of the content has increased the business multifolds.

Management of Digital Archive and Digital Knowledge Bases

The digital archiving system needs certain management tricks and tips to be followed:

1. The document to be entered in to the digital archive is to be evaluated before doing so, weighing the pros and cons from the knowledge distribution perspective as well as the business relevance.

2. The financial impact of procuring a document as well as its maintenance needs to be considered.
3. There should be well defined procedure for the distribution of the content, subscription etc. There can be different packages or subscription modes such as annual, life time, corporate, individual etc to cater for a variety of classes.
4. The pros and cons of taking the venture of translating analog information or the one available in hard copies in to digital form has to be worked out depending up on the relevance and the investment.

The digital archives have opened up new avenues for the online education. The study material can reach the student community through the digital library supply chain, often span the globe. There are many other avenues and issues for the future developments of DAs:

- Before placing the document in the archive, it is important that the document does not violate copy rights and non controversial.
- It should be procured legally
- Collaboration among the distributed archives will provide more benefits for the subscribers
- Classification of the documents is an issue. It can happen based on the domain such as techno logy, science, arts etc. the classification should also support cross referencing and easy search using keywords.
- Integration of the digital archive with the supply chain is a challenging task.
- Marketing of the libraries to the general public, educational organizations etc is challenging.

Data Backup

In a supply chain, data archives (Talawar V G and Biradar B S, 2004) often require the backup of the information. It is a protection mechanism for the data. It is required to take out the data from the production system until it changes, preserve it and make it easily accessible for referencing. The data is removed from the archive after the retention period.

It provides a simple solution to retain the data for long, often on the disk itself! Based on the access pattern, the data is often moved out and placed in the shelf.

The data signals (Nicholas Chase, 2000) from the source to the destination are transferred over 10/100BaseT LAN. The control signals adhere to the IP protocol.

Metadata Association

Metadata of the archive data provides (Baru, C, 1998) the attributes of the archive (Marco, David, 2000). The attributes include the retention period of the document, its physical location, access permissions etc. It is associated with the file rather than with its content. The metadata is generated automatically during the archival in a batch mode or individually. User can assist by defining a few parameters of the metadata such as the author of the file, its source etc. The metadata is very useful for the retrieval of the required file from across several documents created through multiple applications.

Features of Archive

An archive system is expected to support a number of good features. It should support fast, easy and the online access as well as the data capture. To make it happen, appropriate indexing tables are to be maintained. The archive needs to be scalable and cost effective with provision to expand without disturbing the existing system. It should adhere to a strong policy to support the management.

Object Grouping

Often, the user applications require a set of objects to be retrieved together. This is facilitated by the optimal and virtual grouping of the objects. By referring to the group, it is possible to operate over the set of the objects in one shot.

The objects in a group share several properties in common. They have the same life time in the active memory. They are generally placed contiguously so that when they are deleted, a continuous memory block is released for use rather than multiple fragments.

In archiving the sequence of storage includes the secondary memory, primary memory, cache and registers. The data transfers among them may be controlled with a classifier. A neural network may be used as a Bayesian classifier. The usage of a neural network as classifier is provided in the part intelligent information management.

An object can belong to multiple groups simultaneously. First, the object is copied in to different groups using the copy-to-group commands. The groups may be placed at different locations at a time, for example on the active memory, on the library, on the shelf etc. When the object is to be retrieved, appropriate group is to be referred based on the context. If no group is specified, the object is retrieved from the group that has the lowest access time.

The groups could be extend to have different abstraction levels and streamed in the order of fastest storage device first to save time.

If the medium on which the objects are stored is sufficiently large, it is possible to store all the objects next to each other on the same medium. It speeds up the processing of the restore command as they are residing on the same medium. It leads to the following two models of the archive.

1. **Associative Archive**: It makes sure multiple objects of the same set are on the same medium.
2. **Associative Staging:** Here, if an object is retrieved, all other objects belonging to the same set are also brought along with it so as to speed up the subsequent restore of these objects.

These functions decide the storage order. The different data with the same level of hierarchy are stored and retrieved at a time and sent. Depending on the commercial model, data with the same abstract level gets bundled together.

Case Study

Archive Medium: RAID

One of the popular medium for the archival of the data is the Redundant Arrays of Inexpensive Disks or RAID. It consists of an array of small and inexpensive drives which perform better than a single large

Figure 2. Pre-specified data clean up

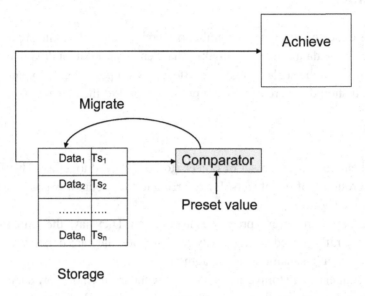

disk drive in terms of cost, speed and accessibility. Because of the presence of small independent drivers in parallel, the system is fault tolerant. Also, maintenance will be easy. Each drive is provided with a data storage space. Additional discussion on RAID is found in (Paul Rogers, et.al, 2005)

Archive Medium: Tape

The tape storage medium consists of both the archive and the backup data. However, there is a difference in the way they are accessed. In case of archive data, it takes a little longer time to access. This is because the data has to be placed in the active memory before being consumed. It calls for speed up of the access of archive data. So, it results in the problem of meeting two different access timing for the access of data from the tape.

Disk Clean Up Mechanisms

There are two ways of cleaning up the disk and free the memory:

1. **Unconditional or spontaneous clean up:** Here the document would be removed from the disc space once the specified retention period of the object expires, unless some process is referring to the object. The data archiving mechanism with pre specified duration is shown in figure 2. A copy of the object is always retained on the tape or the DVD.
2. **Watermark Clean up**: Here the object may be retained on the disk even after the expiry of the retention period as long as there is enough space on the memory. The watermarking of data with the archiving is shown in figure 3. The data exists till another wave of data arrives for the replacement. There are two different watermark levels:
   a. *High watermark*: The archive starts the housekeeping activities once this level is reached. The activities involve transfer or deletion of the expired files based on the pre-defined policy.

Figure 3. Data archiving with watermarking technique

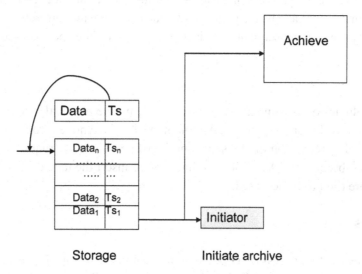

If the retention period set for the documents has not been expired, the documents are to be retained and can not be deleted. The disk space in use can go beyond the watermark level. The application software or the user, through the configurations has to take care of the watermark level and the rate of filling in the memory space.

b. *Low watermark*: Once this level is reached, the deletion or transfer of files stops in the archive.

ISSUES AND SOLUTIONS

Access Speed

Data access speed is the main issue with digital archives. The abstract levels of the data may be mapped on to the storage hierarchy. Objects placed in the archive may be stored on different types of physical media. The access speed of archive is a little longer then the one with a disc. However, the data archival and retrieval can happen automatically without the intervention of the operator, justifying the investment. Automated libraries and juke boxes have become popular for a safe storage. Each media has its own merits and drawbacks in terms of cost, access time and retention period. The archive allows to make the best use of them and to use any media type according to requested quality of service.

The archives make use of disk memory either as a primary storage or as a temporary storage used to cache the data. In primary storage, the documents are meant to be retained over a long duration. In an archive, data gets moved to the secondary storage when it is created on the primary storage. This transfer can also be triggered by an event such as the time to move after the specified retention period on the disk. With the documents getting entered in to the primary memory, soon it gets full. Water mark techniques are often used to remove the documents from the memory when the available memory falls below a value.

Information Access time is a problem in the archive calling for a kind of pre-fetch. The algorithm has to understand the users' access and usage pattern of the data archive and pre-fetch the data, assuming it would be accessed by the user subsequently. This would save the time spent on accessing.

Large Storage

Handling of large volumes of data and archiving is a problem. The physical media such as tapes, DVD are quite often used for the library or jukebox. Although the data is removed from the active storage once the memory gets filled, information on the same and its whereabouts are required to be maintained to support their access subsequently. A notification message to insert the tape or disc has to be generated when such objects are tried to be accessed.

Random Access

In order to support the random access of a document in the archive, the attributes of the document such as name or category are made use. Although there can be several document with the same name or category, the combination of these two attributes is unique in the archive system. These attributes are assigned by the archival system and the applications using them are not concerned about it. When the documents are entered, their whereabouts are maintained by the system.

In order to retrieve the files, the attributes such as the ID of the media used to store the document, the position of the document on the storage media, the size of the document etc are stored by the archival system. It helps in the retrieval of the documents. This information is generally not available or requested by the user. However, it is available over the archive API or the archive Control GUI (A Keyton Weissinger, 1999). However, this is not the actual metadata of the document.

In general, the files are not in proprietary format. So, it is possible to get them on to the local device and consume the content. The tape reading utility ensures interoperability as all the devices usually support the same.

Access Scheduling

With multiple users are accessing the archive simultaneously, sequencing them for the data transactions is a tough task. They are not permitted to disturb the ongoing processes. A smart algorithm is called for scheduling the data sources for archiving. Scheduling is done by the archive manager based on the availability of the resources, the data sources who request them, their priorities, load on the resources, nature of the request such as copy, retrieve, retrieve etc.

A similar issue of scheduling is encountered and negotiated by the ingest unit during the archival of the data. Often, a service quality or a class parameter or a priority tag is associated with the source of the data and the same has to be considered for scheduling. The sources would have different data rates, different priorities and heterogeneous. The storage of information in the archive, accomplished by archive storage unit, needs intelligence to organize the data in a hierarchical fashion of varying degree of abstraction. The different levels of the hierarchy will have different access time as shown in figure 4.

Figure 4. Data access time over the archive.

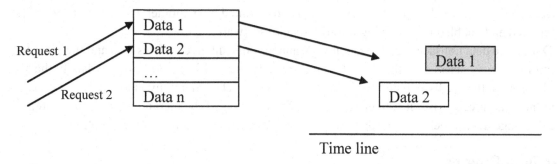

Time line

Archive Management

Achieve management involves the technical and management aspects provided in the listing 3.

Listing 3. Archive management:

1. It has to support the existing archival system. Signal processing is required for the translation and handle this issue.
2. The archive system is to be Scalable and support the expansion. Hierarchical storage of the data would provide requisite scalability and extensibility.
3. Choice of the evolving storage technology is critical to make sure that it does not get obsolete in a short span of time. Hierarchical storage helps to migrate and use all brands of the tools. The hierarchies may be easily mapped on to the changing storage technologies. The hierarchies also render a set of commercial models depending up on the abstraction of the data provided and access permissions for the data.

Archive Security

Maintenance of the security of information in an archive is an issue. However, there are different processes to achieve the same. The archive is to be backed up regularly on a tape for disaster recovery or to handle data corruption either outside of the library or with in. The backup may be carried out manually or with the help of a utility automatically (George Koch and Kevin Loney, 1997). Manual backup works if the archive is small and dedicated human resources are available. The archive catalogue is to be separately maintained by a DBMS (Database Management System) on a RAID sub-system.

Fault Tolerant Archive

To support seamless accessibility an archiving system has to be fault tolerant. If the physical medium such as the tape fails, it is to be disconnected from the archival system. Depending up on the data transaction scenario during the fault occurrence, appropriate measures are taken.

During the migration of the data, if an error is detected on a tape, the operation continues over another tape. The first tape is to be accessible for read and delete operations. If a failure is detected during the read operation, the same has to be cancelled with immediate effect. If the tape fails during the delete operation, the same is to be stopped and abandoned. During the write operations over the tape, if a failure is detected in the drive, the operation gets stalled and resumed over another drive. The failed drive is to be repaired and enabled for archiving through special software.

During the data transactions, if the archive Manager fails, the live updates stop and the same have to be informed to the users over the GUI. The multiple and hierarchical storage of the data in the archive would provide the requisite fault tolerance. Even if one level of hierarchy is lost, it may be generated from the other levels. Also, it is likely that the different levels of the hierarchy would get stored in different storage device technologies that are possibly placed at physically distinct locations.

Handling Queries

In the OAIS model, the data management module is responsible for the execution of queries and maintaining a queue for the pipeline of the queries. Based on the agreed service quality, the queries need to be shuffled in the queue. This is achieved through the usage of a scheduling algorithm to line up the queries in the queue.

Operational Issues

- **Access rights:** The rights management and the access control may be blended with the document access function. The users of archive can have different levels of access permissions. A rule base algorithm maps the right permission to the abstract levels of the storage.
- **Format conversion:** The storage of heterogeneous digital information often requires format conversions. This is predominant in the storage of video. Transcoding is done to put the data in requisite format. The transcoding is done for meeting the demand of a certain data format over the other, reduction in storage space, migration of the rest of the world away from the outdated technologies etc. The archival of multiple data formats is shown in figure 5. It is often required to cater for different classes of users.
- **Data migration:** Migration in the storage is often required to handle changes in the storage technology, access time etc. Hierarchical storage of information on different physical devices such as CD, tape etc helps in the migration of particular information rather than massive data transfers. The hierarchy of storage devices is shown in figure 6.
- **Data classification:** Classification of data is a task quite involved. Automated classifiers are often required to sort the huge database around the supply chain. The end users will be happy only with a reduced access time. To facilitate this, only the relevant documents are to be placed in the fast memory. Today there ate tools to indicate the access patterns of the documents. Depending up on their frequency of access and the access policies in force, some of the documents may be required to be shifted to the lower tier in the hierarchy. This will svae the time required for classification of documents by other means of input. Examples of such archiving include e- mails storage, document storage depending how often they are requested.

The best ways to determine if the data under consideration is a candidate for archiving is to make use of the data pattern assessment with the usage of intelligent elements. It helps to take a decision if it is getting accessed frequently and if it requires an assurance of the service quality during the access.

Figure 5. Archival of multiple formats.

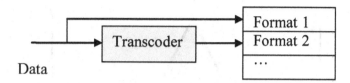

FUTURE TRENDS

In order to support the standards with temporary storage, disk cache enables etc, it is required to translate the data field representations and data formats. It calls for the following changes:

- **Adaption of the Data transmission rate**: It is required for matching the network connections with the tape drive speeds. A feedback neural network may be used for rate adjustment. It takes a large set of previous values as additional input for decision making. This is going to make the system to attain stability fast.
- **Parallel data transfers:** It involves the transfer of data on to the archive system, in spite of the media drives being busy.
- **Temporary storage for the repack:** The data from fragmented tapes is required to be temporarily stored on a disk until a new tape is created and the data is deleted from the initial one.

Data Access

With a powerful signal processing model, the predicted and shifted signal can be generated as feedback to the user based on the watermark status. Once disk object instances have expired, the application may need to force the creation of a disk instance again for a specified object, if it forecasts that some operations will require fast access to this particular object. It calls for an intelligent element to predict the access plan. The characteristics of the archival media are shown in figure 7.

With the growth in the users of the archive, the applications in future can request a pre-fetch of an object to copy an instance from a live media to disk through an API command. The retention period of these instances will be defined in the Storage Plan. The feedback signals from the user such as fast,

Figure 6. Hierarchy of physical devices.

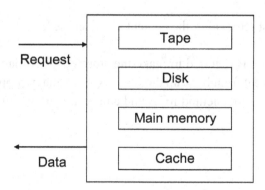

Figure 7. Characteristics of the archival media

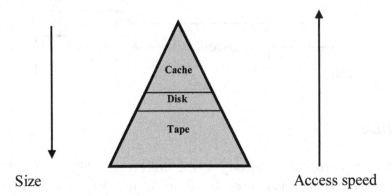

Size   Access speed

slow, good, not so good etc serve as useful input to manage the data transfers, reserve the resources and prefetch the data. A shifted version of these signals work as the feedback signals and help in optimal resource management.

Data Backup

Data backup is different from the archive even if the same vendor or software maintains the same. While the back up of the data is done for its protection, archiving is carried out for its improved accessibility. Quite often, the organizations choose the same vendor to provide both the backup software and the Archive software. This is because the same process and policies that are familiar to the users and interoperable are being practiced. It is also possible for them to share the same storage devices and mechanisms for both. However, if the vendors are different, it is difficult for the media to be partitioned for providing access to the different vendors separately. The interoperability of backup and archival software can help in fast translation of the backup data to archive.

CONCLUSION

In this chapter,

- The issues and techniques of the best practices in the archive policies being followed are discussed.
- Mechanisms for the fast retrieval of the content are discussed.

Effective archiving method is required to make the stored data available to the right people at the right time. Archiving is different from back up though they share many properties on common. Industry standard for archiving provides the method for sound and secure archiving of the data.

QUESTIONS

1. What are the differences between the archive and storage?
2. What are the factors to be considered for the archival of the data?
3. How do you speed up the data retrieval process from the archive?
4. What are the factors up on which the medium for the archiving depend?
5. What are the different house keeping activities that take place in the archive?

REFERENCES

Marco, D. (2000). *Building and managing the metadata repository: A full life cycle guide*. Chichester, UK: John Wiley & Sons.

Murthy, T. A. V., et al. (2005). *Multilingual Computing and Information Management in Networked Digital Environment: organized by CUST and INFLIBNET*, (3rd International CALIBER). Chase, N. (2000). *Active Server Pages 3.0 from scratch*. New Delhi: QUE, Prentice Hall of India Private Ltd.

Rogers, P., Janssen, R., Otto, A., Pleus, R., & Sokal, V. (2005). Redundant array of independent disks (RAID). *ABCs of z/OS System Programming* (Vol. 3). Armonk, New York: IBM Press.

Strebe, M., & Perkins, C. (1998). *Internet Information Server*, (1st ed.). New Delhi: BPS Publication. Gundearloy, M. (2000). *Visual Basic Developer's Guide to ADO*. New Delhi: BPB Publications.

Talawar, V. G. & Biradar, B. S. (2004). *Digital Resources and Services in Libraries: Organized by Kuvempu University and ASSIST, 4th ASSIST National Seminar.*

Weissinger, A. K. (1999). *ASP in a Nutshell*. Mumbai, India: O'Reilly, Shroff Publisher & Distributors Private Limited. Baru, C. (1998). *Archiving Metadata*. Paper presented at the 2nd European Conference on Research and Advanced Technology for Digital Libraries (poster), Crete, Greece. Petroutsos, E. (1998). *Mastering Visual Basic 6*. New Delhi: BPB Publications. Soni, Er. S.K. (1997). *Multi-media Archival for Technical Education in Indian Ocean Region Countries An Indian Proaction*. XXVII, Annual Convention of ISTE, MACT. Koch, G. & Loney, K. (1997). *Oracle 8i - The Complete Reference*, (3rd ed.). New Delhi: TMH.

Witten, I. H., & Bainbridge, D. (2003). *How to Build a Digital Library*. San Francisco: Morgan Kaufmann Publishers.

Wyke, R. A. (1999). *Pure JavaScript*, (1st ed.). New Delhi: SAMS, Techmedia Publication.

Chapter 13
Information Storage Security

ABSTRACT

The primary goal of the information supply chain is to provide access to the right users to share the data. So, a framework is required to define the rightful users. This chapter provides the mechanism and algorithms to do the same. The hierarchical representation of data introduced here, map on to the different degrees of permissions enjoyed by the customers throwing open new business opportunities.

INTRODUCTION

The previous chapter explained the need of archiving the data. This data is to reach the "rightful" users based on the privileges they enjoy for the consumption of the data. Here the mechanism for the description of these rights is provided.

The data exposed to the different players of the supply chain will be under the risk of information security. In this chapter, the security of information has been taken as a parameter describing the quality of service (QoS) and methods are suggested for the minimum agreed guaranteed value for the same. Simulation results have shown that the signal processing model based on the user feedback is highly efficient in handling this parameter. The service guarantee would be readily met with the help of a feedback parameter from the receiving end of the information to the source of the information. The technique has been reused in the chapter on Information Transmission with quality of service. This reduces the stranded time of the information or information loss along the communication channel from one business unit to the other unit along the supply chain.

DOI: 10.4018/978-1-60566-888-8.ch013

Figure 1. Digital content carrying copyright

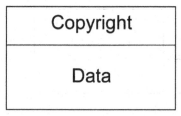

It is very difficult to control the proliferation of the content once it has been broadcast over the medium. In the absence of appropriate security mechanisms, it would be possible to record the songs off the radio and copy the TV programs and pay-per-view movies. Broadcasting to computers makes it even easier for the end users to create the digital copies that can be preserved and passed around. Content providers have used existing Digital rights management (DRM) solutions to restrict the distribution of the content and prevent the users from recording the broadcasted content. But these solutions are often cracked. A large number of third party software packages exist over the internet that can copy or record a digital broadcast. In this chapter the method of providing security for the contents during the distribution is discussed. It is expected to throw light on the techniques used to create and distribute the digital content that adhere to the copyrights. New business models are discussed to support the effective distribution of the content.

BACKGROUND

The sophisticated method of introducing security for the information at the time of content creation and storage is through the digital rights management (DRM). It is covered extensively in MPEG-21. Although the DRM is extensively used with the multimedia content, the underlying concept may be used for any information content, services or the software. DRM is used in e-commerce, e-learning, conferencing, libraries etc. It can be used for music distribution.

Digital rights management (DRM) is a technology that supports the distribution of the online content (Lawrence Lessig, 2004) with copyright, such as Music and documents. The technology provides a mechanism for the content creators to safely distribute and sell the contents online. It takes help from different technologies to realize the access control policies for the software, music, movies, or other digital data, services and the hardware.

The rights management paradigm existed since ages in different forms and size. The focus of earlier versions of the DRM was confined to the security and encryption of the contents to prevent the unauthorized copying. The digital content used to get encrypted with the help of a key. The secret key was distributed only to those who pay. The content is blended to the copyright as shown in the figure 1.

The activities of rights management covers the description, identification, trading and protection, monitoring and tracking of all forms of the rights. It includes the usages, specification and management of rights holders' relationships. The supply chain starting from the creation of the content up to the consumption by the end user is covered under DRM.

Figure 2. Data access permissions: Read.

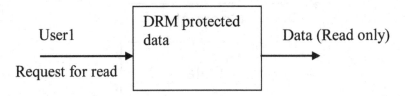

Case Study: E-Book

The usage of digital rights management may be illustrated with the example of an e-book (TinHat, 2006). The author places the soft copy of the book in the e-book store and provide "Read" and (or) "Print" permissions for selected pages and specifies the pricing and security options for the book. In addition, as an attraction for the readers, a number of pages may be provided as a free preview.

The on-line payment made for using the e-book may be shared by the multiple authors, editors and the e-book vendors in an agreed. All these transactions are automated and the money from the readers of the book straight away reaches the authors' bank account! The mechanism to enable all these transactions is covered under DRM. This information is encoded in a Meta language such as XML, specifically using the rights description language such as ODRL. With the encoding in XML, it is possible to exchange the information with the other e-book vendors supporting the same language semantics. It results in the complete and automatic interoperability.

The DRM software consists of 2 parts- Setting selective permissions for the usage of the book and the automation of the bank transactions. With the help of a graphical user interface (GUI) the author can change the permissions any time depending up on the demand for the contents of the book. Another GUI displays the revenue distribution among the authors, publishers etc and not necessarily visible for the readers of the book. Generally the authors do not have permission to edit this. Figure 2 and 3 illustrate the different access permissions.

Components of DRM

The usage of a specific component of DRM depends up on the application (Rosenblatt, B, et.al, 2001). The difference lies in the degree of interactivity required by the application. For the music content, the interactivity is less, about once per song. The same is true with the e-book. In contrast, interactive games require the user intervention for every stroke. Each time, a new content is to be transferred from the server.

Digital Rights Management (DRM) consists of three major components:

Figure 3. Data access permissions: Edit

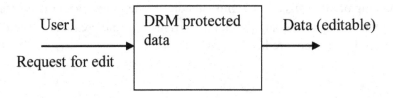

- Description or expression of the digital rights, similar to the copyrights.
- Authorization to access and consume the content, happening through password or otherwise.
- Enforcement of the rights through encryption mechanism.

These components are applicable at different levels of the network. The entire network between the distribution server and the client device need to support and interpret DRM. The enforcement is to be content specific. DRM flow makes use of the four players:

- The content provider
- License server
- Distribution server
- The end user.

The content provider encrypts the content or the data and places the same in the distribution server. The copyright and license information of the content are to be placed in the license server. The content protection software is to be installed in the client. The UI for viewing the content and the transactions would be called in the end user application.

The content encryption happens with the help of the license keys placed over the license server. Multiple licensing options are possible throwing open different commercial models. The license may be granted for a fixed duration of time or it can be permanent; for a single PC or multiple PCs, for a fixed number of 'download and play' or unlimited usage etc. Depending up on the security algorithm being used, the license key on the server changes the value periodically calling for the synchronization with the content provider and the end user.

In order to use the content, the customers need to get the license keys first. In e-commerce based model, the URL of the license server would be included in the header of the media file or the content. The key may be downloaded from the license server after an appropriate payment that happens through the e-transaction. The license server also maintains the databases of the users, the permission modes etc. Watermarks run all along the content without being noticed by the end user. They carry information about the content creators and prove the authenticity or originality of the content. The users should be happy for what they pay.

The online distribution of the contents happens through streaming or downloads. The content delivery mechanism in general, is independent of the underlying DRM technology. In addition to displaying the content, the client software that resides at the user terminal takes the responsibility of communicating with the license server and gets the key. It also handles the online payments etc.

The key from the license server and the content from the distribution server are to be transferred over different protocols. A lower data rate is sufficient to transfer the key. Secure and error free transmission is the goal here. On the other hand, the actual content from the distribution server can withstand a few packet drops depending up on the protocol being used. Quite often, real time transmission is the goal here.

The rights are described through a Meta language. The usage of XrML for assigning rights is given in the chapter on Metadata. The need of Metadata to enforce DRM is described in (Norman Paskin, 2003). The authorization for the distribution of the content may be provided at multiple levels. Generally, the owner of a service or the content provides access to a set of distributors by providing the appropriate license. They in turn provide the access permission or licenses to a set of customers. They work as agents or brokers. For the end user, they are responsible to ensure the authenticity of the content.

DRM Implementation

The DRM may be implemented (K . G. Saur München, 1998) with the agent-based technology. DRM Agent implements a trusted entity in the client device. It oversees the consumption of the content and the enforcement of the digital rights. The agent starts working the moment the rights protected content is launched on the client device.

DRM is often enforced through the operating system (Hofmeister, C, Nord, R, & Soni, D, 2000). The system first checks the file headers. If the files contain unauthorized content, the content of the files would not be played. To protect the data on the page file from copying, the operating system blocks the access to the page file or erases the data from the page file before the copying of the page happens. In addition, to enforce the selective permissions for the usage of the contents, the operating system has to ensure a tamper proof clock running over the device.

From the implementation perspective, the DRM software development happens at two places - the client and the server. The client software includes decryption software, drivers for the content memory and the players, delivery software, e-commerce software and communication software. The communication software transfers the appropriate rights and permissions to the end user and back to the license server.

The server software includes two components: content creation software and the distribution server software. The content creation software consists of encryption software, optional watermarking software, rights expression and the copyright. The content management software, delivery software and the license software are to be executed on the distribution and license servers.

The components of a typical DRM system are shown in figure 5. It goes well with the typical content supply chain model shown in figure 4.

The authorization information is described in the right expression language (REL). MPEG-21 (MPEG REL) provides the standard for the Right expression language (Carl A. Gunter, Stephen T. Weeks, and Andrew Wright, 2001). The REL defines the security of the content as well as techniques for creating new commercial and business models.

The contents are required to carry the complete authorization information. The rights expression includes the following components:

a. The consumer-to whom the rights are transferred.
b. The content or service –For which the rights are applicable.
c. The conditions- When the rights are to be exercised.
d. The issuer- who provides the license.

Figure 4. Supply chain model

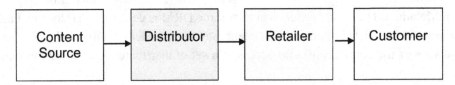

The mode and duration of the license is specified with the help of REL.

As the data gets streamed over the Internet freely, security features and rights management are to be fused to the data at the time of content creation and storing

Digital Asset Management

Digital asset management (John S. Erickson, 2001) spans the exact hardware and software used in the content creation, the production rights, the steps involved in the content creation, the permission rights for content distribution etc. The asset management system will have seamless access to the original data and resources required to create the contents. Storage of such a massive data for thousands of processes and content objects is a challenging task.

Storage Security Standards

The generally used storage security standard protocols include the Fiber Channel Security Protocol (FC-SP) and the Storage Network Industry Association's Storage Management Initiative Specification (SMI-S). Both of them will help to promote interoperability by linking the vendors of the products and the standards for the implementation.

Symmetric Key

Symmetric keys are basically private keys used for the secure storage of the data. The keys are to be maintained with strict confidentiality. Hence they are generally used with the data at rest. There are various standards to support the symmetric key encryption.

IEEE P1619: It supports the data on the disk.

IEEE P1619.1: It supports the data on the tape.

Figure 5. Working of a DRM system

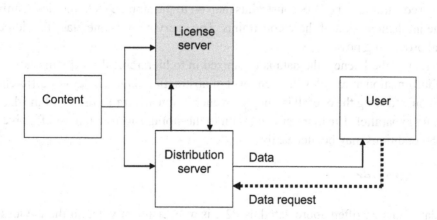

Asymmetric Key

Asymmetric keys are composed of the pair of a public and a private key. The private keys are not shared while the public key is made available to the general public. There will be no simple mechanism to extract the private keys from the public key. Any effort would involve a lot of computations and time. In the usage of the asymmetric key, the data will get encrypted with the public key. The decryption is possible only with the help of the private key. Thus, asymmetric keys are used when the content is to be shared especially over the internet.

Key Hierarchy

A hierarchy of keys is maintained in order to ensure additional security. In a two level hierarchy, there is a data encryption key and a key encryption key (KEK). The KEK is used to store the key in the encrypted format. The keys are often authenticated with Key Message Authentication Code (KMAC). The key contains the secure hash (or HMAC) signature. The hierarchy of keys provides better security at the expense of the computation. The combination of KEK and KMAC are used at each level of the hierarchy. When a key is created, it is associated with KMAC so that it can be authenticated later.

In KEC, a certain set of keys is used for the encryption of only keys and not data. Such keys do not get exposed to the hacker at all. This hierarchical organization helps in the recovery of the keys when they are "lost" or destroyed. The hierarchy of keys map on to the probability of the security threat at each level in the hierarchy.

Depending up on the application and the scenario, right of the encryption is to be selected. For storage security, where the data is stationary, symmetric keys may be used for better performance as they need less memory. The advance encryption standard is popularly used because of its strength.

The encryption can happen at the document level, directory level or disk level depending up on the abstraction supported. The encrypted data may be further encrypted depending up on the sensitivity of the data.

QoS for Data Access

Scalability and the reliability of the network can be improved significantly by imposing stringent quality of service (QoS) constraints. The QoS constraints map on to the storage technologies. Timing issues are involved in the implementation of these constraints. The encryption, frame classification etc take time and substantial processing power.

In order to reduce the latency, the data is organized in to hierarchical form with varying degrees of abstraction of information at each level. Each level of abstraction required keys of different complexity for the encryption, reducing the overall latency with encryption and transmission of the data of different layers happening in parallel. The hierarchy maps on to the storage abstraction for effective usage of the keys. The QoS conditions may be met easily.

Peer to Peer Transfer

Peer to peer data transfer, often abbreviated as P2P, is a mechanism wherein the devices directly exchange or share the data as well as the services over the network unlike a client server model where the resources on the server are available for the client applications only up on request. P2P supports both push as well as the pull of the content while the Client server architecture is more of a pull mechanism for the transfer of the content. Internet has provided backbone for the P2P paradigm.

The data transfer over p2p architecture has resulted in several cases of violation of the digital rights. More information on DRM issues with p2p are available in (Bill Rosenblatt, 2003).

Since the devices can directly and freely share the content, Digital rights management has to be enforced over the P2P networks. The DRM has to protect the rights of the genuine users of the content and permit the transfer of the same if the users are authorized to do so under the rights agreement.

There are various issues associated with the implementation of the DRM.

- The weak control of content creator over the definition of the rights.
- Connectivity of the user to the network to maintain uninterruptible P2P connectivity.
- The license can be a part of the content or it can be a separate file.
- Linking the authorization process with financial transactions.
- The authorization software sits on the playback device.
- The authorization for the consumption of the content is to be made on the basis of user's identity or device's identity or both making it very difficult to maintain individual credentials.

P2P networks support seamless transfer of data and resources between computing machines directly. In a client server model, however, the resources are placed on the server and would be made available for the client machines only up on request. With the growth of internet, P2P transfer also has grown and become popular.

Issue of authorization in peer to peer network is a problem. Although the p2p architecture aims at the direct resource sharing among the machines, it often results in the illegal transactions and the violation of the copyrights.

Authorization is to be handled by the server machine at the content distribution side instead of the network transferring the same (Bill Rosenblatt, 2003). The network handles and interprets the digital rights over the content specified in ODRL or MPEG-REL. The content in encrypted format as well as the license describing the rights for the consumption of the content is transferred over the P2P network. The license interpreter resides over the client machine. Depending up on the authorization the user is having over the content, it can be played, copied or distributed further. More information on DRM issues with p2p is available in (Bill Rosenblatt, 2003).

Integrating DRM with P2P Networks enables the online content business models. The multimedia web services of the Service oriented architecture would get integrated with the secured access of the rights management. The permissions to use web services run much similar to the rights to use the content. Web services extensively make use of the P2P network to offer the cost effective protected services. Web services description language (WSDL) provides a standard model for the web services. It supports P2P services. With the interoperability and open standards in place and with the help of P2P network, it would be easy for the content creators to sell the content through a website.

Hierarchical Data Organization

The security parameter associated with different levels of data organization hierarchy could be different and proportional to the information content or abstractness of the hierarchy. Depending up on the choice of the user, the associated data could be transferred appropriately.

Figure 6. Hierarchical usage of keys

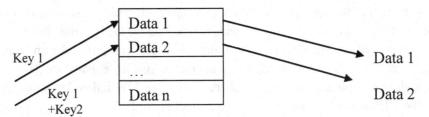

The hierarchical representation of data allows the content distributor to selectively issue rights for different levels of abstractions. The hierarchical representation of digital rights is shown in figure 7. It may be specified in REL. By adding an additional layer to the same contents, multi lingual licenses may be issued increasing the profit multifold. This calls for careful structuring of the hierarchies. The run time and the online permission granting will be a feature of the license. The sophisticated authorization technologies will enable a variety of business models in the web services. The revenue model would be different for different levels of the hierarchy.

The hierarchy of keys follows the hierarchical representation of the data as shown in Figure 6. To access higher order hierarchies, more keys are required.

As the hierarchies are modular by default, the scalability and extensibility of the contents require online granting of the permissions that get updated periodically. This hierarchy may be reflected in XML or REL. The rights may be issued to intermediate agents selectively. There are different ways of granting permission. This determines the security QoS while storing the data and is fused with the data as metadata.

Figure 7. Hierarchical representations of digital rights

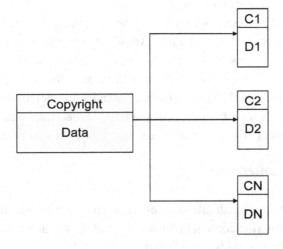

ISSUES AND SOLUTIONS

A feedback of information to the source on the traffic status will bring down the resource constraints while meeting security constraints. The feedback model optimizes the resource utilization while meeting the security constraints. The hierarchical representation provides higher degree of fault tolerance.

TCP and UDP Connectivity

The data transfer from the distribution server on to the client device can happen through a connection oriented protocol such as TCP or through a connection less protocol such as UDP. In UDP, there is always a risk of the firewalls rejecting the data packets. However, in TCP,, each packet is associated with a TCP connection. The firewall checks the connection for each of the packets and allows them if the connection is registered and known to be secure.

To implement a similar strategy over UDP, the firewall has to check the address of a UDP packet and check if a similar packet has been encountered in the past, as these packets do not maintain a connection identity. This is not a safe method as it is possible for a hacker to tamper the originating address of the packets. Hence, handling of UDP packets is a security issue. Hence TCP based data transfers are preferred by the content distributors.

The TCP based transfer is not free from problems. It consumes the bandwidth with retransmissions of the timed out and lost packets, often unnecessary for the multimedia traffic. However, the compression technologies and the large available bandwidths have made it feasible to realize. Alternatively, a workaround is possible for the data to pass through the firewalls by using the TCP port 80.

Interoperability

The rights management system is to support interoperability for a seamless data transfer. The interoperability is to be assured for the CODEC types used, the business models and the DRM system. It is defined through the extensible media commerce language (XMCL), a variant of XML. The content streaming adheres to the RTP protocol. The usage of open standards such as ODRL (ODRL, 2004) or MPEG REL (ISO/IEC, 2004) improves the interoperability (LTSC, 2004). Today, DRM is turning in to proprietary. A translation across different DRM systems is required. To ensure the interoperability, a common procedure is to be followed for the encryption of the content, specification of the rights etc. More options are to be provided for the CODECs and the media players.

The DRM largely depends up on the availability and adoption of the open standards, ease of implementation of multiple CODEC technologies, ease of e- transactions etc. It takes time for the technology to catch up and become popular.

Implementation Issues

The use and control of DRM tools pose a major limitation. The entire system would be continuously subjected to hacking if not for attacks. The final content depiction would be in analog form that might be re-captured or copied at least with a reduced quality. It calls for effective watermarking at the final output devices such as speakers and screens. The technology for the effective implementation on DRM is provided in (William Rosenblatt; William Trippe Step, 2001).

The users of music content often prefer to load the content on to a portable device and play the same in leisure. This activity is prone to piracy. It calls for innovative techniques to prevent further copying of the content from the memory card of the portable device on to the other devices. It may be implemented by encrypting the license key before being transferred to the portable device with a key unique to the portable device memory card. The key is placed at a random location over the card not easily accessible for the user. The content may be played only with this unique card. Networked devices that consume the streaming content however do not face this problem. The license would be valid one time and generally there is no scope for store and play.

In a network environment, the DRM may be enforced with the help of the MAC address of the device. Permissions to use the content would be tied to a MAC address, captured at the time of obtaining the license key from the license server. Since the MAC address of the client machine in a network cannot be tampered or changed easily, it ensures that the permission would be granted only for the specified device.

DRM is associated with content streaming, data compression technologies, Internet, web services, server, memory, cryptography, encoding, operating system etc. Extensive usage of DRM in future opens door for wide opportunities (Duncan, Barker & Douglas, 2004) for the development in these areas. The problem of digital piracy has created new business opportunities for the content creators as well as the software service providers, who provide a mechanism to enforce the digital rights of the contents.

Regulatory Issues

The DRM system needs to be scalable as it gets commercialised with many new users flooding in every day. Often the existing infrastructures put a major restriction on the same. With the Internet available across the globe, the contents travel over different geographies. The DRM has to support multiple currencies and the currency conversions have to be done carefully. Generally, there is a transaction fee involved in every transaction of the credit card. It makes the option of pay per download less attractive, especially when the payment is made through the credit card. The content has to cater for a variety of end users, calling for a multilingual support. Often the contents are placed over geographically distinct locations. The availability of different laws at different regions poses a major challenge for the interests of the content providers. It calls for the enforcement of a global copyright law.

FUTURE TRENDS

Providing and maintaining the digital rights for the content is a volatile topic where the strategies keep changing subjected to the government regulations, technological advancements etc. However, some of the topics that show directions for the future are captured here.

Rights Description

MPEG-21 provides the description of the rights data dictionary (RDD) where the rights of the expression and the access and distribution permission of the content are defined. It attempts to blend the service quality of the data with the security at different levels of abstraction to provide one integrated directory for security and service quality.

It may be used to provide the different levels of security and permissions to the same hierarchical level as viewed by the different agents. RDD also describes the scalability of the directory.

With Digital Information Declaration (DID), it is possible to render the different presentations of the information for different users depending up the access rights. This is possible by separately maintaining the description part and the information part. With DID it should be possible to link the descriptions to the different hierarchical levels of data representation, depending up on the commercial models.

The quality of information is related to the security parameter associate with the data and may be achieved by selecting the requisite abstraction level as appropriate. The content usage rights are closely associated with the access permissions of the data. The rights description language is to be flexible enough to define them separately to cater for unforeseen business cases in the future. Hence the model defining the rights is required to be modular and hierarchical in lines with the service quality.

Conditional Authorization

Providing multilevel authorization is also possible in lines with sub-contracting the sale of the content. The abstract levels of data map on to the levels of encryption in the data. During encryption, information redundancies are added. The resulting spectrum gets whiter. The stack of security levels differ in much the same way as the abstract data levels. The data will be scrambled and then organized as hierarchical form to meet encryption as well as the selective permission and abstractions.

In future the content owners and creators can decide when, where and how their contents need to be published and who can use the same. The end users will get pointers for getting the contents of their choice and will be able to get more contents by paying more. The consumer electronic companies provide interactive devices and software to enable various business models. The different business models associated are unlimited access, pay per view, pay for more quality, flat rate, rent, multi tier model etc. The service provider would offer many facilities like entertainment, bill payment e-transactions etc.

Mobility

Support for the DRM over the mobile environment is challenging. For example, the transfer of logos and ring tones require DRM protection. The protection requires disabling the forward of the same to the other devices. If the content is music, further copying or playing on any other device has to be blocked unless the DRM supports the multi-device and multi-channel capabilities as well as the interoperability among the different devices.

The industries involving Content creation and distribution would be largely benefited with DRM. The typical applications include

- Audio: music, audio clips and books
- Video: movies and music videos
- Publishing: e-books/digital libraries and achieves, documents, news articles etc.
- Computer games
- Software: Applicable for all software
- Web sites
- Health care
- Education

- Finance
- Law
- Research

The finance and legal consultations as well as transactions can happen online over a secure network making use of the DRM. With DRM. The research organizations can sell the Intellectual property (IPs) through their web site, simplifying the process.

For the applications requiring only a selected part of the contents such as one or two songs from a bunch of eight to ten songs residing on a CD or DVD, DRM provides a feasible solution that is otherwise not possible to realize. The users needs to pay only for the contents of their choice. The aim of DRM is not confined to the detection of piracy in the usage of the contents. It would provide with the end users just what they need.

The presence of data in electronic form has enabled many services over the internet. With this it is possible to explore new opportunities. With the contents available in digital form, it becomes easier to distribute, share and copy. The DRM is not confined to media and entertainment marketplaces although it has a lion's share in this domain. The DRM applications have started entering in to other industries including health care, education, finance, law, software and research.

Potential Players in DRM Space

There are different players in DRM market space.

1. The Toolkit vendor provides the requisite software and the tools for the content owners to prepare the secure contents through encryption and concatenate the rights information on to the content.
2. The Player software vendor provides the content transfer mechanism for the player running on the client device. The data transfer mechanisms depend up on the server technologies.
3. The hardware vendors provide memory cards that can store the contents along with the key for local encryption and prevent the content being copied on to the other portable devices. Crypto enabled processors have started entering in to the market with the capability to detect the piracy in the software running on the device.
4. The embedded software providers offer a tamper proof approach for the host and device software and firmware to provide protection for the content buffers, persistent state, key stores etc.
5. The Government Agencies are interested in controlled viewing and sharing of the highly secure and confidential documents, audio and video data. They take a role in enforcing and amending the law over the infringement.
6. The private Organizations are interested in controlled distribution of the proprietary information; keep track of the access and any modifications made for the same.
7. The Content owners are interested in the reward in terms of revenue through sales and promotions. Their concern is mainly for the copyright protection of the content.
8. The service providers and the content distributors are concerned about minimizing the cost of providing services and try to refrain from getting in to lawsuits over illegal distribution of the content.
9. Producers of the end user equipment such as PCs, media players and memory cards are interested in minimizing the design and production costs and provide maximum interoperability.

10. The end users are interested in immediate access to the desired content with minimum e-transactions.

DRM is closely associated with IPTV. IPTV is expected to get rolled out in millions across the world by the end of 2009. It open up new issues and opportunities for the content protection (Gartner report, 2005).

CONCLUSION

In this chapter,

• The relevance of digital rights management is introduced for the content distribution
• Hierarchical data organization is proposed for the easy distribution of the data in the content stream.

The huge databases maintained by the modern enterprises often face with the problem of data inconsistencies and data security. Recently, the expenses over secure data transactions have increased multifold. In this chapter, the data security issues are addressed and solutions are provided through a smart organization of the data. A hierarchical data organization is proposed to solve most of the issues. Such an architecture throws open different commercial models with different degrees of data security. The anticipated trends in this area are captured.

Distribution of content has been challenging ever since the content has been placed on the internet. As a solution for this approach, Digital Rights Management methodology has been evolved. A brief introduction to the DRM technology is provided here with emphasis on the issues being faced and the future directions. The tools and techniques are generic and no specific assumption has been made on the nature of the content.

QUESTIONS

1. Why rights are to be 'imposed' over the digital content?
2. How does the storage of the data influence the choice of rights management strategy?
3. How does the DRM maximize the profit for the different players along the supply chain?
4. What are the challenges involved in the implementation of the DRM?
5. How does the mobility of the data source or the end user affect the DRM?

REFERENCES

Duncan, Barker & Douglas. (2004). *Digital Rights Management Study: Interim Report June 10, 2004. JISC, 2004.* Retrieved June 27, 2004, from http://www.intrallect.com/drmstudy/Interim_Report.pdf

Erickson, J. S. (2001). Information Objects and Rights Management. *D-Lib Magazine, 17*(4).

Gartner (2005). *Maintaining data quality*[Report]. Retrieved 2005 from http://www.ebizq.net/views/download_raw? metadata_id =6210&what=feature

Hofmeister, C., Nord, R., & Soni, D. (2000). *Applied Software Architectures*. Reading MA: Addison-Wesley.

ISO/IEC (2004). *Information technology -- Multimedia framework (MPEG-21) - Part 5: Rights Expression Language*. ISO/IEC 21000-5:2004.

Lessig, L. (2004). *Free Culture*. New York: Basic Books.

LTSC. (2004). *IEEE LTSC Digital Rights Expression Languages – Requirements for Learning, Education, and Training Technologies. IEEE Learning Technology Standards Committee submission to ISO/IEC JTC1 SC36*. Retrieved July 10, 2004 from http://jtc1sc36.org/doc/36N0709.pdf

ODRL. (2004). *Open Digital Rights Language Initiative*. Retrieved May 28, 2004 from http://www.odrl.net

Paskin, N. (2003). Components of DRM Systems Identification and Metadata. *Digital rights management*, (LNCS Vol. 2770, pp. 26-61). Berlin: Springer.

Rosenblatt, B. (2003). Integrating DRM with P2P Networks: Enabling the Future of Online Content Business Models. *DRM Watch*, November 18. Retrieved from http://www.cbronline.com/research.asp?uid=DMTC1190; Retrieved in January 2006 Gunter, C. A., Weeks, S. T. & Wright, A. (2001). *Models and Languages for Digital Rights* [Technical Report]. InterTrust Star Lab, Santa Clara, CA.

Rosenblatt, B., et al. (2001). *Digital Rights Management: Business and Technology*. In *An overview of DRM technology, business implications for content publishers, and relationship to U.S. copyright law*. New York: M&T Books; John Wiley & Sons.

Rosenblatt, W., & Trippe Step, W. (2001). *Digital Rights Management: Business and Technology*. Chichester, UK: Wiley.

Saur München, K. G. (1998). *Functional Requirements for Bibliographic Records*. IFLA Study Group on the Functional Requirements for Bibliographic Records.

TinHat. (2006). eBooks *and Digital Rights Management (DRM), for ePublishers*. Retrieved May 28, 2008 from http://www.tinhat.com

Section 5
Information Retrieval

Chapter 14
Information Retrieval

ABSTRACT

The demand of the end user for the information is to be fulfilled by the supporting supply chain. The search queries for the data are to be appropriately handled to supply the content seamlessly. The users finally have to get what they want. This chapter explains how the quality of search results can be improved with a little processing on the queries.

INTRODUCTION

In the previous chapter, the data storage and distribution mechanisms are discussed in detail. To provide the required data for the user, a powerful search mechanism is required. Here, the content search algorithms for providing the 'right time' data for the user are explored.

As the network bandwidth has increased and the cost of storage media has drastically come down, audio and video have become key means for communicating the information in addition to the text. It calls for more intelligence for the browsers. In this chapter, the required extra intelligence would be explored. It throws light on the alternative database search mechanisms, search engine architectures etc. The focus of this chapter is on the reduction of the query time with the help of smart algorithms. The present day distributed nature of the documents call for the efficient data communication and integration, especially when it is required to access particular information in the multiple files through a query. This calls for the real time and on-line decisions. The relevance of information retrieval in conjunction with the on-line decisions would be explored in this chapter.

DOI: 10.4018/978-1-60566-888-8.ch014

Clustering of the data is required for the effective Retrieval of information (Singhal, Amit, 2001). First, the attributes of the data to be retrieved may be compared with the attributes of the cluster. It shows the degree of fitment of the elements of the cluster with the requirements of the data to be retrieved. Further search would result in the required data from the cluster. The clusters are arranged in the form of a hierarchy. The hierarchical system provides a mechanism for the fast search. Also, it requires less storage.

Most of the documents available over the web, such as the digital libraries, are in the textual form. To enable interoperability for the retrieval of the data, the description and representation of these documents is done in XML form (Erik T. Ray, 2003). Often the description consists of the metadata, annotations and multimedia information.

In general, both metadata and the data are requested by the end user. The access pattern can be of several types- the whole document or a part of it or a cluster of the documents. It can be the attributes or the document itself.

BACKGROUND

Information retrieval (IR) is the technology for providing the required content based on the request from the user. It involves the searching of the content based on the keywords, with assistance from the metadata. To facilitate the retrieval, the documents are clustered based on some commonalities (Levene, Mark, 2005). Identification of these commonalities is quite involved. The documents are described with the Metadata. Fusion of the Metadata available in various forms is challenging. To ease the issue of interoperability, XML is generally adopted for the metadata description.

Information routing or filtering is the process of retrieving the required information from the data streams such as the news feed. Here the keyword search happens over individual documents or stream unlike the conventional information retrieval where a large number of stored documents are used for the retrieval of the relevant information. The documents or portion of the stream matching with the required features or profiles will be rendered as the search result. The browser support for query is discussed in (Kent Wittenburg and Eric Sigman, 1997)

Performance

The search performance is typically measured using three numbers:

1. *Number of queries handled per second*: It can be very large depending up on the underlying search engine, from tens to hundreds of queries.
2. *Average search time per query*: The query response time is typically tens to hundreds of milli seconds.
3. *Size of the data transactions*: It will be of the order of several Gigabytes.

The parameters characterize the search engine. The efficiency may be improved with parallel search over multiple servers.

Case Study: Rule Based Search Engine

The data from different sources are extracted with rule based engines. Rule based engines infer the results from the known facts and get updated to form an automated reasoning system. In this work, both forward chain rule and backward chain rule architectures are considered. In a forward rule chain rule, the system starts with a known initial knowledge base of experience and more facts are gathered and added by applying rules until no more rules apply and then a query is made on the data base. A backward chain rule starts with a query, attempts to pop up some results and proceeds from the query towards the database. Both of these setups can be realized with appropriate signal processing techniques explained ahead.

Case Study: Natural Language Search Engine

The natural language search engine supports the exact sentences or often semantics for the search. Unlike a keyword based search engine, result of the search is context sensitive. For example, the phrases "power hunting" and "hunting power" render different results in a natural language search engine although the words combination is the same. A key word based search engine may produce the same result for both.

To enable natural language processing, summaries of the multimedia content is to be created. The content is divided in to several parts or scenes. A short summary, called story is to be assigned with each segment. There can be a story covering several segments. A hierarchy of stories at multiple levels of abstraction may be maintained. For example, in News-on-demand, short summaries of the news are created to cater for a variety of users providing the information of their choice. The segmentation of the content is however challenging. More information on the query over natural language based engines is provided in (Walter Liggett, Chris Buckley, 2005). The query on such a data is to provide the data at different abstraction depending up on the users' interest captured through persistent queries. The more the queries on the same topic, the better should be the resolution of the retrieved result.

In images, the segments are extracted based on signal processing techniques such as object extraction. In video, the key frames provide the required summary. Identification of the key frames is challenging. The browser in future are to support image based keyword search, meaning, image may be used in the place of the keyword for content search.

Speech recognition technology is useful for the recognition of the spoken words and converting the same in to text automatically. Although it can be done manually with a high degree of accuracy, automation of the same is often sought to speed up the process. However, the accuracy of the automated system is yet to be improved. This is because the technology as such is error prone. The conversion to text greatly helps the search process with textual key words. In all the queries where end user is a human being, user feedback is given due weightage. The response to query process improves and gets strengthened with the user feedback.

Case Study: Statistical Search Engine

Keyword matching is used for the selection of the appropriate document in response for the query. The matching provides all the related documents. So, before providing the relevant documents, the similarities in the different documents are to be identified to remove the redundancies in the information. In statistical search, the duplicates are removed by assigning a weight for the match or relevance. Hence, each record will have an associated relevance. This information is often rendered to the end user. The user feedback or behavior is very helpful in providing the better results next time for the same choice of the keywords. Based on the relevance, only a few documents are provides to the user in the search window.

Document Indexing

The documents and requests are described using index language. The index terms are derived from the text of the document or otherwise, but provide a description of the content of the document. There are two ways of assigning the index terms to the document:

- **Pre coordinated:** Here the index terms are coordinated at the time of creation.
- **Post coordinate:** Here the index terms are coordinated at the time of the retrieval of the document.

Classification of the documents under a label is very helpful for the retrieval of the right document. By grouping the similar documents in hierarchical fashion, retrieval turns very fast.

The queries from user are mapped with the index terms and queued in the index buffer. Each of the index terms is examined and duplication of the data fetches is avoided with effective queue management. Time windows are defined to observe the index terms present with in the window of the queue.

Document Classification

Classification of the documents is used for keyword clustering and document clustering.

Clustering happens based on the similarity between the objects in some domain or with respect to some parameters.

Scalability is a very important feature desired for the classification of the documents. Addition of document for already classified group should not be difficult. It is desirable to avoid running another iteration of classification over all the documents including the one being added.

Composite Queries

Some of the proprietary technologies allow the streaming of the results even when the query process is still running. The applications are fed with the partial results before the total result is available. The composite queries ate often broken in to several queries that can run in parallel. Finally their results are collated and presented to the calling application. The server in turn, assigns one thread for each of the queries and gets the result the earliest. The gain will be reasonable if multiple data sources are involved in resolving the query.

Markup for Retrieval

The markup provides tags for the effective and fast retrieval. The quality of the results in terms of the relevance and the abstraction of the information largely get influenced by these tags.

XML supports the association of the XML tags with the documents. It is especially useful when the content search is difficult. With markup, it is possible for the users to add constraints to the queries.

Figure 1. Data refinement with progress in time

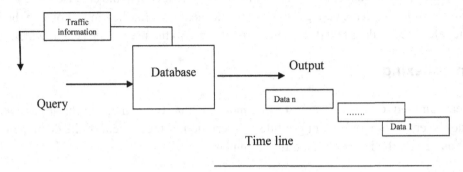

Multimedia Data Retrieval

Because of a large customer base, there is a huge demand for the innovation in the multimedia content retrieval. It involves the retrieve of the images, video and the audio content without a describing text. Depending up on the application, indexing of the document based on one of the features may be used for the retrieval of the document. For example, indexing of the images based on the color distribution will help to retrieve images with a particular shade of the color. It may not be of much use in all the general applications. Better features such as face of an individual may be associated with the document. The search results in all documents containing the same face that makes sense for most of the applications.

Retrieval of speech and video documents based on the text would be a common future requirement. MPEG-7 standard describes the framework leaving the implementation details specific to the product.

The multimedia data is generally stored in the compressed form in order to save the disk space and the transmission bandwidth, although it requires some processing power to do that. It is economical and relatively to easy to afford the same, than the expensive resources or bandwidth over the network.

Relevance Based Feedback

One of the most important but difficult operations in the information retrieval is the formulation of the appropriate query to retrieve the required document (T. Qin, T.-Y. Liu, X.-D. Zhang, Z. Chen, and W.-Y. Ma, 2005) from a pool of millions of available documents. In general, it does not happen in one shot and requires several iterative steps. In each step, the query statement is to be altered based on the documents retrieved in the previous step. Relevance based feedback method is one such technique for refining the query iteratively (Steve Lawrence; C. Lee Giles, 1999). A query can be iteratively improved by starting from a composite query term or a query vector and adding the terms from the relevant documents, while deleting the terms from the irrelevant documents. Figure 1 shows how the data gets refined as time progresses.

Relevance feedback improves the quality of the search results. Statistics has shown an improvement between 40 to 60% in a single iteration. However, the drawback is that, looking at a a document and the keywords, it is not possible to say what makes it relevant or irrelevant unless the user steps in.

On the other side, the relevance feedback may be used to update the index terms associated with a document and used to fetch the same. Subsequently, it would be fetched only when it is very relevant. Thus, the iterative process with user feedback would help to get the right document t for the right query. Also, a document would be fetched only when it is appropriate for the query.

Figure 2. Architecture of relevance feedback based query system

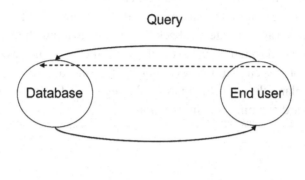

Blended with the user behavior is the probabilistic query, where the probability that a document matches for a query is estimated. It depends up on the composition of the relevant irrelevant documents for the query. It may be noted that a document may be relevant for a query and irrelevant for the other. Modern search engines provide this value to the user along with the search results. Further discussion on query procedures is provided in (Fabrizio Sebastiani, 2004) and (Yunjie Xu, Michel Benaroch, 2005). Query over graphical data is discussed in (Steve Jones.1998).

The relevance of information (Saracevic, T, 2007) in the data as seen by the end user may be used as a feedback factor to improve the quality of the information subsequently. Generally it is performed off line. The end user experience may be added to the retrieval process through statistical and interactive learning models. The interactive retrieval system is discussed in (Eric Lagergren and Paul Over, 1998). Architecture of the relevance feedback based query system is shown in the figure 2.

The evolving user behavior will have profound impact on the query results. The feedback based learning process may be implemented with feedback neural networks for multifold improvement in the performance. Based on the feedback the learning system in turn provides the information for the queries. I.e. it learns how the interactive user fine tunes the queries till the search gets completed.

For a given search with a set of keywords, the web pages of the search result are ranked based on their relevance for the search. Page rank represents the drgree of relevance of a web page for a given set of key words. The relevance will be different for a different choice of keywords and the search. The abstract levels of data storage may be linked to the page ranking.

ISSUES AND SOLUTIONS

Search Time

The search time happens to be the major problem in the query process calling for algorithms to reduce the same. The query process starts from a known initial knowledge base that corresponds to zero feedback.

A feedback system retains the previous history. A higher order estimator is derivable by adding a few terms to the lower estimator. Each estimator is a feedback system taking query as the input providing the data as the output. Subsequent application of the assertion of rules results in a spectrum of estimators. An estimator can implement the forward chaining rule engine.

The set of estimators may be replaced by an estimator that happens to be the weighted average of these estimators. I.e. by providing an appropriate feedback from output to input, though redundant information, it is possible to avoid traverse through all the estimators or data bases and save the query time.

The equivalent estimator is such that, whatever may be the starting estimator structure, it is possible to arrive at the requisite plane through the appropriate degree of feedback. Thus, a feedback neural network can take a backward chaining rule in to action.

Merging the Rules

The search result could be rendered with different resolutions by stopping the query process corresponding to the appropriate estimator. This is useful especially in time constrained or probability searches or pattern matching and decision making. The preset search time or probabilities are mapped on to the requisite estimator. The superposition of estimators further explains that, a feedback neural network can combine multiple rules that are involved in the query process. Thus a differentially fed query process enjoys both the forward and the reverse chain search procedures simultaneously making it more effective.

Neural Network Based Query Engine

The usage of neural network for queries is a matured practice explained in (KWOK, K. L., GRUNFELD, L., AND LEWIS, D. D, 1994). The problems of lengthy period associated with such a network may be reduced with the usage of feedback neural network. The usage of probability theory for retrieval has been explained in (KWOK). It relates the probability of relevance before and after observing the documents. The feedback system provides a minimum variance and minimum bias estimator.

QoS Based Query

The interactive query process calls for the stringent quality constraints such as delay to be imposed on the query engines and the data transfer networks (Xie, M,, 1998). The cost of this quality based information paves way for different information marketing business models. The concept of QoS based query is shown in figure 3.

Maintaining the query information consistent, timely and relevant is a tough task. The quality process includes fixing the missing and often inaccurate data calls for information estimators.

Figure 3. QoS based query

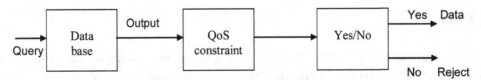

Figure 4. Architecture of QoS based query

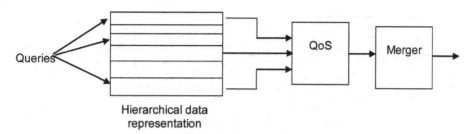

Hierarchical data
representation

The scheduling of queries from multiple sources need to be arranged efficiently based on the quality of service parameter associated with each of the queries. These service parameters map on to the data organization. If the hierarchy level of the data is too deep, it calls for more search time. The output rate of the results of a query may be made to follow the QoS constraints by advance prediction of the probable rate of the query. Architecture of a QoS based query is shown in figure 4. This feature decides the scheduling and order of the queries. Scheduling will have decisive impact on the query results.

When the rate of queries is too large and buffering is not possible, it leads to shedding by the query manager. Under these circumstances, hierarchical organization of the data can provide at least a limited output. The mirroring of servers further helps to achieve the same. Depending on server loads, the agents have to divide and route the queries. This load may be predicted in 'k' steps advance. This imparts QoS features to load shedding. The loss of queries under busy servers also predicted 'k' steps advance and indicated to the source. AJACS provides a kind of this indication through tool bar.

Figure 5 shows the hierarchical representation of data for queries. The data formed at different time gets merged in to a result of better quality.

FUTURE TRENDS

For various reasons, information retrieval has turned probabilistic. The specific kind of query from the source calls for appropriate interpretation of the problem and search the records statistically to choose the most appropriate solution. This in-time solution is possible with an intelligent element.

Differential Response

The incremental data set captured from the data sources may be thought of as the different abstract levels of the data. This is true because the old data will be archived in to data warehouse and the most recent data serves as the source of the data. When a query is made over such a database, the ratio of information content of the different abstract levels remains the same. In the chapter Information measurement, it has been shown that any of the estimators is expressible in terms of other estimator as a weighted sum. This is important to ascertain the value of the information delivered as a response to the query. The difference in the information between any two estimators that represent the two abstract instances of the information gives a measure of distance between the two. Thus the sampling interval of the data has an impact over the response to the queries in terms of the quality of the information delivered. More the sampling interval more will be the distance and difference in the quality.

Figure 5. Merging of search results

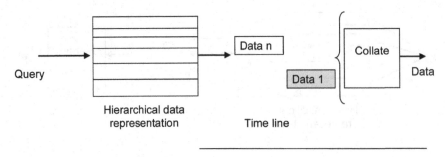

Multilingual Support

Support for multilingual searches would be increasingly used in future. It caters for global supply chains. This can be accomplished by replacing the English syntax with the appropriate natural language word. The basic search engine can be in English and perform the appropriate translations through the wrappers. As the information is stored in the hierarchical fashion, natural language search engine can easily access the same. As we navigate along the hierarchy in a natural language search engine, the required results are popped up at each level of abstraction, allowing the user to further narrow down the search. At each level in the hierarchy there will be a match at different degree of abstraction and accuracy. Query support for multilingual data is given in (Aitao Chen, Fredric C. Gey, 2004).

This goes well with the user behavior for searching. The user tends to narrow down the search and arrive at the precise requirement of information with the progress in time. This allows the search engine to traverse deep and deep in to the hierarchy. The progress of query as well as the degree of abstraction of the popped up result may be indicated on a graphical user interface (GUI).

Aggregated View

With the documents and the associated metadata being scattered across hundreds of servers in distinct physical locations, search and merge engines would take a new form in future (X. Liu and W. B. Croft, 2004). They are required to merge the search results meaningfully calling for more intelligence and expertise. Such an engine builds the expertise based on the user queries, requirements, and behavioral patterns over a period of time. In addition to the key words or the natural language sentences, the user may be required to interactively specify the merging rules or the way the search results or data needs to be integrated.

One immediate application will be the super search engine triggering several available search engines (Ross, Nancy; Wolfram, Dietmar, 2000), at a time and merging the results meaningfully.

With the data being organized in to the multiple abstract levels, the users can have the freedom of choosing the suitable information at the desired level of abstraction that is meaningful for them. Often the user will not be interested in too much of details, but only in the relevant information.

Multi-Pass Query

The query process (F. Diaz, 2007), will be iterative over many passes. A two pass query is shown in figure 6. The method requires user feedback to improve the procedure in each iteration. The method may be improved by providing differential feedback i.e. the weighted sum of a set of consecutive feedbacks. Finally a single query can replace multiple passes.

Hierarchical Search Engines

Search engines could be hierarchical (Gandal, Neil, 2001). I.e. there will be a set of distributed search engines each of them performing search over different hierarchical levels of the data. A Meta search engine combines the results of these search engines. This mechanism works effectively when the storage of the data is hierarchical. The design of the search engines for different levels of hierarchy could be different both in terms of the index term databases as well as search permissions and search speeds over the storage media. While integrating the data especially corresponding to the different keywords that are to be concatenated, the abstract level of the resultant data would be the weighted sum of the abstract levels of the results of the queries

Hierarchical Representation of Data

The impact of query process on the hierarchical representation of data may be illustrated with the help of an AJACS enabled web page displaying the cricket score. Generally the primary interest of the end user is in the score. The score gets refreshed very frequently. The next level of interest is in the players. The one time interest is in the web page. Accordingly, frequency of the query gets changed. The abstract or hierarchical arrangement of the data has to consider the same for effective blending with AJACS and make it useful. The score has to be mirrored more times. This calls for an intelligent data fusion.

Figure 6. Multi pass query system

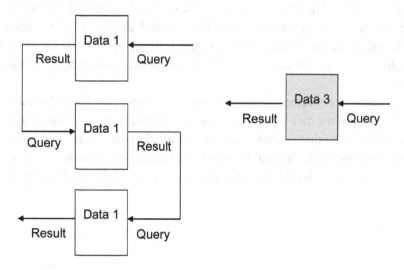

Data Caching

The data to be retrieved may be made available in the cache for fast access. An algorithm may be used to determine who has to be placed when. Especially if the data is compressed for the sake of space or ciphered for the sake of security while storing, it is more challenging to search in real time and required pre fetching to reduce the search time. The search technology goes with the storage as well as the security policies. These two parts may be blended with the heretical storage with different levels of abstraction where compression of the data and grading of the information happens across various planes. These planes or estimators appropriately follow the different security policies and may be brought in to the cache subjected to the QoS as well as the frequency of their access. The frequency of access of each abstraction level depends up on the commercial model i.e. number of customers trying to retrieve or having permission to retrieve the specific level of abstraction in the data. In this way, the quality of service of data gets blended with the retrieval.

The gap between the speed of the CPUs and the speed of the data streaming devices is increasing. As a result, the latency and the bandwidth requirement observed with the streaming are limited by the performance of the storage devices and the underlying network providing the connectivity. These limitations are addressed in Distributed caching techniques. It requires further refinement before the large scale integration in to the network.

In adaptive caching scheme ACME, multiple experts are used for managing the replacement policies within the distributed caches. It improves the hit rate significantly compared to static caching techniques. The static caching techniques are less adaptive reducing their performance. However, the cluster of nodes is easily scalable as they are isolated and no data or messages are exchanged among them.

On the other hand, Machine learning algorithms may be used to select the appropriate best policies or a mixture of policies with weightage proportional to the recent success. Each of the cache nodes updates itself based on the weight and the workload. An intelligent agent can be used to predict the cache behavior.

Multimedia Query

The multimedia information or documents have associated Metadata and some search engines can do their job based on the metadata. The other technique in the retrieval of the documents containing speech is to convert the entire speech to text and use a text based search engine. This can also happen during the search time if the requested conversion is fast enough. It happens to be a tradeoff between the processing power and the storage. In any case, the technique happens automatically requiring the usage of speech to text converters.

Bayesian classifiers can be conveniently used for querying, especially for audio and video searches. The conditional probability of the data within the closely matching regions or data clusters is taken and the matching results above a certain threshold value are returned as search results. While integrating the data especially corresponding to the different keywords that are to be concatenated, the abstract level of the resultant data would be the weighted sum of the abstract levels of the results of the queries.

CONCLUSION

In this chapter,

- It has been shown that the information redundancy can be implemented with differential feedback.
- The technique for improving the time response for the queries is provided.

Redundancy in the information results in fusion of applicable rules and results in faster integration of the data. A feedback neural network works as a Bayesian estimator that fuses various searching and data mining rules providing the advantages of all of them. The issues associated with distributed searching or queries are addressed with a solution based on the feedback neural network.

Moving forward, the data would be available in multimedia form over the web. The search engines have the complicated task of searching audio and video information. It gets further complicated with the semantic search within the data calling for the usage of intelligent elements.

QUESTIONS

1. How does the storage architecture affect the data retrieval?
2. What are the differences between the rule based search engine and the natural language search engine?
3. How do you improve the access speed of the data?
4. What is the relevance of the' relevance based feedback'?
5. How do you implement multilingual query over the common database?

REFERENCES

Chen, A. & Gey, F. C. (2004). Multilingual Information Retrieval Using Machine Translation, Relevance Feedback and Decompounding. *Information Retrieval*, 7(½), 149-182.

Diaz, F. (2007). Regularizing query-based retrieval scores. *Information Retrieval*, *10*, 531–562. doi:10.1007/s10791-007-9034-8

Gandal, N. (2001). The dynamics of competition in the internet search engine market. *International Journal of Industrial Organization*, *19*(7), 1103–1117. doi:10.1016/S0167-7187(01)00065-0

Jones, S. (1998). Graphical query specification and dynamic result previews for a digital library. In *Proc. of UIST'98, ACM Symposium on User Interface Software and Technology*, San Francisco, CA, November 1998.

Kwok, K. (1989). A neural network for probabilistic information retrieval. *ACM SIGIR Forum, 23*(SI, June), 21-30.

Kwok, K. L., Grunfeld, L., & Lewis, D. D. (1994). Trec-3 ad-hoc, routing retrieval and thresholding experiments using PIRCS. In D. K. Harman (Ed.), *NIST Special Publication 500-226: Overview of the Third Text Retrieval Conference (TREC-3),* Gaithersburg, MD, November, (pp. 247–255). Washington, DC: U. S. Dept. of Commerce, National Institute of Standards and Technology.

Lagergren, E., & Over, P. (1998). Comparing interactive information retrieval systems across sites: The TREC-6 interactive track matrix experiment. *Proc. of the 21st Annual Int. ACM SIGIR Conference,* Melbourne, Australia, (pp. 164-172).

Lawrence, S., & Lee Giles, C. (1999). Accessibility of information on the web. *Nature, 400,* 107. doi:10.1038/21987

Levene, M. (2005). *An Introduction to Search Engines and Web Navigation.* Upper Saddle River, NJ: Pearson.

Liggett, W., & Buckley, C. (2005). System Performance and Natural Language Expression of Information Needs. *Information Retrieval, 8*(1), 101–128. doi:10.1023/B:INRT.0000048493.67375.93

Liu, X., & Croft, W. B. (2004). Cluster-based retrieval using language models. In *SIGIR '04: Proceedings of the 27th annual international conference on Research and development in information retrieval,* (pp. 186–193). New York: ACM Press.

Qin, T., Liu, T.-Y., Zhang, X.-D., Chen, Z., & Ma, W.-Y. (2005). A study of relevance propagation for web search. In *SIGIR '05: Proceedings of the 28th annual international ACM SIGIR conference on Research and development in information retrieval,* (pp. 408–415). New York: ACM Press.

Ray, E. T. (2003). *Learning XML.* Sebastopol, CA: O'Reilly.

Ross, N., & Wolfram, D. (2000). End user searching on the Internet: An analysis of term pair topics submitted to the Excite search engine. *Journal of the American Society for Information Science American Society for Information Science, 51*(10), 949–958. doi:10.1002/1097-4571(2000)51:10<949::AID-ASI70>3.0.CO;2-5

Saracevic, T. (2007). Relevance: A review of the literature and a framework for thinking on the notion in information science. Part II: nature and manifestations of relevance. *Journal of the American Society for Information Science and Technology, 58*(3), 1915–1933. doi:10.1002/asi.20682

Sebastiani, F. (2004). Introduction: Special Issue on the 25th European Conference on Information Retrieval Research. *Information Retrieval, 7*(3/4), 235–237. doi:10.1023/B:INRT.0000011242.39361.cb

Singhal, A. (2001). Modern Information Retrieval: A Brief Overview. *Bulletin of the IEEE Computer Society Technical Committee on Data Engineering, 24*(4), 35–43.

Wittenburg, K., & Sigman, E. (1997). Integration of browsing, searching, and filtering in an applet for Web information access. In *Proc. of the ACM Conference on HumanFactors in Computing Systems, Late Breaking Track,* Atlanta, GA.

Xie, M., et al. (1998). Quality dimensions of Internet search engines. *Journal of Information Science.*

Xu, Y., & Benaroch, M. (2005). Information Retrieval with a Hybrid Automatic Query Expansion and Data Fusion Procedure. *Information Retrieval, 8*(1), 41–65. doi:10.1023/B:INRT.0000048496.31867.62

Chapter 15
Intelligent Information Processing

ABSTRACT

The data stored in a database exhibits a certain pattern at different degrees of abstraction although by nature it is random. The availability of patterns in the data would be useful in classifying the same with a tag and clustering the same. Query over such a data cluster would provide a quick response. Ina huge database, it is difficult to come out with exact patterns. The result of classification and clustering is often probabilistic. As a result, the estimation would turn statistical calling for the merger of the responses. In this chapter, the clustering and classifier algorithms are explained along with the decision process to merge the results.

INTRODUCTION

In the previous chapter, the application of the pattern matching in the data for the retrieval of the required content is discussed. To make it happen, the data needs to be organized and grouped in to clusters based on the similar patterns. Here, the methods used for the identification of patterns in the data are explored.

Pattern refers to the ability to depict a certain known features in the observed data or information. The algorithms and applications making use of pattern matching work on the assumption that the patterns remain invariant when they undergo transformations. Specifically, human observers take it for granted. The typical transformations include shift, rotation and scaling in a plane. In spite of these transformations, a human observer is able to recognize patterns in the handwritten characters, faces, voices etc, with different size, position and orientation.

DOI: 10.4018/978-1-60566-888-8.ch015

Like biological systems, neural networks have the ability to learn and recognize patterns in the data. They are capable of generalizing the results (Arun K.Pujari, 2000). I.e., they are able to find out the right class of the patterns, to which they have not been exposed in the training phase. The output provided is invariant to the distortions produced at the input. For a complex task such as face recognition (J. Dahmen, D. Keysers, H. Ney, and M. O. Gǖuld, 2001) a large number of neural networks are required to be used collectively. It is a tough task to collate their results and inferences, calling for the use of an intelligent element.

By providing historical data to a neural network, it is possible to train the network towards an ideal estimator. It happens by imparting feedback of various degree where by the network will learn adequately to generalize the inferences or observations.

Pattern recognition (Ripley B. D, 1996) is the science and art for looking for patterns in the data. It makes use of features extracted from the data, data clustering and classification, comparison and error analysis. It is used in automation applications including character recognition, image processing, speech analysis and speaker recognition, person identification etc. Statistical approach and the artificial neural networks are popularly used for pattern recognition application. (Bhagat, P. M, 2005). A variety of models are supported depending up on the complexity. If the data and the patterns are simple, simple models are sufficient. The conclusions derived and the decisions made are largely dependent on the model. (A.Krause, 2002). Complex models are required to learn complex patterns. The complexity of the model may be increased by adding more variables. It helps in capturing the contribution from each of them and increases the accuracy. Depending up on the model, various techniques are employed to improve the scalability and complexity. For example, in a neural network model, the number of hidden layers controls the complexity, while in a regression model, the number of polynomial terms and the interactions take the role. The complexity of a tree based model depends up on the number of branches. All these models are highly scalable.

Today, databases used for supply chain management are too large and grow at a faster rate making it difficult for the algorithms to analyze the data completely. In this chapter the tools, techniques and algorithms are introduced to find the patterns of interest in large databases and data streams.

For some of the applications, the requisite background knowledge can be provided through a Bayesian network. This background knowledge is integrated with the discovery process to get a new set of patterns in addition to the one known already. A neural network with a good background knowledge acquired through historical data is able to handle arbitrarily large databases and Bayesian networks that are too large for the exact inference to be feasible.

This chapter is concerned with the simple optimization problem of the applications around clustering. It is expected to provide insight on pattern recognition techniques making use of a feedback neural network.

BACKGROUND

Today, the different players generate information in heterogeneous format including video, audio, speech and machine generated data formats all along the supply chain. It is very difficult to synchronize and organize this information. The help of automated programs and machines intelligence are sought for the same.

Like human beings, a pattern recognizing machine also looks for certain patterns in the data (Dietrich Paulus and Joachim Hornegger, 1998) before clustering or grouping the same (Christopher M. Bishop, 2007). For example, it can be as simple as placing all the files containing the keyword "information" under the folder called "information". More intelligence is required for a better classification with increased depth or hierarchy. There are two techniques for data classification: supervised classification and unsupervised classification. Both of them are used for the pattern recognition applications. All the pattern recognition techniques are to define the classes first. Then the patterns of each class are to be characterized. The data to be classified is sampled and its features are extracted. Depending up on the features, the data elements are clustered and placed in one of the classes. The classifier updates its knowledge based on the performance and learnings of the classification.

Probabilistic models are used in statistical pattern recognition, to assign the elements to a predefined class. In the recognition of digits, the object is assigned with on of the numbers 0 to 9. In the character recognition, it is from a to z and so on. In the image processing and face recognition applications, the known image patterns or the faces are mapped on to the classes. The principle of maximum entropy or the maximum likelihood estimation is a powerful framework that can be used to estimate class posterior probabilities for pattern recognition tasks. It is a conceptually straight forward model that that supports the accurate estimation of a large number of free parameters.

Patterns in Multimedia Data

In multimedia data, a certain degree of patterns are evident. For example, in the color based classification of JPEG images, the DC or average values of Discrete cosine transform of Cb & Cr (color components) falling in a specific range are used. Different colors would have different average values. The same is true with audio and speech. The formants or peaking frequencies associated with the speech are characteristic for the individuals. Based on the previously stored values, the speech segments may be categorized as belonging to specific individuals. In these examples, the multimedia classification happens in the transformed domain.

The translation of Information to knowledge and then to wisdom provide a metamorphic evolution of the understanding of the data. With a better understanding of the nature of the data, context independence increases from the information to knowledge and from the knowledge to wisdom. Information paints contextual meaning and relation for data. It is however not concerned about the pattern. The pattern digs out a relation in the tons of raw data. It happens by virtue of knowledge. The underlying mechanism of pattern formation refers to wisdom. Based on the same principles, it maps a set of unfamiliar patterns to another set of unfamiliar patterns in the data.

Moving forward, the knowledge base queries would consist of image, video and speech samples in the place of the keywords. The data retrieval system is required to support multimedia pattern matching. Based on the outcome, which is of a 'yes' or 'no' kind in some applications, decision is taken to trigger an action. Such knowledge bases would be used in Banks, industries, Airport surveillance systems, crime detection and prevention etc. It can prevent the unauthorized entries. It requires real tome pattern recognition, which is challenging in terms of complexity and resources.

A portion of the challenge data is taken for training and the other part is synthesized with a neural network. The framework for pattern matching is shown in figure 1. The pattern is scaled first. It is then matched with the actual data. Later, the difference is computed. By setting a threshold on the difference, the speaker identity may be endorsed. Alternatively the challenge data may be sieved through a

Figure 1. Pattern extrapolation and matching

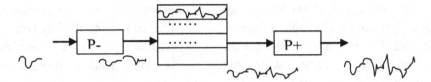

feedback neural network. The same would be compared with the data stored in the knowledge base for every level of the abstraction. If the challenge data is the distorted version of the data in the knowledge base, the lower order abstraction match better as they carry more information. The degree of matching falls with the increased abstractions or with the higher order estimators. By setting a threshold for each level, it would be possible to endorse the identity of the challenge data. The degree of distortion may be provided.

Automatic speaker identification would be more commonly used in future applications. There are some cases where the signal or the pattern matches for the shape and not for the value. In such cases the signal needs to be scaled appropriately calling for the preprocessing. In addition, the signal matches with one of the abstract levels of the original pattern indicated by the abstract level of the hierarchical data organization. This scenario would be common in speaker identification and verification.

Neural Networks for Pattern Recognition

Although conventional computers can be used for the pattern recognition, artificial neural networks have built in advantage in their architecture to support adaptive learning. They can learn and implement the conventional pattern recognition algorithms as well (Bishop, C. M, 1995). In a conventional computer, direct comparison is made for a match between the data object and the predetermined and anticipated patterns. The outcome is an 'accurate' match or no match. If a noisy input 'close' to the anticipated pattern is applied, the computer program does not provide a satisfactory result. However, neural networks can work with noisy inputs and unknown patterns providing a 'close match' in some statistical sense.

One of the problems in the pattern recognition and data mining is the presence or noise or missing data in the input, making it difficult to classify. It compounds the problem if an unknown input is applied with missing data and the noise. Although support vector techniques can be used to address this problem, the discrete data makes it inefficient. A Bayesian neural network can be used for recalling previously unknown patterns. The feedback neural network can work as a Bayesian neural network. It can afford to work with small SNRs as a result of the feedback or data history. Noise associated with the inputs reduces the accuracy of generalization in a bigger way then the noise in the reference output.

- For the input values where the function being learnt is relatively flat, the input noise will have little effect.
- For the input values where the function being learnt is steep, input noise severely degrades the generalization.

However, the previous history associated with a feedback neural network enhances the power of generalization.

A multilayer Neural networks may be trained to learn the nonlinear algorithms (D. Keysers, F. J. Och, and H. Ney, 2002) for classification using the feature extraction. Although the architectures and algorithms are different, frequently used neural network models are equivalent to the various statistical pattern recognition methods used in practice. Hence, the parallel architecture of the neural networks may be exploited to implement the existing feature extraction and classification algorithms. (Ripley, 1996) discusses the relationship between neural networks and statistical pattern recognition.

The identification of patterns in the knowledge is important to take the information towards wisdom. Artificial neural networks are useful to bring out the hidden patterns. The feed-forward networks are generally used for pattern classification and recognition applications. It includes the multilayer perception and Radial-Basis Function (RBF) networks. The Self-Organizing Map (SOM) or Kohonen-Network are useful in data clustering and feature mapping applications.

The neural networks contain the input layer, the output layer and hidden layers in between them. Depending up on the complexity of the learning [pattern, there can be one or more hidden layers or it may be totally absent.

The learning algorithms with the neural networks involve updating of the network architecture or the weights in each iteration based on the comparison with a specific value or meeting of a condition. Later, the trained neural network is deployed to perform a particular task of classification or clustering in the field.

As the neural networks are less dependent on the actual domain knowledge and largely rely on the input output training patterns, they are widely used in classification and clustering applications in multiple domains. They do not require system models or differential equations governing the evolution of the system and the system behavior. All they need is the optimal set of training data. They follow n\ more of rule base approach instead of model based approach.

It is often expensive or difficult to label a training Input output pattern with its class.. Unsupervised classification is used when the unlabeled training data is available. Unsupervised classification (D. Miller, A. V. Rao, K. Rose, and A. Gersho, 1996) is also known as data clustering. Here a group of objects with similar pattern are grouped or clustered together. The membership of the objects in different classes is assigned using the Classification trees (N. Ye and X. Li, 2002).

In pattern recognition applications, weight of the feature index plays an important role. The weight reflects the importance of the feature index. The weight is composed of two components.

- **Subjective weight:** It is based on the knowledge and experience gained by the experts or individuals. A neural network can adaptively optimize this weight through the inherent learning capabilities with historical data.
- **Objective weight:** It is based on facts determined by the statistical properties and measurements carried over the data.

Hierarchical Pattern Matching

With the increase in the usage of machines for intelligent information processing, several pattern matching activities have to be processed at a time. Pattern recognition or matching can happen at multiple levels of hierarchy if the data is stored as hierarchies of multiple abstractions. In such cases, the pattern matching algorithms may be implemented in parallel reducing the matching time. Finally the results from different levels of matching may be collated and a decision may be taken. In another type of implementation,

Figure 2. Neural network based classifier

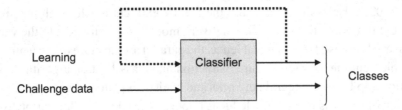

the lowest abstract level may be matched first. Only up on a satisfactory match or with an acceptable degree of matching, the other levels in the hierarchy may be traversed.

Classifier Architecture

Depending up on the speed and load requirements, to cater for different applications, various classifier architecture (Richard O. Duda, Peter E. Hart, David G. Stork, 2001) are being used in practice (C.M. van der Walt and E. Barnard, 2007). For the classification and clustering of data originating over a supply chain, neural networks of large size are required. However, it is difficult to get such large size neural networks with a large number of neurons, in spite of advancements in the VLSI technology.

Optimal Architecture

In general, there are many different classes of network architectures. All of them require extensive inter-connections between the source nodes and the neurons, and/or between the neurons. For each of these connections, the knowledge acquired through a learning process is stored as the synaptic weight. As the number of input nodes and hence the neurons increases, the number of interconnections and synaptic weights also increase. A neural network based classifier is shown in figure 2.

To overcome this difficulty, a new reconfigurable artificial neural network architecture has been developed for the data classification application. It makes use of a learning algorithm based on maxi-mization of the mutual information. The architecture is realizable through the usage of multi-layer feed forward network. Unlike a back propagation neural network, where the knowledge learnt in the training period is stored as synaptic weights, here the knowledge is stored as evolving circuit structure that gets refined in each of the iterations, with increase or decrease in the number of neurons. For every neuron, the threshold values required to activate the neuron are stored. The output signals of the hidden layers are processed using logic circuits before passed on to the next layer as the input. Based on the statistical analysis performed during learning process, only the important features required for the classification are selected and grouped in to subsets, which form the input space for the neural networks. In the hidden layers, only the outputs of important neurons are forwarded to the next layer.

For the final decision, the intermediate decisions made for the subset of the features are to be collated. This merging of the results happens through another network trained optimally. The architecture of this network is a combinatorial circuit, reducing the interconnections. It consumes less memory in spite of a large number of inputs and nodes.

Estimators

Classifiers generally make use of estimators. The output of each of the estimators is a class. As the data size increases, the number of estimators also increases. Each of the self-organized neural networks used in the classifier may be thought of as an estimator. It has been shown that a large number of estimators can be replaced by a single one with a feedback neural network. Thus a bunch of self organized neural networks forming the feature space can be replaced by a single feedback neural Network to get a similar performance. The order of feedback is computed based on the mutual information.

A feedback neural network can be used as a maximum likelihood estimator. In the superposition of the outputs of multiple estimators, the resulting output shifts towards an ideal estimator where the entropy is the minimum and correspond to the maximum likelihood estimation.

Classification Tree

Data retrieval and data mining (R. Duda, P.hart and D.Stork, 2002) systems extensively make use of the classification tree analysis (Lee, C.Lin.C and Chen, M, 2001, Linn, W.Orgun, M. and Williams, G.J, 2002). The classification tree predicts the value of a dependant variable similar to the conventional techniques such as non linear estimation, discriminant Analysis, statistics or Cluster Analysis. They are more flexible than anty of these methods.

The hidden patterns from the past data are to be extracted. The extracted patterns are then transformed in to a set of rules (Karimi, K. and Hamilton. H.J, 2002, T. Scheffer and S. Wrobel, 2002). The rules need to be consolidated and merged (S. Thrun, 1995, T. Scheffer, 2005). These rules will be able to predict the decisions for the similar events in the future.

Data Clustering

The logical extension of finding patterns in the decoded information calls for clustering of the data based on some inferred as well as observed similarities. The clustering problem basically involves optimization of certain cost function with the partition of the training set or the actual data when deployed. The average value of variance among the members of a cluster can be a cost function. Data clustering are extensively used in the pattern recognition applications. When a data set from an unknown source is available, the use of data clustering is to categorize the underlying statistical structures in the data by extracting similar the components in the mixture. Clustering is a typical example for the class of unsupervised learning problems (A.K.Jain, M.N.Murthy and P.J.Flynn, 1999). Here only input samples of the system under design are available for the training. The target system output will not be available.

Clustering involves the logical partitioning of a group of items or data points into subgroups, retaining a maximum similarity among the members of the group. The mechanism of clustering is shown in figure 3. As a result of clustering, the output can be different from the output of standalone sets. When no advance information is available on the data distribution clustering will be the useful technique for grouping and subsequent analysis of the data. In this chapter, pattern recognition is explored as a method of organizing and translating information in to knowledge.

Clustering algorithms based on quantum mechanics would speed up the process several folds. The algorithm based on Eigen states is popularly used.

Figure 3. Data clustering

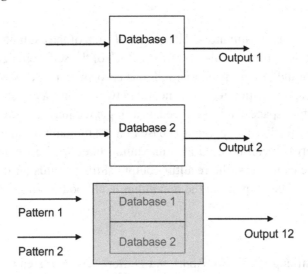

Pattern with Information Feedback

The output of a system with a differential feedback from the output stage to the input stage exhibits a certain known behavior. The autocorrelation of the output of such a system would be self similarity to different scales of time. This is due to the fact that the output of such systems will have a long range dependency. I.e. the output at any point depends up on the previous outputs.

The internet is one such system, where the autocorrelation of the traffic exhibits self similarity for various time scales. For an artificial neural network, it would be relatively easy to predict such an output. A feedback neural network models such systems as the output is long range dependent. Once the self similar pattern in the information or data is identified, other properties of the differential feedback would follow. It would be possible to identify the abstract levels in the information. The characteristics of the information sources can be made known and the rate of information or knowledge acquisition from each of them may be controlled. For an expert system, if the information on the degree of self similarity in the data pattern is provided, it can predict the disasters such as network breakdown, earth quake etc in advance. Figure 4 shows pattern matching over a hierarchy of data.

ISSUES AND SOLUTIONS

Duplication in Data

Removal of duplication in the data is an issue in the cleaning process of the information or knowledge. To identify the duplication of a data, it is applied to a Bayesian (S. Jaroszewicz and T. Scheffer, 2005) classifier. The class with lowest conditional probability is selected as the disjoint data. The two data patterns share the least information in common. In the feedback neural network classifier, it corresponds to the highest information or lowest entropy state. Alternatively, if the data corresponding to the class

Figure 4. Pattern matching over Hierarchy of data

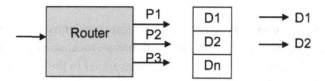

of maximum conditional probability is more than a specified threshold, the data may be treated as the duplicate of the matching class and it may be discarded.

Data Over Fitting

The entropy minimization technique is often used in pattern recognition. It is a matured concept in statistical thermodynamics. Tin information theory, it is used to reduce the redundancy in the content by identifying the similar patterns. The same concept is used in pattern recognition, language modeling and text classification.

From the probability distribution or the available training data of the set, it is required to satisfy the constraints of classification for the data with lowest possible entropy. Minimization of the entropy is a condition to avoid over fitting in the data. A further advantage of the minimum entropy approach is that it is scalable, extensible and provides a self similar model. A feedback neural network is one such implementation of the model. With this, new features may be easily added to the classifiers.

Randomness in the Data

The time series often exhibits regular patterns in spite of their inherent randomness. The statistics of such a sequence shows known patterns. For example, the peaks of the autocorrelation function falls asymptotically. If the time series is a collection of observations of a naturally occurring phenomenon, the autocorrelation function exhibits a kind of self similarity. This is because of the long range dependency associated with the samples. Typical examples are the earthquake and the flood records. A feedback neural network basically absorbs the long range dependency by taking historical data in to computations or decision making. It makes these networks an ideal candidate for the prediction of the time series. Each observation of the data is correlated in the resulting output time series. As the system gains more knowledge through the historical data, the accuracy in the prediction would turn better.

Noisy Data

Identification of noise in the data pattern is a tough task. The spectrum of the distorted signal, obtained by subtracting each of the corresponding estimators and then taking the Fourier transform, would fall under different regions. Depending up on the distribution of the noise energy in these regions, it is possible to identify the source of the corrupting noise.

User Experience

In the recovery of data based on user requirements, appropriate mechanism to incorporate the feedback from the user is expected. A conventional neural network has no mechanism to handle this. A feedback neural network can however use the user input as additional signal in the process of searching and fine tune the search based on the user interests.

FUTURE TRENDS

Data Classification & Clustering

Data classification (R. O. Duda, P. E. Hart, and D. G. Stork, 2001.) is the backbone of data mining. A couple of techniques being matured in the recent past and likely to get in to the products are provided below.

Bayesian Learning

A classifier generally makes use of the Bayesian network. The classification happens based on the data patterns. The conditional probabilities of various classes are computed and the class with the highest conditional probability will be selected as the pattern matching with the specified input. The network is initially trained with the known patterns. A feedback neural network reduces the training period. The class selected by the same will have the highest probability or lowest information. This corresponds to the estimator with the entropy lowest among all. It also happens to be the global or generalized behavior or solution for the applied pattern.

Reinforced Unsupervised Learning

Reinforced or unsupervised learning is increasingly being used in classification applications. It plays vital role in the classification of data or information in to useful knowledge. In the classification applications, the neural network has to handle data with higher degree of randomness. So, the neural networks with fixed weights may not be of much use as their performance to the untrained data is less satisfactory. A Self organized neural network works well in such situations. Compared to the conventional neural network architecture, self organization greatly reduces the interconnections by making use of local interconnections based on the statistical analysis. It gets rid of the storage of a large number of synaptic weights. The network has the feature of the adaptive hardware structures and adjustable threshold values based on the mutual information selection criteria.

Competitive Learning

Competitive learning often makes use of the data clustering. Here the correlated information with similar attributes in the input space is grouped together. In a typical artificial neural network, a set of training data is provided for learning. In each of the iteration, the output of the neural network is compared with the target output. Based on the error or the deviation, the weights are updated. In a self organizing model, the past experience or exposure to the pattern and the response for this input will be made use.

Competitive learning can be achieved through multiple means depending up on the applications, each differing in the way it is implemented. Typically, for clustering problem, feature mapping architecture is employed to find out the correlations in the data in the high dimensional input space. The size of the self organizing network grows with the iterations. The network size is not predefined and the neurons get added or deleted adaptively during the learning process. The addition and deletion of neurons is achieved by changing the orders of differentiation. A higher order differential feedback obviously covers the entire learning process. The strategies in modifying the network topology during the learning process (adding, deleting and clustering neurons) are to improve the pattern identification in the data and at the same time to try to reduce the total entropy. Also, entropy starts reducing with increase in the order of the feedback and reaches a minimum when the order is infinite.

Self Learning

As the training starts, the nodes of the network are presented with the input pattern and allowing them to compute their weights. A threshold is placed on the outcome of the training to eliminate some of the nodes. However, the winning node and the ones close to it are allowed in to the next iteration and the process continues. These nodes are the neighborhood of the winner.

To start with, all the nodes of the network are treated equally and are scattered around the winner node. As the training progresses, the size of nodes in the neighborhood of the winner gets reduced linearly. Finally, in the last iteration, only winner node would be left out. As the training progresses, the constraint on adaptation becomes rigorous and learning becomes more perfect. That is why the nodes start getting dropped out finally leaving the winner. The degree of adjustments that can be made for the weight get reduced linearly with the time. Thus, in each of the iteration, only the nodes more close to the winner would survive.

The changes to each element in the weight vector are made in accordance with the following equation.

$$\delta w_i = \alpha(w_i - i_i) \tag{1}$$

where α=Learning rate, δw= Incremental change in the weight. i = Input.

The neuron with the weight vector closest to a given input pattern will be the winner for that pattern and for any other input patterns to which it is the closest. All input patterns in the set for which the same node is the winner are taken to be in the same group. A line will be drawn in the map to enclose them to represent their relationship.

However, self learning networks do have some drawback of the requirement of a large data set for training. Although the neurons that get closely placed in the output space represent similar input patterns, they not necessarily follow the same. Conversely, the neurons that are far apart in the output space not necessarily the indicative of the measure of the different input patterns proportional to quality of a SOM, average quantization error etc. In an adhoc network, due to a restricted parameter space, input output pattern cannot be learnt accurately. In such scenarios, self-organized neural networks are widely used.

CONCLUSION

In this chapter,

* Pattern recognition techniques are introduced
* The usage of artificial, neural networks in highlighted.

In pattern recognition, depending up on the nature of the data, multiple algorithms are used. It calls for flexibility of the system to absorb the changes. The system has to be flexible enough to adapt to the changes. Pattern recognition involves algorithms for sensing the data, feature extraction, classification, clustering, decision making, learning and adaptation. The intelligent information processing algorithms discussed in this chapter address all of them.

Pattern recognizers make use of a variety of signal processing concepts at single or multiple-layered perceptrons, functional link nets and radial basis function networks; techniques like learning vector quantization networks, self-organizing maps, and recursive neural networks.

QUESTIONS

1. How does the neural network help in the recognition of the patterns in then data?
2. What are the steps to be followed for the identification of the handwritten data?
3. How does an estimator classify the data in to patterns?
4. How does pattern matching happens over a hierarchy of data?
5. What is the impact of noise on the pattern recognition and classification?

REFERENCES

Bishop, C. M. (1995). *Neural Networks for Pattern Recognition*. Oxford, UK: Oxford University Press

Bishop, C. M. (2007). *Pattern Recognition and Machine Learning*. Berlin: Springer.

Dahmen, J., Keysers, D., Ney, H., & Gʺuld, M. O. (2001). Statistical Image Object recognition using Mixture Densities. *Journal of Mathematical Imaging and Vision, 14*(3), 285–296. doi:10.1023/A:1011242314266

Duda, R., Hart, P., & Stork, D. (2002). *Pattern classification,* (2nd ed.). New York: John Wiley.

Duda, R. O., Hart, P. E., & Stork, D. G. (2001) *Pattern classification* (2nd Ed). New York: Wiley.

Jain, A. K., Murthy, M. N., & Flynn, P. J. (1999). Data clustering: A Review. *ACM Computing Surveys, 31*(3), 264–323. doi:10.1145/331499.331504

Jaroszewicz, S., & Scheffer, T. (2005). Fast discovery of unexpected patterns in data relative to a Bayesian networks. In *Proceedings of the SIGKDD Conference on Knowledge Discovery and Data Mining.*

Karimi, K., & Hamilton, H. J. (2002). *Discovering temporal rules from Temporally ordered data Lee Notes on Computer science.* In H.Yin, N. Allinson, R. Freeman, J. Keane, S. Hubbard (eds), (Vol 2412, pp. 25-30).

Krause, A. (2002). *Large scale clustering of protein sequences.* PhD thesis, Berlin Bhagat, P. M. (2005). *Pattern Recognition in Industry.*

Lee, C., Lin, C., & Chen, M. (2001). Sliding window filtering: An efficient algorithm for incremental mining. In *Proc. Of the 10th international conference on Information and knowledge management,* (pp 263-270).

Linn, W., Orgun, M., & Williams, G. J. (2002). An overview of temporal data mining. In S.J.Simoff, G.J.Williams and M. Hegland, (Eds.), *The 1st Australian Data mining workshop. ADM02* (pp. 83-90), University of technology, Sydney, Australia.

Miller, D., Rao, A. V., Rose, K., & Gersho, A. (1996). A global optimization technique for statistical classifier design. *IEEE Transactions on Signal Processing, 44,* 3108–3122. doi:10.1109/78.553484

Paulus, D., & Hornegger, J. (1998). *Applied Pattern Recognition* (2nd ed.). Wiesbaden, Germany: Vieweg, Verlag. Keysers, D., Och, F. J. & Ney, H. (2002). Maximum Entropy and Gaussian Models for Image Object Recognition. In *22.DAGM Symposium for Pattern Recognition,* Zurich, Switzerland.

Povinneli, R. J. (1999) *Time series data mining: Identifying temporal patterns for characterization and prediction of Time series events.* PhD Thesis, Marquette University, WI.

Pujari, A. K. (2000). *Data mining techniques.* Universities press (India) Private limited.

Ripley, B. D. (1996). *Pattern Recognition and Neural Networks.* Cambridge, UK: Cambridge University Press.

Scheffer, T. (2005). Finding association rules that trade support optimally against confidence. *Intelligent Data Analysis, 9*(3).

Scheffer, T., & Wrobel, S. (2002). Finding the most interesting patterns in a database quickly by using sequential sampling. *Journal of Machine Learning Research, 3,* 833–862. doi:10.1162/jmlr.2003.3.4-5.833

Thrun, S. (1995). Extracting rules from artificial neural networks with distributed representations. *Advances in neural information processing systems.*

van der Walt, C. M., & Barnard, E. (2007). Data characteristics that determine classifier Performance. *SAIEE Africa Research Journal, 98*(3), 87–93.

Ye, N., & Li, X. (2002). A scalable, incremental learning algorithm for classification problems. *Computers & Industrial Engineering, 43*(4), 677–692. doi:10.1016/S0360-8352(02)00132-8

Chapter 16
Knowledge Base Systems

ABSTRACT

A dumb information system in the information supply chain can provide data that is often difficult for the customer to interpret and use. To help in this regard, machine intelligence based on some learning rules is introduced in this chapter. Architecture of the knowledge base and the rule base are explained. The acquired knowledge from the different sources is to be consolidated.

INTRODUCTION

The last chapter deals with the identification of patterns in the data. The occurrence of the patterns in the data takes it to a higher level of organization, clearly indicating it is not junk. Based on a chain of reasoning and inferences, these data patterns provide a solution for complex problems. Here, the architecture to build a system that provides expert solutions for the domain specific problems is discussed.

In a traditional computing system, there is less scope for providing the solutions for the problems based on the previous learning. The solutions are hardcoded with a rigid program language and remain the same always. On the other hand, in an expert system, the solution is coded in the database rather than being provided by a program. This architecture is advantageous in several ways.

In an expert system, the information is modeled at a higher level of the abstraction. To build the model resembling the human reasoning, support from different tools and symbolic languages is sought. The language used for modeling supports rule-based programming, where a set of rules are used to represent heuristics or actions under s certain context or situation. A Rule has two portions:

DOI: 10.4018/978-1-60566-888-8.ch016

1. An **if** portion where a series of conditions or patterns or stimuli are specified. These patterns are to be matched with the input pattern to excite the appropriate condition.
2. A **then** portion where the effects or the consequences are described when the **if** portion turns out to be true.

The usage of a neural network for pattern matching has been given in the chapter on intelligent information processing. The architecture of expert systems with the organization of data in to abstraction levels in place is the topic of discussion here.

Expert systems are useful for getting specific solutions for the problems in domains as diverse as mathematics, medicine, business, law, military, education etc. Although the knowledge stored in an expert system is specific to a domain, it can provide solution for any problem with in the domain. In this chapter, the components of the expert system are discussed in detail. The architecture of the expert system in turn determines the design of the applications calling the same. The different services that need the help of an expert system are e- governance, portals, knowledge management (Liebowitz, J. & Chen, Y, 2001), etc. Generally, the queries focus on:

- **Diagnosis:** Used to find the faults in the data when it is difficult to carryout manually. For example, design of a million gate integrated circuit.
- **Data Interpretation:** When it is difficult to analyze a large volume of data, for example, geological data, the help of an expert system is sought to find the patterns and interpret the data.

In an expert system, the solution provided depends more on the problem type than on the domain of the problem. In its simple form, it takes the queries from the user or the invoking applications, provides the required information as well as *clarification* required to solve the problem or help in the decision making (Power, D. J, 2002). Often it is iterative providing more precise answer in each of the iterations. Thus it is much powerful than an ordinary search engine.

An expert system is designed to address the requirements of a specific domain with a much focused objective. This is because they perform well and maintain the knowledge base of a single domain when they have a narrow focus rather than maintaining information on all the areas that are generally not requested by the users of the system.

Expert system is strongly coupled with the knowledge or the knowledge base. The knowledge base provides the capability to handle any query and render the expert suggestion. The knowledge base is to be scalable and adaptable with provision to add learning and experience. The updating of the system has to happen periodically without keeping it down and change in the architecture. The same would be reflected in the quality of the solution rendered by the expert system. The different mechanisms used for the storage and retrieval of knowledge are provided in a separate chapter.

Knowledge base alone will not be of much use. The expert system has to make use of the knowledge in the reasoning processing to arrive at the logical inferences.

BACKGROUND

Expert systems (Joseph C. Giarratano, 2005), are the intelligent computer programs meant to provide solution for the problems in a specific area making use of the knowledge base it can read and understand.

The expert systems are used for various activities such as prediction, analysis, debugging, diagnosis, planning, monitoring etc. Expert system consists of sophisticated programs (Peter Jackson, 1998), authored using Artificial Intelligence (AI) (Poole, David; Mackworth, Alan; Goebel, Randy, 1998).

Machine intelligence spans the cognitive skills such as continuous learning, recollection and the capability to analyze and solve the problems (Russell, Stuart J, Norvig, Peter, 2003). In general, the AI applications are interested in problem solving, the methodical approach for building the problem to arrive at a solution, than the solution itself.

Expert systems include the AI programs (Luger, George; Stubblefield, William, 2004) having competency in a particular domain to solve the problems through reasoning by making use of the knowledge in the domain. These programs show intelligence in reasoning and symbolic inferences (Nilsson, Nils, 1998). They are helpful to understand how the knowledge may be symbolically represented inside a machine. In the expert systems, the knowledge base contains the information that is useful for human experts. In Artificial intelligence applications, expert systems (ES) and knowledge-based systems (KBS) are interchangeably used.

Expert system architecture consists of two components: the knowledge base and the reasoning or inference engine.

Knowledge Representation in Expert System

Knowledge representation is much more difficult than the information representation discussed in the earlier chapters of this book. The important component of the expert system is the knowledge base. It is this knowledge base that differentiates one expert system from the other in the same domain. Today, tools also provide an explanation for the decisions taken or reasoning of the expert system

There are two distinct ways of representing the knowledge:

1. *Rule based*: It makes use of the IF-THEN statements for the representation of the knowledge. The IF part gives the condition or the constraint while the THEN part provides the consequence of exciting this condition. The IF and THEN parts may be nested in a complex rule or a separate set of rules may be stated.
2. *Frame or schema based:* Here the entity to be represented is associated with a schema. It encodes the attributes and their values for the entity. The relationship among these entities is also defined both qualitatively and quantitatively. Finally, the entities may be represented hierarchically.

The system knowledge is almost heuristic, probable or uncertain subjected to experience or exposure. Hence it is associated with a weight factor. To complicate the problem, the data supplied for the reasoning is also uncertain. The concepts from fuzzy logic may be used to handle such data and use the knowledge for reasoning and arrive at an inference.

In the expert system, in the representation of knowledge as the set of IF- THEN rules, the rules actually reflect the experience and learning for different conditions or situations. The rules themselves are of little help. The real power of an expert system lies in how these rules are sequenced and traversed in arriving at a partial result or inference. The rules represent the degree of certainty of the conclusion if that particular scenario or situation is encountered. The certainties are determined by the statistical techniques. The choice of rules taken while traversing and arriving at the conclusion provides the input for providing an explanation for the inference.

Figure 1. Training of expert system

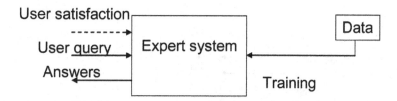

The programs driving the knowledge bases implement the laws of reasoning and provide the inference subjected to certain rules. Merging of rules and prediction of the missing parts of the knowledge base happen to be the important task in the implementation. This chapter addresses these problems.

The knowledge base contains two forms of knowledge:

- **Factual knowledge**: This form of the knowledge is based on the facts. It is acquired from the sources such as text books, journals, widely circulated and agreed beliefs and facts. It remains consistent and similar in all knowledge bases
- **Heuristic knowledge**: It is based more on the judgmental knowledge of the individuals. Hence, it is gathered more from the experience and individual specific, difficult to model and characterize. It spans good practices, judgment, analysis and reasoning.

Components of Expert System

Expert system architecture is composed of the following components:

- **Knowledge base:** It is a database composed of the acquired knowledge. In an expert system, there can be one or more knowledge bases depending up on the architecture and the domains supported.
- **Reasoning engine**: Based on the knowledge base and the rule base, provides the mechanism to infer from the chain of thoughts or reasoning.
- **Knowledge acquisition subsystem:** It helps in the acquisition and maintenance of the knowledge. The knowledge base architecture is to be scalable and extensible. Figure 1 shows the training process involved in updating the knowledge base.
- **Explanation subsystem:** It reasons out the steps taken by the expert system or the inferences arrived at the inference engine or the request made for the additional data to provide the solution.
- **Rule base:** It maintains a set of rules being used for arriving at a conclusion. It resembles the human reasoning.
- **Inference engine**: It arrives at the inferences made based on the rules being excited.
- **Integration unit:** It combines the inferences made by the inference engine towards arriving at a final conclusion.
- **User interface**: Provides a communication channel between the end user and the expert system.

Figure 2. Architecture mapping learning rules to conclusions

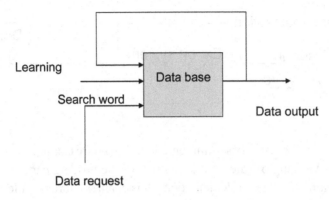

Rule Base

A rule base consists of several rules required for decision making; similar to the way the human beings make decisions. The rules are separate and not directly related to each other. However, during inference phase, the inference engine logically connects them together and provides the conclusions based on the problem in hand and the context. The architecture of data generation with learning rule is shown in figure 2. The rules may be added or deleted independent of the presence of the other rules providing a scalable architecture. However, the conclusions reached would strongly depend up on the presence or absence of certain rules

The complex applications and problems require a large set of rules and resources to simulate the human reasoning process for the decision making. The rules are traversed in a complex way demanding a huge processing power and the main memory to store the partial results. Aggregation of the inferences is also a challenging task demanding additional intelligence such as a Bayesian network for consolidation. Simple applications on the other hand arrive at the conclusions making use of only a few rules and the information. The rule base is also a data base frequently subjected to queries. It may be organized in to multiple hierarchies as shown in figure 3. To excite the full "rule", all levels in the hierarchy are to be accessed.

In order to reduce the complexity of the traversal over the rules, the rule base is partitioned in to essential and non essential parts. The required part consists of the rules that are required to be applied to arrive at the conclusion. All other rules are discarded. This partition is totally dependent up on the application and

Figure 3. Rule base organization

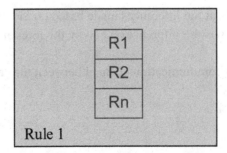

is virtual. This partition allows the systems with smaller main memory to load the smaller set of rules required for the application. The segmentation or partition can be done in several ways supporting the solution to render results at different degrees of accuracy or abstraction based on the application, context, requirement and the audience. For example, is it really required for an ordinary user to have a precise answer for the question "How many molecules of water are present in a cup of coffee?" The sequencing of loading the segments is to be well managed to optimize the paging or memory transactions.

In addition to the rules, the main memory is to retain the partial results as well, calling for optimal usage of the memory. The results are often interlinked and require to be retained for a long time. For example, in the implementation of the decision tree, often there will be a jump to the parent node to explore the alternate path. The data at this node is expected to be present in the main memory when the roll back happens. When a different segment is loaded in to the main memory, the partial results of the analysis or inferences over the previous segment are to be made available. More memory is required to support a rollback to a node in the previous page.

Knowledge Base

The knowledge base, the database where the information is stored, can be built in any programming language.

Shell

Most of the transactions between the knowledge base and the external world happen through the Shell. It sits between the end user interface and the operating system of the expert system. The main functions performed by the shell are provided in the listing1.

Listing 1 Functions performed by the Shell of an expert system

- It helps in the creation of the knowledge base.
- It interprets all the commands over the knowledge base.
- Processing the query information entered by the end user, gets the additional data and relates the same to the concepts stored in the knowledge base and provide the solution.
- It manages the UI, screen capture, representation of the objects, routing of the data to and from the knowledge base etc.

Shell is often sold as the end product facilitating the organizations to build the knowledge base separately from the scratch. Even the knowledge base system may be procured separately. However, their integration is a tough task.

Operating System

Operating system is an important component in the architecture of the expert system. It provides the capabilities and resources of the machine to the expert system, reducing the dependency on the external programs. The typical resources and the utilities include the memory and file system management, rudimentary User interface, interface to the external world and keyboard and mouse in put from the external world etc. However, too much of dependency on the operating system reduces the performance.

Figure 4. Architecture of the knowledge base

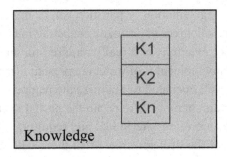

In a conventional computer, algorithms are extensively used to solve the problems. The solution for a problem may be found out if there is an algorithm or a **known** way to solve the same. However with an expert system, the solution is more of judgmental and would have provided a similar solution for a similar problem in the past. The effectiveness of the solution may be used to correct it to provide a better solution in the future. If the solution space is too large, it is not possible to visit all of them. The solution based on the previous experience and heuristics need to be provided. The knowledge base is often organized hierarchically similar to the rule base as shown in the figure 4.

The Rules of a knowledge base help in providing a probabilistic solution rather than the definitive or concluding solution. To make it happen, the objects of the knowledge base themselves are stored with the associated probabilities. The inference engine consolidates these results and provides a probabilistic solution. In general, the output of the system contains the data that is probabilistic or some data may be missing.

The resolution of problem in all application areas requires some data, unique to the domain and the problem in hand. This data required by the expert system keeps changing. Often, the user provides the requisite data to the expert system at the time of querying the system. It happens through a user interface that takes the data and places the same in the working memory for further processing and decision making.

Knowledge Integration

An expert system happens to be the fusion of several appropriate knowledge sources (Ahmed, P. K. et Al, 2002). The integration of knowledge bases is challenging especially when there are abnormally large number of knowledge sources. Many issues such as duplication of work, consolidation of work, global optimal decisions etc would crop up. Basically the generation and the usage of knowledge stems up from the collective behavior of the multiple sources. The behavior of the individual knowledge sources has to be translated on to the global and collective behavior through an effective communication among the knowledge sources. The inconsistency between them has to get resolved automatically. The sources start aligning themselves towards a global behavior through the feedback signals that get exchanged among them and aid in the growth of the knowledge base without a centralized server. This behavior of the knowledge bases may be linked to swarms. Such a model for the knowledge fusion is totally scalable and extensible.

Case Study: Knowledge Integration in Swarms

The conceptual similarities of distributed computing and the hierarchical memory organization paradigm together with the natural phenomenon of swarms has resulted in the notion of swarm computing having parallels with knowledge management. In knowledge swarms (Maurice Clerc, 2006), a group of knowledge units each with a specific mission perform a common task and store its own contribution to the knowledge base and exchange the data over an adhoc network. There will not be a centralized server to control them. Each of them would leave some information to communicate with the others. The feedback may be applied for the intended utilization of this information for the communication among the individuals of the swarm. The model translates the information left out by the individuals to the collective behavior (Parsopoulos, K, E., Vrahatis, M, N., Natural Computing, 2002) of the swarm. The entropy or disorder in the knowledge gets minimized with increase in the order of the feedback.

To represent the information, the ants use the chemical signals called pheromones. Those insects of the group that are ahead of rest of the swarm would leave behind the relevant coded information for the detection and alteration by the others that follow them. The swarm members start changing these pheromones continuously. Each member while passing over the footprint of the other one will overwrite with its own interpretation. It distorts the message in its own way. What is left at the end will be having the contribution from all the authors who interpret the information in their own way; i.e. a long feedback or history.

The signal used for information exchange in a swarm comprises of two components, namely the Gaussian part and the impulsive part. The Gaussian part of the signal corresponds to the aggregate of information over a period of time, whereas the impulsive part models the information contribution by the individual source of the information. The Gaussian component imparts long range dependence (LRD) to the signal, whereas the bursty component gives rise to spikiness. The investigation of random processes characterized by long range dependency or wide range of timescales is becoming increasingly important in many experimental fields ranging from the investigation of earthquakes in earth science, to turbulence in fluids or the price fluctuations in financial markets and demand-supply variations in the supply chain. In particular, many random processes exhibit a scale invariant structure. A feedback neural network can accurately model such a data.

Information Organization

The information to be organized as knowledge or in the worst case, the solution given out from an expert system consists of two components- the structured knowledge and unstructured knowledge. The structured part may be thought of as made up of a Gaussian component while the unstructured random part of the knowledge may be thought of as made up of a bursty component. The composition of knowledge in to structured and unstructured is largely due to the way the feedback signal gets exchanged among the knowledge sources at the time of learning and the formation of the knowledge base. A connection-level analysis of signal at coarse time scales (time scales greater than a round-trip-time in the exchange of the signals) reveals that a single pair of knowledge sources dominatingly contribute during the period of the burst. The number of dominating connections that cause bursts is found to be a small fraction of the total number of knowledge source pairs.

Integrated Data Representation

In the previous chapters, it has been discussed that the centralized integrated representation of data in a modern enterprise has many advantages. On the same lines, the advantage of having a single expert system is that it will have the collective information, the sum total of knowledge from all the individuals. It happens to be the scaled or enhanced form of individual expertise. The feedback of information among the knowledge sources would be extremely useful for building up a crisp data base. The feedback provided makes the system resistant for over training. Hence, a small training set is sufficient for global learning with the required degree of accuracy.

The information feedback architecture that operates on multiple scales is useful for modeling this problem. The forecasting strategy is implemented by dividing the prediction task into elementary tasks. The model sieves the input signal into detail signals and a residual so that the original signal can be expressed as an additive combination of the weighted differential series, at the different resolution levels. The latter provide the accurate representation of the signal or the time series, so that the tiny temporal structures may be resolved and observable.

Data Arrival Pattern

In future, the data arrival pattern (Gachet, A., 2004) would almost turn real time making the system to work seamlessly. Any information that is to represent the complex sequences or events must be able to store and update context information spanning the possibly unlimited temporal intervals. In the above example, for the swarm footprint to remember some aspects of the past, one has to build into the system as much knowledge of the past as possible. A general approach involves deliberate inclusion of delays in to the system equations. In such a system, due to domain translations, multiplicative interactions of scalars are substituted by temporal convolution operations necessitating a time-dependent weight matrix. A general formulation of the delayed system in continuous time is an equation of the form.

$$T\frac{dv(t)}{dt} = g(u(t) + i(t)) \tag{1}$$

$$u(t) = \int_0^t W(t-s)\,v(s)\,ds \tag{2}$$

v(t) and *u(t)* are the N-dimensional vector activity and internal inputs of the units at time *t*, *W* is a N x N time-dependent matrix of weightage of present inputs and previous outputs. T is a diagonal matrix of conveniently chosen positive time constant, and *i(t)* is the input data vector. The sigmoidal function *g(h) = (1 + e^{-h})^{-1}* absorbs the associated non linearity. The above formula yields a solution in the discrete domain

$$v_k = g(\sum_{d=0}^{D} W_k^{dT} v_{k-d}) + I_k \tag{3}$$

This is nothing but the information feedback model. As it has been explained, it contains two terms-one is data dependent term and the other one is data independent term. It is resistant for over fitting (or overloading of information in whatever the means) and spans over different time scales. Such a state space model is preferred for input-output black box model as they require a smaller number input space. They are less prone to over fitting especially when small training sets are available.

Requirements of the Web Based Information System

The intelligent system happens to be an intelligent search engine that does 'Data mining' over the available data. It is capable of responding to the customer over voice, e-mail, image keyword etc and hence uses powerful pattern matching algorithms. The data mining concepts are provided in a separate chapter.

Based on the experience gained by the customer interactions and the patterns in the acquired or the updated data, better results may be delivered for subsequent queries, much the way like the human operator who gets the knowledge improved with time. Armed with such a system, the customers may be provided with solutions for the problems instead of mere data. It also reduces the data transfer over the network.

ISSUES AND SOLUTIONS

Large Rule Base

The set of rules to be traversed by an expert system before outputting meaningful and useful information are increasingly large. As a result, the performance tends to be sluggish and may not meet the real time constraints. A feedback neural network may be used to merge the rules and reduce the decision overhead. Because of this, the response time gets reduced. It is significant especially for mission critical applications. The outcome of each rule may be thought of as estimation performed by an estimator. A feedback neural network takes the estimation towards the ideal estimator with increase in the order of the feedback. An alternative approach for learning the rules in the absence of the supervisor is the swarm computing.

Relevance of Search Results

Retrieval of the relevant data from a large knowledge base expert system (Abraham, A, 2002) is a tough task. The users would find it difficult to collate the results extracted from multiple repositories over multiple search engines. They often provide irrelevant results wasting the precious time and the resources. The data thrown out by these search engines contain both structured and unstructured parts. This is in spite of the manual tagging of the documents for facilitating the search engines to retrieve them easily.

ESPs (enterprise search platforms) solve this issue by providing the search results in integrated form. They are composed of content search and data integration components. As a result, the response to the queries will be very precise with a high degree of relevance. It helps in then auto archiving and indexing of the documents. It provides customized search results making use of the concepts from natural language processing, auto-categorization etc.

Figure 5. Effect of feedback on reasoning

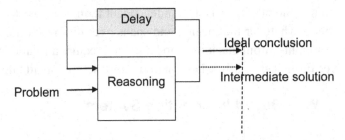

Reasoning from the Data

The reasoning in the expert system involves a set of IF-THEN-ELSE rules. The rules are required to be sequenced for the appropriate reasoning and invoking a chain of thoughts. There are two approaches for the chaining or taking the reasoning ahead.

1. **Forward chaining:** Here the reasoning or chaining starts from a set of rules and finally converge at a conclusion.
2. **Backward chaining:** Here the end result or the conclusion is known in advance. But the reasoning to arrive at this result is to be explored.

These approaches of reasoning are fused with the inference engines. They exploit the knowledge stored in the knowledge bases for reasoning before they start inferring.

In practice, both these chaining techniques are relatively slow. A feedback of information may be used to solve this problem. The feedback converts the model in to a mixed chaining problem solving model. In this model the chaining starts from a known state and proceeds towards the conclusions. The conclusions may be intermediate or permanent and compared with the known conclusions. The error or difference may be used as an additional input or condition to the model in the next time slot. Higher ordered errors may be generated and used as in a feedback neural network. The problem solving may be made very fast as the feedback improves the rate of learning of the system. Other benefits of the feedback would follow. Figure 5 shows the influence of feedback on the conclusion. The solution space is also hierarchical and asymptotically moves toward the ideal solution with differential feedback.

FUTURE TRENDS

System Model

The outputs of information feedback model are central differences which are generated with shifts. Shift for predicted samples amounts to generating samples with future and the past values. The idea here is to use the near future prediction of the loss probability as the control signal that is fed back to the input. The usage of several previous values is equivalent to sieving the signal through multiple time scales. Hence, when differential model is used, it is equivalent to scale the time by a factor function of the exponential power of the order of feedback. Differential model produces same results of scaling. Shift in the feedback

Figure 6. Data fusion in expert system

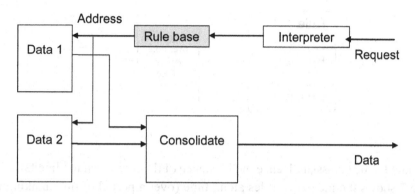

signal amounts to scaling the model. One effect of scaling is that the number of events gets reduced. Thus, the abstract or hierarchical representation of information in the data sources produces the same effect of providing the historical information that is a prerequisite in a knowledge database.

The IF-ELSE rules may be mapped on to the different estimators explained in the second chapter. In IF-ELSE rule, based on the condition, some of the target or output variable would undergo changes. In some cases the number of options would be more than 2. Even in these scenarios, the output variable changes according to the decision taken. Another rule that enforces the decision would act up on this variable that acts as the input. Based on the outcome of the rule, another output would be produced. This way, the chain of rules produces finally a single output that happen to be the outcome of the historical decisions.

In a modified version of a feedback neural network, the output of each decision would serve as an additional parameter to take up decision in the next step. Such a decision network inherits all the properties of the conventional feedback neural network. Each of the rules represents an estimator. As the set of estimators may be replaced with a single estimator, the set of rules may be replaced by a single rule. The architecture using hierarchical search and fusion of result is shown in figure 6.

Decision Making

The different representations of the decision making (Power, D.J, 2003) such as trees may be mapped on to the modified feedback neural network (Abraham, A, 2001) with the nodes representing the estimators. As we go down in the tree, the rule with which we started the tree will be more and more abstract and the local outputs would be determined by the local rules. This factor would be extremely useful is the business models and to evaluate the relevance of a rule at any point of timer down the line; meaning, the next position is more strongly influenced by the present rule than by a previous rule.

Representation of Decision Rules

The translation of models in to the symbolic representation of rules is getting increasingly complicated. Each of the estimators may be approximated from any of the estimator by adding the suitable terms to the Gaussian pulse of an appropriate abstraction or scale. This is because the estimators are Gaussian distributed as explained in the first chapter and the result of addition of these terms to Gaussian pulse

Figure 7. Merging of rules

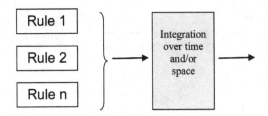

may be approximated to be Gaussian. Hence the influence of the rule down the line falls off as a Gaussian pulse. Figure 7 shows the merger of rules along time (over a period of time making use of history or differential/delayed feedback) or along space (at any time, the estimators used for learning rules replaced by a single estimator that can learn all rules. Such an estimator is realizable with differential feedback). Each rule is realized with an estimator. The merging or integration of rules can happen in temporal or spatial domain.

Interestingly, the first rule determined the course of action where the decision has been taken without any feedback output, will have the constant influence across. This is because any of the estimators consists of two parts- a fixed part ands a spurious part. The fixed part, corresponding to the bias, is determined by the very first rule. This is in agreement with the principles from chaotic physics where the initial position has a strong say down the line. Any deviation from this position would have increasingly large deviation in the future as the system evolves. This is because the initial estimator with few feedback terms is added with a series of feedback terms to get the Gaussian pulse corresponding to the higher estimators. Interestingly the result of this addition of term would also be Gaussian. The same reasoning replaces all the estimators with an equivalent estimator. The fixed part contributes for the bias in the output. Hence the output of the IF-ELSE rule would be strongly biased by the initial selection choice. As the chain of the rules gets longer, the resulting output tends to be noisy. This is because, with the increase in the order of feedback, the output becomes more and more flat resembling the ambient white noise. In addition, the information content gets reduces with increase in the order of the feedback or equivalently with increase in the length of the IF-ELSE chain. The entropy starts reducing. This is in consistent with the earlier observations.

The estimators are mapped on to the IF-ELSE statements of prolog. A neural network may be used as a pre-processor for processing the signal data for the expert system. The neural network acts as a transducer for these signals and converts them into symbolic information that can be understood by the expert systems

CONCLUSION

In this chapter,

- The architecture of an expert system towards solving the domain specific problems is provided.
- The mechanism of knowledge representation with organizational learning and decision making are discussed.

Knowledge base forms an important component of the knowledge management. It is popularly called expert system and happens to be the amalgamation of the related information. Uncertainty in the expert systems can be handled in a variety of approaches. In this chapter the usage of feedback neural network has been provided.

QUESTIONS

1. What are the components of an expert system?
2. How does the expert system architecture help in the supply chain management?
3. How does the knowledge get represented in an expert system?
4. How does the choice of rule base affect the performance of an expert system?
5. How does the knowledge integration happen in an expert system?

REFERENCES

Abraham, A. (2001). *Neuro-Fuzzy Systems: State-of-the-Art Modeling Techniques, Connectionist Models of Neurons, Learning Processes, and Artificial Intelligence*, in Lecture Notes in Computer Science, Vol. 2084, (eds. Mira., Jose and Prieto., Alberto) Springer Verlag, Germany, pp. 269–276.

Abraham, A. (2002) Intelligent Systems: Architectures and Perspectives, Recent Advances in Intelligent Paradigms and Applications, in *Studies in Fuzziness and Soft Computing*, Springer Verlag, Germany

Ahmed, P. K., et al. (Eds.). (2002). *Learning Through Knowledge Management.* Oxford, UK: Butterworth-Heinemann.

Clerc, M. (2006). *Particle Swarm Optimization.* ISTE.

Gachet, A. (2004). *Building Model-Driven Decision Support Systems with Dicodess.* Zurich: VDF.

Giarratano, J. C., & Riley, G. (2005). *Expert Systems, Principles and Programming.*

Jackson, P. (1998). *Introduction to Expert Systems.*

Liebowitz, J., & Chen, Y. (2001). Developing Knowledge-Sharing Proficencies. *Knowledge Management Review, 3*(6), 12–15.

Luger, G., & Stubblefield, W. (2004). *Artificial Intelligence: Structures and Strategies for Complex Problem Solving (5th ed.).* Menlo Park, CA: The Benjamin/Cummings Publishing Company, Inc.

Nilsson, N. (1998). *Artificial Intelligence: A New Synthesis.* San Francisco: Morgan Kaufmann Publishers.

Parsopoulos, K. E., & Vrahatis, M. N. (2002). Recent Approaches to Global Optimization Problems Through Particle Swarm Optimization. *Natural Computing, 1*, 235–306. doi:10.1023/A:1016568309421

Poole, D., Mackworth, A., & Goebel, R. (1998). *Computational Intelligence: A Logical Approach.* New York: Oxford University Press.

Power, D. J. (2002). *Decision support systems: concepts and resources for managers.* Westport, CT: Quorum Books

Power, D.J, (2003). A Brief History of Decision Support Systems. Retrieved May 31, 2003 from DSS-Resources.COM, (Version 2.8).

Russell, S. J., & Norvig, P. (2003). *Artificial Intelligence: A Modern Approach (2nd ed.).* Upper Saddle River, NJ: Prentice Hall

Chapter 17
Information Mining

ABSTRACT

The data in its raw form may not be of much use for the end customer. In the attempt to extract the knowledge from the data, the concept of data mining is extremely useful. This chapter explains how the data is to be filtered out to extract useful information. Often, exactly this information is requested by the players of the supply chain towards decision making. They are not interested in the binary data.

INTRODUCTION

The previous chapter explains how an expert system provides solution for complex problems. The solution largely depends up on the queries and the data provided by the user, much similar to the retrieval of the data with keywords. However, the data fetched would get filtered with another layer of intelligence. Here, the contextual and intelligent retrieval mechanism of the data, called data mining, is explored to solve the problems specific to a particular domain of expertise.

The huge volumes of data getting generated over the supply chain require the assistance of machines for the conversion of same in to knowledge. It involves extensive data analysis and intelligent interpretation. Data mining refers to finding patterns in the data and fitting suitable models for the same. The model derived from the data is used to infer the knowledge. The usage of machine intelligence (Green, C. L., & Edwards, P., 1996) for the retrieval of knowledge based on patterns and inferences is increasingly becoming popular in digital archives. It calls for the storage of data in machine readable forms that includes text, pictures, audio, video etc. In response to the customer requests, Knowledge retrieval systems provide the closely matching items from the collection of the data based on the 'patterns' and

DOI: 10.4018/978-1-60566-888-8.ch017

the 'inferences'. The knowledge discovery in database (KDD) (Matheus, C., Piatetsky-Shapiro, G.; and McNeill, D, 1996) uses the concepts from Machine learning, pattern matching and statistics to find the requisite data patterns (Xingquan Zhu, Ian Davidson, 2007, Xingquan Zhu, Ian Davidson, 2007a).

BACKGROUND

Data mining (Han, J., Kamber, 2001) involves the collection and analysis of a large volume of data that is generally not feasible to carryout manually and the help of machine intelligence is sought. Eg., analysis of the hourly variations in the stock prices of a company based on the data gathered over 15 days. This data will be helpful for predictions of the future values and decision making.

Data mining architecture comprises of (Mierswa, Ingo and Wurst, Michael and Klinkenberg, Ralf and Scholz, Martin and Euler, Timm, 2006) archival, retrieval, analysis and usage of the data. The algorithms and concepts borrowed from the Artificial intelligence, neural networks, Fuzzy sets etc are used for the realization of the same.

Data mining (Ethem Alpaydın, 2004) runs the statistics and machine learning algorithms over different data formats. While the data is getting translated in to usable knowledge, patterns will be identified in the data. The patterns enrich the knowledge model.

Knowledge fusion is an important part of knowledge management that consolidates and brings in the knowledge distributed across in to one integrated platform. Bayesian networks are proposed for the fusion of the knowledge. The usage of Neural Networks for Bayesian decision to facilitate data mining is the topic of discussion in this chapter. It brings in the required automation for information sorting, classification and clustering.

Data Mining for Knowledge Discovery

Statistical methods are used for the discovery of knowledge in the data. The uncertainties, inferences etc are quantified through the statistics and used for comparison. However, even if a random data is taken and searched, one can always find some patterns which add to the "hits" and improve the statistics. But that is actually not the case in reality as it bears no meaning. It makes the usage of statistics a bit difficult for data mining applications. Data mining is an important technology to retrieve the required information based on certain patterns in the data. The search for patterns can happen at different levels of abstraction as the pattern itself may be organized hierarchically and composed of clusters of clusters of the patterns. With the increased usage of the knowledge, the data mining tools traverse the hierarchies and produce more precise results in each of the iteration. Figure 1 shows how patterns are discovered in a random data. A part of the data may not fit with any pattern.

Data Clustering

Data mining is useful for extracting knowledge from the data (Kantardzic, Mehmed, 2003) by uncovering the patterns in the data not visible for human eyes. This translation happens by dividing data in to chunks of clusters. Figure 2 shows clusters in the data of figure 1.

Figure 1. Patterns in a random data

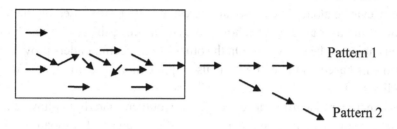

Figure 2. Clusters in the data

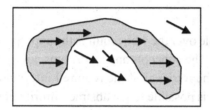

Items with the similar characteristics belong to the same cluster. Any two clusters are to be different with distinct characteristics. Clustering requires identification of patterns in the data. The architecture of a clustering algorithm is shown in figure 3.

Data mining often helps in decision making by predicting the future values of the data. The data is often mined with textual entry with the support of natural language processing. It helps in the automation and works with pre indexed data. The natural language process also helps in interfacing the knowledge base with the user feedback or behavior.

Information Filtering

Information filtering (Lang, K., 1995) and recommenders learn and analyze the user behavior, improve the performance of the information retrieval and provide a personalized touch for the results rendered. Information retrieval results in tons of documents depicted based on their relevance. A filtering mecha-

Figure 3. Clustering algorithm

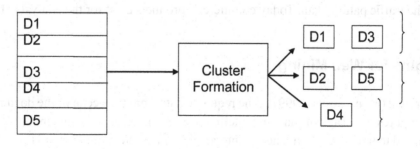

Database

nism provides the selection of these results by understanding the personal interest of the user rather than totally based on the relevance alone. The personal interest may be learnt based on the user feedback or ratings. For example, if the user always rates horror movies as high, the search result obviously ranks them first for a given choice of the keywords. On the other hand, recommenders provide a list of similar articles or advertisements based on the content the user application is running, assuming the user will be interested in similar stuff.

When the user is a member of a group or reflector, the grouplens paradigm allows the recommendation of the articles or documents, what the other users of the group are downloading. Software agents can be used to realize the same.

Web Mining

The enormous knowledge available over the web requires the appropriate knowledge representation and retrieval tools to tap out the same. The concepts and algorithms developed in machine learning and Web mining are extensively used for the retrieval of the required information from the web. From the web mining and web usage patterns, it is possible to get abstract information on the customers of a company as well as the business interests.

The web mining involves three major steps:

1. *Preprocessing*: It covers the cleansing of the data. The issue with the data over the web is that it is difficult to identify the users of the data and their sessions from the available logs.
2. *Pattern discovery*: It involves the machine learning techniques of classification and clustering to associate the patterns in the data.
3. *Pattern analysis*: It involves rule mining where rule based reasoning is used for thr analysis and arrival at the inference.

Mining multimedia data is a challenging task over stretching the resources, adding to the memory requirement, browser complexity etc.

Applications

Web mining is used for a variety of applications including the knowledge discovery process (Delmater & Hancock, 2000), for mining marketing intelligence from the data available on the web (Buchner, A., & Mulvenna, M. D, 1998) etc. The performance of a website or portal may be improved significantly by analyzing the traffic pattern data. Today commercial products exist for the analysis of logs and huge databases.

Search Engine for Web Mining

Search and retrieval (Mena, Jesus, 1999) of the requisite data from the ocean of the documents available over the web requires the usage of machine intelligence (Buchner, A., & Mulvenna, M. D, 1998). The agents are required to have the intelligence to interact with the system, understand the environment and adapt to the changes by means of continuous learning.

Figure 4. Search operation over the clustered data

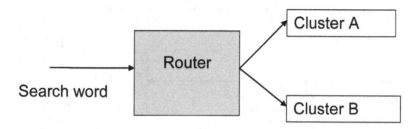

The user behavior on the request for information may be analyzed using the Search engine transaction logs. They throw light on the most popular key words being used, most popular websites, length of search queries etc. While rendering the results, the usage of Boolean operators with the keywords, the relevance of the results etc need to be considered. The search operation over a cluster data is shown in figure 4

Case Study: Wireless Web

Today, majority of the Web content exists in the traditional Web pages such as HTML documents. In the near future, more and more documents on the Web will be written in the formats suitable to cater for the handheld devices such as PDAs (Personal Digital Assistants) and cellular phones. These formats include CE-HTML, WML (Wireless Markup Language) and HDML (Handheld Device Markup Language). The information carried over a wireless network is typically localized. Assuming the wireless infrastructure is available, the information mined over the wireless network is generally time critical. Often it supports personalized services as authenticity is a default feature of the wireless network.

ISSUES AND SOLUTIONS

Adaptation of the information agent for different environments is a challenging task requiring fast learning algorithms. When multiple agents rules (Langley, P., and Simon, H. A, 1995) are used for data mining, fusion of the information gathered from them is challenging. Each of them work as an element in a swarm and requires a Bayesian neural network for merging with the concepts borrowed from the swarm computing.

Interoperability of the data acquired from these agents is a task. Semantic web, where the data is already stored in interoperable or integrated and ready to use form, will be able to handle this.

The timing and the related QoS issues of for supporting real time responses is handled through scheduling algorithms. Depending up on the requirements of data from an agent towards contributing an integrated solution, its data transactions are prioritized and evaluated periodically. A Bayesian network is used for knowledge fusion. Any missing information, dropped while meeting the QoS constraints, may be synthesized.

As in information retrieval, relevance feedback based on the user's response (Peng, Y., Kou, G., Shi, Y. and Chen, Z, 2006) for the data provided may be used here as well. A feedback neural network may be used to implement the same. However, the level of knowledge expected from them is much higher (Ian

Figure 5. Classifier based on data hierarchy

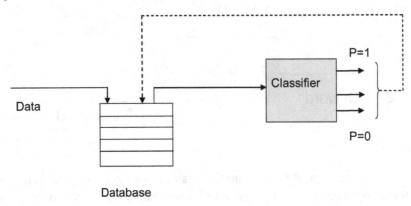

Witten and Eibe Frank, 2000), that is achieved through adaptive learning (Mannila, H.; Toivonen, H.; and Verkamo, A. I, 1995). Semantic web provides considerable help for the web mining over semantics rather than syntactic keywords.

Limited Training Set

Clustering of the data is carried out when the degree of membership of the data belonging to the set of predefined classes is not available (T. Zhang, R. Ramakrishnan, and M. Livny. Birch, 1996, V.S.Ananthanarayana, M.Narasimha Murthy and D.K.Subramanian, 2001). Clustering makes use of unsupervised learning since the training data is not available. A feedback neural network may be conveniently used for unsupervised learning. Hierarchical clustering results in a hierarchy of clusters. The dendrogram describers how these clusters are related to each other. The classifier based on data hierarchy is shown in figure 5. There are two ways of clustering the data:

- **Agglomerative algorithms:** Here the small clusters are iteratively merged in to larger ones and used widely.
- **Divisive algorithms:** Here the large clusters are appropriately split in to smaller ones.

The clusters of data are obtained by cutting the dendrogram at any level in the iteration of the algorithm. A feedback neural network can bring out the relation of the hierarchies in the cluster.

FUTURE TRENDS

Clustering

Being unsupervised, it is difficult to classify and cluster the data because different algorithms result in the distinct results. i.e., clusters of data with different sizes. In addition, the number of clusters and the way of grouping of data depends up on the number of iterations of the algorithm being carried out. A feedback neural network however can be used both as supervised or unsupervised classifier depending up on the context and availability of the training data. The network is adaptive and is capable of continuously learning.

Moving Clusters

The data grouped under a cluster based on some observed patterns or the similarities tend to vary with time. Such a time varying cluster forms a moving cluster. As a result of this variation, the members of a cluster start resembling more with the other clusters than the members of the same cluster. With lapse of time, the resemblance of a member of a group with the other members of the same group becomes more and more abstract. The potential join or match between a pair of moving clusters because of the changed commonalities is to be explored. The commonalities can happen at the abstract levels enabling them to be grouped under some level of the hierarchy. The required degree of abstraction can be brought about by the different estimators of a neural network. A moving cluster can record the location of its members.

Processing of a large volume of data in the organization requires intelligent algorithms (Huang T.-M., Kecman V., Kopriva I, 2006). In practice, a set of algorithms are made use. The outputs of these algorithms need top be combined by weighing the output of each algorithm and clustered appropriately.

After clustering, an object hierarchy is formed. The object in the hierarchy also depends up on the probability of access so that retrieval of the data happens at a faster rate. Prediction of the access pattern and cache behavior also helps in the organization of the hierarchies.

CONCLUSION

In this chapter,

- The need of intelligent web miming tools for the retrieval of the domain specific information to solve complex problems is explained.
- The model of semantic search is discussed.

In order to retrieve the requisite information over the web from large databases, automation techniques based on pattern matching are made use. The automation supports batch processing to search in large documents. To make it happen signal processing techniques are made use.

QUESTIONS

1. What are the differences between the data mining and the data retrieval?
2. How does signal processing algorithm help in the data mining?
3. How does data mining help in the discovery of the required knowledge?
4. How do you support personalization of search in data mining?
5. What are the applications of web mining in supply chain management?

REFERENCES

Alpaydın, E. (2004). *Introduction to Machine Learning (Adaptive Computation and Machine Learning)*. Cambridge, MA: MIT Press.

Ananthanarayana, V. S., Narasimha Murthy, M., & Subramanian, D. K. (2001). Efficient clustering of large datasets. *Pattern Recognition, 34*, 2165–2563.

Buchner, A., & Mulvenna, M. D. (1998). Discovering Internet marketing intelligence through online analytical Web usage mining. *SIGMOD Record, 27*(4), 54–61. doi:10.1145/306101.306124

Delmater & Hancock. (2000). *Data mining explained: A manager's guide to Customer centric business intelligence*. Woburn, MA: Digital Press.

Green, C. L., & Edwards, P. (1996). Using machine learning to enhance software tools for Internet information management. *Proceedings of the AAAI-96 Workshop on Internet-Based Information Systems*, (pp.48-55).

Han, J., & Kamber, M. (2001). *Data Mining: Concepts and Techniques*. San Francisco: Morgan Kaufmann.

Huang, T.-M., Kecman, V., & Kopriva, I. (2006). *Kernel Based Algorithms for Mining Huge Data Sets, Supervised, Semi-supervised, and Unsupervised Learning*. Berlin: Springer-Verlag.

Kantardzic, M. (2003). *Data Mining: Concepts, Models, Methods, and Algorithms*. Chichester, UK: John Wiley & Sons.

Lang, K. (1995). News weeder: Learning to filter Netnews. *Proceedings of the 12th International Conference on Machine Learning*, (pp. 331-339).

Langley, P., & Simon, H. A. (1995). Applications of Machine Learning and Rule Induction. *Communications of the ACM, 38*, 55–64. doi:10.1145/219717.219768

Mannila, H., Toivonen, H., & Verkamo, A. I. (1995). Discovering Frequent Episodes in Sequences. In *Proceedings of the First International Conference on Knowledge Discovery and Data Mining* (KDD-95), (pp. 210–215). Menlo Park, CA: American Association for Artificial Intelligence.

Matheus, C., Piatetsky-Shapiro, G., & McNeill, D. (1996). Selecting and Reporting What Is Interesting: The KEfiR Application to Healthcare Data. In U. Fayyad, G. Piatetsky-Shapiro, P. Smyth, & R. Uthurusamy (Eds.), *Advances in Knowledge Discovery and Data Mining*, (pp. 495–516). Menlo Park, CA: AAAI Press.

Mena, J. (1999). *Data mining your website*. Woburn, MA: Digital Press.

Mierswa, I., Wurst, M., Klinkenberg, R., Scholz, M., & Euler, T. (2006). YALE: Rapid Prototyping for Complex Data Mining Tasks. In *Proceedings of the 12th ACM SIGKDD International Conference on Knowledge Discovery and Data Mining (KDD-06)*.

Peng, Y., Kou, G., Shi, Y., & Chen, Z. (2006). A Systemic Framework for the Field of Data Mining and Knowledge Discovery. In *Proceeding of workshops on The Sixth IEEE International Conference on Data Mining Technique (ICDM)*.

Witten, I. & Frank, E. (2000). *Data Mining: Practical Machine Learning Tools and Techniques with Java Implementations*.

Zhang, T., Ramakrishnan, R., & Livny, M. Birch (1996). An efficient data clustering method for very large databases. In *SIGMOD*, (pp.103–114).

Zhu, X., & Davidson, I. (2007). *Knowledge Discovery and Data Mining: Challenges and Realities* (pp. 163–189). Hershey, PA: Idea Group Publishing.

Chapter 18
Knowledge Management

ABSTRACT

The data in its raw form can make some meaning as information after being subjected to a variety of processes. With the available information, it is possible further to extract the contextual meaning by translating the same in to knowledge. In this chapter, the paradigm of knowledge management is introduced. The acquired knowledge is useful as a tool for the players of the supply chain. Internet plays a crucial role in sharing the knowledge. The different web based techniques for knowledge management are provided here.

INTRODUCTION

The previous chapters explain how the data may be organized and retrieved in an intelligent way to solve the problems in a knowledge domain. It opens up a need for transforming the available information to knowledge in a domain and enhances the quality of the solution through the organizational learning and best practices. Here, the lifecycle of the knowledge management is introduced.

The rapid explosion of information on the internet has created a new promising and challenging platform for the media. As the volume and complexity of the online information grows, retrieval of the requisite relevant information in a time bound fashion has become a major challenge. It adds to the problem of the controlled distribution of information, to be addressed in the last leg of the supply chain. The automation of this supply chain is not an easy task. The mismatch between the natural language and the computer systems semantics is growing.

DOI: 10.4018/978-1-60566-888-8.ch018

The search queries and the online resource information may be represented and communicated through natural language. The natural language has two components: syntax and semantics. Syntax gives the structure of the language. The semantics provide the contextual meaning extracted from the language. Today, the conventional search engines render the requisite information based on syntax match only. The end user or a program has to filter out the contextual relevant results from the output of the search engine.

The knowledge base in an organization also contains the best practices and learnings (Ahmed, P. K. et Al. (Eds.), 2002) being observed or followed in the organization. The repository needs to be updated periodically, say, after the successful completion of a project in the organization. It happens with the intervention and rigorous evaluation from the experts in the field (Wenger, E., McDermott, R., Snyder, W.M, 2002). As the best practices are context and time dependent, they keep changing to catch up with the ecosystem of the organization. It requires continuous unlearning and learning cycles, which is to be a part of the business process of the organization (Argyris, C., 1999). In this chapter, the cycle involved in the conversion of information to knowledge and its distribution is introduced. It is expected to be useful in the design and sharing of the knowledge and best practices across the organization.

Knowledge management deals with the creation, acquisition, organization, access and distribution of the matured information in an Organization (Malhotra, Y, 2000a, 2000b, 2000c, 2000d). In the business world, it is manifested as continuous learning, collaboration and adaptation. Knowledge management calls for collaboration for sharing and enriching of the information. The information is assimilated from distinct and distributed sources in different forms. The fusion of this heterogeneous knowledge can happen in lines with the information fusion, with a difference that it happens at an abstract or higher level. The objective of knowledge management is to drive the maturity of the organization through collaboration and sharing the information.

BACKGROUND

One of the drawbacks with the conventional knowledge management models is that, it is defined in terms of the abstract parameters such as the data, information technology, best practices, etc. They fail to capture the dynamics accurately because these parameters themselves depend up on the variables such as attention, motivation, commitment, creativity, and innovation, that is required to be included in the model. The input of the model needs to capture the dynamics of the organization.

The capability of human beings to interpolate, extrapolate, generalize and learn the patterns enable them to infer the knowledge from the templates not being exposed previously (Brown, J. S. & Duguid P, 2000). As a result, the inference turns out to be personalized depending up on the context, time and relevance (Belbin, R.M, 2000). With this being the situation, storing the individual knowledge in static or standard templates in the databases will not be of much use (Brown, J. S. & Duguid P, 2002).

Knowledge management basically deals with the extraction of the relevant information (Malhotra, 1998, Malhotra, 1999) from the data through data mining and business intelligence. It spans the knowledge extraction, collaboration, technology transfer etc. The lifecycle of a knowledge management system is shown in figure 1.

Knowledge management provides the up to date information required for taking decision. Simultaneously, it opens up enough space for the predictions of the future. For Knowledge management (Little, S., Quintas, P. & Ray, T. (Eds), 2001) the focus is on the current usage of the data. Beyond the knowledge or

Figure 1. Lifecycle of knowledge management system

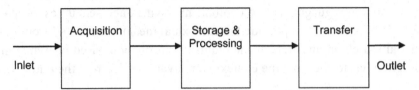

the current usage of the data is the wisdom. With the help of wisdom, a user can make future predictions in the data based on the present knowledge and the previous information of the data. Such a prediction will be done by an intelligent element with built-in expertise fused.

Knowledge Management System

The goal of a knowledge management system (KMS) is to provide the right time information rather than the real time information through Artificial intelligence and expert systems (Malhotra.Y, 2001a). The required knowledge for driving the fluctuations in the business still calls for human intervention (Malhotra, Y, 2001b, 2002a). Finding such patterns is challenging (Collison, C. & Parcell, G, 2001). Artificial intelligence and expert system provide a seamless interaction between the human experts and the machine. The KMS provides the required data for the decision making. The human experts in turn feed the learning in to the KMS so that they can provide a better dataset next time.

Data Transformation

The raw data as such is not useful. It can come in multiple forms such as numbers, words, taste, smell etc. Only some of them can be stored and retrieved multiple times for future use. It would find use only when someone tries to make 'sense' out of it.

Information provides a meaning for the data. It imparts the required sense. The sense is perception based and varies from person to person. The associated meaning is not absolute. Temperature in Europe is 50 degree centigrade makes meaning for some and would have personalized impact. Repeated information on the European temperature would lead to 'expertise' over European climate.

Knowledge provides the expertise in all walks of life. It is the amalgamation of repeated and all relevant information on a particular topic. Knowledge itself is not the end. It just reflects historical relevant data and fails to predict the future or interpret the problem. With the help of knowledge it is possible tell the temperature of any city in Europe ten days back. But what is its relevance? Is it an outcome of global warming? With knowledge alone, such questions cannot be generated in the first place. The translation of data to knowledge is shown in figure 2.

The future prediction is very much essential in real world scenarios. A commander moves the troops or aircraft carriers not only based on the information till that point, but based on the wisdom anticipating that some thing may happen in the future. He makes use of the knowledge and has the wisdom to think more of it.

There are various tools and techniques for knowledge management. The different strategies used for knowledge management include:

Figure 2. Translation of data to knowledge

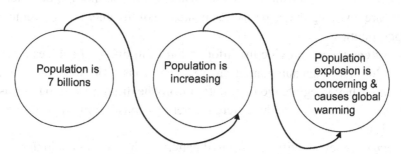

- Connections – It provides the mechanisms for connecting the people to form a network. It makes use of the gadgets such as the mobile phone, wireless enabled laptop etc.
- Communications –It comprises of special interest groups such as forums, e-group, listserv etc.
- Conversations – It spans interactive communication tools such as chat.
- Collaboration – It includes the tools for sharing knowledge over a wider group. E.g. wiki.

These different activities use the components of the knowledge base in common (Brooking, A. F, 1999). The system supports direct usage of the data in activities such as teaching, distance learning, computer based training etc. Alternatively, an expert system can make use of the same for updating its knowledge through the learning objects. The Learning objects are described through the learning object is the learning object metadata (LOM). The usage of LOM has been standardized to promote interoperability and reusability of the learning objects in the data base across the database.

Knowledge may be thought of as the information viewed at an abstract and integrated level. Knowledge bases are highly specific and confined to a specific field such as education, health, agriculture etc. A specific part of the knowledge providing requisite answer to the user query or requirement is the information. Conversely, raw data or pockets of information would be bundled together with appropriate patterns, relations and meaning associated to result in a knowledge base.

Web Based Knowledge Management

In an organization today, internet is extensively used for handling knowledge management issues (Wellman, B., Boase, J. and Chen W, 2002). As a result, the knowledge management architecture is turning web centric (Wellman, B, 2002). The heterogeneous and distributed information sources smoothly get integrated over the web (Wellman, B, 2001). The internet plays an important role in every step of the knowledge management, including the knowledge extraction from distributed sources, transfer and sharing. It helps in capturing the data and information, binds a network of experts (Van Wijk R. Van Den Bosch. F., Volberda. H, 2003) to the acquired knowledge, aids in sharing the knowledge and best practices, maintains the expertise and finally links the knowledge with the business. The integration of knowledge provides a unified view of the end to end process in the supply chain.

The web based knowledge management systems (Prusak, L, 2001) consist of the following techniques:

- **Web services:** It is a mechanism to provide business solution through the internet. The applications or software invoking the web services make use of the internet as a vehicle, providing new business opportunities.
- **Intelligent systems:** They provide the information from different sources (Siew lan Neoh, dan Yu-N Chean, 2003) through autonomous agents. They consist of three components:
  - ◦ *Mediators:* They integrate the information from the different heterogeneous sources.
  - ◦ *Facilitators:* Help to locate the different heterogeneous information sources and their access mechanisms
  - ◦ *Data miners:* They identify the required pattern in the data and help in retrieval.
- **Resource description framework:** The knowledge and the structured information can get exchanged between different platforms and programs in an enterprise through XML. The XML also supports queries over the database wherein the search operation often covers the semantics.
- **Mediator architecture:** It works as service broker and binds the application with the right data source. With this, it is possible to seamlessly exchange the information between the heterogeneous data sources without having to integrate the data. Integration can happen later to provide the right response to the queries.

Representation Model

A knowledge management system is to support a hybrid representation of the knowledge as the knowledge is specific for the domain and so also is the reasoning. Hence, it requires multiple inference engines as well as the retrieval systems. In general, the knowledge about the cause and effect is because of the relation they bear. For example, if you put your hand in the mouth of a lion waiting for food in the cage, you are likely to lose it. It is more of the rule based representation than the knowledge about the food habits of lion. Contrarily, in some applications, the domain knowledge is demanding. For example, suggestions for the hybrid type of paddy to be grown in a particular soil type and the sowing seasons. It is more of the fact based representation.

Knowledge representation most of the times grows by experience and builds a library of the learning. Today there is a weak linking between the knowledge representation and it applications. It is believed that, Meta knowledge descriptors are required to build a library of links between the domain knowledge and its representation.

Knowledge Dissemination

There are various knowledge transfer techniques available in the modern communication world including face to face communication, Internet (As the user gets deep & deep towards the information & wants more & more detailed information, the knowledge organization in to abstractions would be helpful . Hierarchical representation of knowledge goes well with this requirement), Chat, Electronic mail, Intranet etc. Intranet provides similar features of internet. The repeatedly accessed or popular contents may be downloaded once and provided in the central repository of the intranet for repeated use (by many people). In addition, the documents need not be in html format. Any archive format will serve the purpose. Intranet can also share the organization information instantly.

One of the techniques for effective knowledge dissemination is to have a good network of collaboration. The different collaboration categories are given in (Siew lan Neoh, Dan Yu-N Chean, 2003).The techniques could be online or offline.

- **Online collaboration:** The online collaboration techniques include meetings & discussion, seminar & conferences, chatting, video conferences etc. Here the transmission bandwidth would be critical and stringent QoS constraints are required to be met. The appearance of picture in video conferencing makes it more interactive and effective.
- **Offline collaboration:** The offline dissemination methods include E-mail, SMS, Fax, Journals, News groups, voice mail etc. In Voice mail, with the speaker recognition algorithms or text to speech algorithms, it would be possible to provide the appropriate information for the appropriate user based on the request. Inter & intra enterprise infrastructure shows layered approach as the mean of knowledge sharing. It maps on to the abstract levels of the data storage. The same information may be streamed on to different categories through different means. Artificial intelligence (AI) techniques will be increasingly used for knowledge dissemination.

Knowledge management with different components such as acquisition, storing, dissemination may be modeled as a supply chain. The behavior of each of them may be controlled by the feedback signals originating from the end user and propagating down the line. It would place the entire supply chain optimal and provides an efficient mean for the knowledge management.

When these components are modeled as independent objects, the overall or global impact of these components may be computed by obtaining the weighted average of the impact of the individual objects on the organization.

Knowledge management spans more and more managerial components like maintaining the skilled resources, competent employees, investment over the infrastructure, competency management and change in the corporate culture (Tsoukas, H., Mylonopoulos.N, 2004). There is a paradigm shift in the knowledge representation from the human readable text to machine readable data, program and code.

For the successful knowledge management, metadata is to be coupled with the ontology. The Metadata is to describe the associated knowledge base. This metadata itself could be organized hierarchically reflecting the hierarchical representation of the knowledge base. Ontology based knowledge management is discussed in (Bechhofer, Sean. et al, 2004).

There are two architectures with knowledge management:

1. *Static representation:* Here the knowledge is meant for reuse and follows pre-defined representation.
2. *Dynamic representation:* It is used for the knowledge creation and provides the active representation of the knowledge.

An adaptive knowledge management system requires capability to find the complex patterns in the business data and use the same to adaptively change the databases as the learning for the decision making in the future. A simple program fails to do that.

Figure 3. Demand for the knowledge hierarchies

Knowledge on the % methane in the atmosphere of Saturn
Knowledge on the atmosphere of Saturn

Knowledge on the solar system

Knowledge level   **Number of people interested**

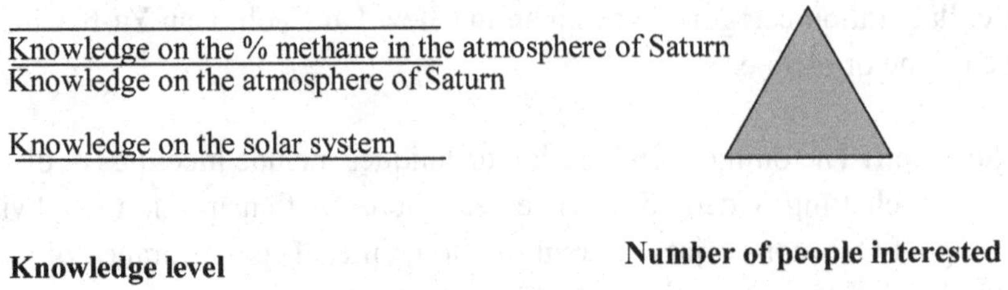

Hierarchical Representation of Knowledge

Like information, the knowledge representation could be hierarchical. The end user of the knowledge generally requires hierarchical knowledge depending up on the interest or taste. Generally in a knowledge database, each of the hierarchical level is self contained with appropriate user group or subscribers for the same. Usually the consumers for each level decreases as the depth of the hierarchy increases. For example, there will be more people interested in biology than in the floral diagram of the myrtaceae family and more people in 'general medicine' than in the working of a pacemaker. The number of users at each level of the hierarchy often follows the direct pyramid as shown in figure 3.

In an information database the hierarchies represent the abstract data. For example, the people of payroll section are interested in knowing the individual employees salary. For the managing committee of the organization (E.g. Chief finance officer) the interest is in the total expenditure of the organization towards salaries than the salary of a specific individual. Probable they never ask for the information on individual salaries.

The information at each level of the knowledge hierarchy may be organized in a hierarchical way, resulting in a fine split of information chunks as shown in figure 4. The information organization at each level of knowledge is self similar.

Another difference between the information and knowledge hierarchies is that, depending up on the availability of the bandwidth and the service parameters, there could be a dynamic transition in the information hierarchies during transmission. The typical example could be the transmission of picture information that is stored in a hierarchical fashion. If the network bandwidth is low, the finer details of the picture may not be required to be transmitted at all, subjected to the service parameters. A typical example is "online surgery". Here an expert sitting at a remote place provides guidance to a team of "surgeons in action" through images transferred over the satellite. The in time transfer of images is more important than the very fine details of the image. In the knowledge transfers, there will not be any

Figure 4. Information organization with in knowledge

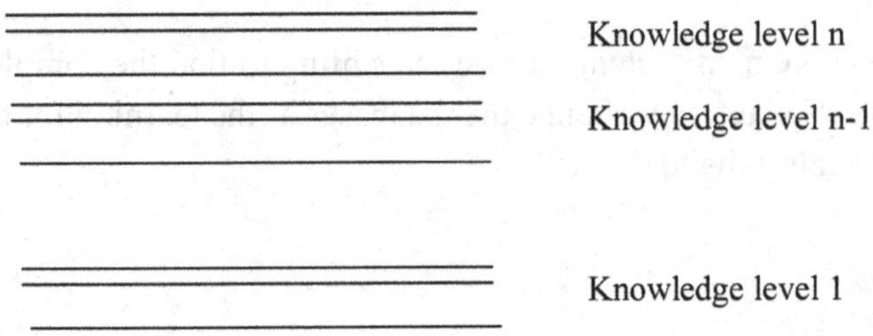

Knowledge level n

Knowledge level n-1

Knowledge level 1

Figure 5. Hierarchical representation ion of knowledge

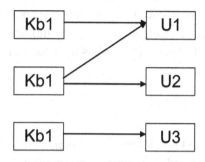

transitions in the knowledge hierarchies. The figure 5 shows different ways of using knowledge base hierarchies depending up on the available bandwidth and resources.

Atomic Representation

New models for the representation of knowledge requirement in a modern industry (are getting popular. One such model is the atomic model. The lowest level of hierarchy in knowledge representation is called atom. There will be a kind of bonding between these atoms. Depending up on the query over the knowledge base, the atoms get bonded to result in a variety of 'compounds'. The compound is isolated and extracted with the help of a compound extractor. This information is passed on to the retrieval layer. Each atom of the knowledge consists of knowledge electrons bound to the nucleus through a force of attraction.

In the atomic model of knowledge representation, the differential feedback between the nucleus and the knowledge electron in the knowledge atom results in further hierarchies in the representation of the knowledge with various degrees of abstraction. Like the atoms, the feedback exists between the hierarchies as well. This representation provides multi resolution model for the knowledge organization with minimal redundancies across the hierarchies. Figure 6 provides the feedback in knowledge hierarchies.

ISSUES AND SOLUTIONS

Organization of the Knowledge Base

The primary issue with the knowledge management is the organization of the knowledge base. There are two choices – Hierarchical and organic knowledge management. The hierarchical knowledge base

Figure 6. Feedback in knowledge hierarchies

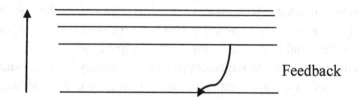

Feedback

has the focus on design and implementation of a set of rule base business processes implementing the production and integration of the knowledge. The rules are implemented by the managers of the knowledge base. The organic knowledge management requires the implementation of the policies supporting the existing patterns being followed in the communities by default. These patterns of knowledge would be well maintained

Management Issues

There are three major issues with the knowledge management. They include location of the knowledge, systematic storage of the knowledge and effective utilization of the stored knowledge or the knowledge database for the benefit of the organization. Here the associated problems include the life cycle of the knowledge management itself.

For converting the raw data in to useful knowledge i.e. for capturing the intelligence in the data, pattern recognition tools and techniques may be used. For classifying and storing the data, effective clustering and classifier tools will be used. For the retrieval of the knowledge and the address the interactive audience, data mining and expert system tools are used. The usage of intelligent elements such as neural networks in all these tools has been explained in the previous sections.

As a part of knowledge sharing, the isolation of information sources and information is required. I.e. the data has to be freely available for some individuals and detached for the others. The hierarchical representation of data provides a mean to implement the same by providing selective permissions at various abstract levels.

Knowledge management usually implies the internalization of the knowledge and data files. I.e., any bit of information must be reformatted, re-classified and some times stored for private use of the system, creating the high impedance between the system and the outside world to further limit the sustainability. This problem is addressed by non-obtrusive metadata strategies

Security

Security of the knowledge bases is a major issue. Any intrusion in to the knowledge base from an unauthorized foreign element has to be detected in time to take the appropriate action. An intelligent element can understand user behavior on the knowledge base and indicate any anomaly or deviation from this behavior. The intelligent element can be used to learn and classify the system call traces in to normal and abnormal. Initially the neural network is trained with the trace corresponding to normal and abnormal behavior. The neural network can also predict the traces based on learning. Any significant deviation observed from the predicted traces represents a possible intrusion. The neural network classifier can indicate the type of intrusion such as misuse of logins, change in documents etc.

Data Inconsistency

Inconsistency of data in the knowledge base creates a major problem down the line. It is required to see that, duplicate objects do not exist in the knowledge data base. It ensures uniqueness of the data and the consistency. Any other indices and links would refer to the unique object.

In general, the specific knowledge management process is strongly coupled with the nature of the application in hand. As a result, the issues getting surfaced need to be addressed uniquely.

FUTURE TRENDS

- **Prediction and interpolation:** Knowledge management has made it possible to predict and perform unheard and unthinkable experiments without laboratory. With a wealth of information and data available, with the help of prediction and extrapolation tools such as artificial neural networks, interesting inferences can be made out of the data. For example, it is possible to predict the chemical properties of a new compound with atomic number 150 based on its predicted structure and the available data.

- **Knowledge management tools:** One of the important factors in knowledge management is the knowledge dissemination and sharing (Liebowitz, J. & Chen, Y, 2001). Web based open source sharing (Preece, J, 2000) is discussed in (Van de Sompel, Herbert, Beit-Arie, Oren, 2001). For collaboration and sharing the knowledge, various tools and techniques are in place. It includes tools like Newsgroup, Mailing list, Faq-o-matic, Wiki and Web logs.

Newsgroup

Newsgroups are off line and non interactive method used for spreading the information. Here the user subscribes to the desired group and "posts" the information to the group. The readers can subscribe to these newsgroups and have the option to read the posts offline in leisure. It is also possible that the users are intimated when a new post is made. They can visit the newsgroup and download the new posts available.

Mailing List

Mailing list is very similar to a PDL (Public Distribution List) or a "group email-id". The difference is in the nature of its operation and the objective. A mailing list is generally created on a specific topic. A mailing list has a moderator (or moderators) who owns the list and controls the information in the list.

Usually entry to the list happens by subscription, which often needs to be approved by the moderator. Once subscribed, a user can send mails to the list. A mail thus sent, reaches all the subscribed users. In addition, mailing list usually has the provision for archiving. Thus all conversation threads will be available for viewing/searching later.

Web interfaces may be provided for the mailing list. It allows efficient and effective list management.

Faq-o-Matic

This is an efficient way to create and maintain FAQs. In a way it provides knowledge the base. Organizations, teams, projects and products have Frequently Asked Questions. They are living documents which need updating. A static document is very difficult to update and more difficult to traverse.

This tool provides a mean to add/insert questions and creating any number of sections/subsections. In addition, it would get modified by any of the authorized users (rather than one individual having to do it).

Wiki

Wiki is a popular concept in collaborative development. It is a set of web pages which are shared and edited by all the users. It allows a group of users to keep information about anything updated independently.

Web Logging

Web logs are a way to share ones' thoughts to a wider forum. This is similar to newsgroups, but accessible through the web.

The management of a knowledge based system consists of three parts:

- Knowledge Base development.
- Knowledge Base deployment and query
- Knowledge Delivery system.

Knowledge Base development consists of an intelligence layer to capture the Semantics of the resource content. It provides a framework for the information delivery. The Knowledge Base is populated through semi automated ontology techniques. This process generally makes use of an intelligent element such as a neural network for hierarchical resource clustering.

The Knowledge Base deployment and query process makes use of an intelligence layer. It looks in to the hierarchies to provide the context and resolve the semantic difference using advanced search techniques. It has two components:

- **An inference engine:** It is useful for the Knowledge Base Object query and navigation.
- **A fusion system:** The multiple hierarchies are to be blended to present the query results.

The Knowledge Delivery system may be designed as a web application, providing the required information to run the application. This can happen through the browsers with built in intelligence to deliver contextual information. The browsers are expected to provide both syntactic and semantic information. With the help of an Ontology Browser the taxonomic tree of the Knowledge Base Objects may be extracted first. An intelligent search filter can narrow down the search field with in the tree based on the user specified preferences and search limiters.

CONCLUSION

In this chapter,

- The hierarchical representation of the knowledge is introduced.
- The mechanisms for seamless sharing of the knowledge are explored.

Knowledge and best practices management is an important activity in organizations thriving for a reasonable maturity. It is directly aligned with the business process and aims toward improving the business performance. The knowledge management system (KMS) promotes innovation in the organization. It matches the business performance of the organization with the knowledge base, competencies, information technologies and best practices in the organization. The knowledge management system has to adapt to the fluctuations in the business. One of the components of knowledge management is sharing of the knowledge across the organization.

QUESTIONS

1. What is the difference between the knowledge and the information?
2. What are the steps to be followed in knowledge management?
3. How does a good data organization help in knowledge management?
4. How does the internet help in the knowledge management?
5. What are the different ways of sharing the knowledge?

REFERENCES

Ahmed, P. K., et al. (Eds.). (2002). *Learning Through Knowledge Management.* Oxford, UK: Butterworth-Heinemann.

Argyris, C. (1999). *On Organizational Learning.* Oxford, UK: Blackwell.

Bartlett, C. A., & Ghoshal, S. (1995). Changing the Role of the Top Management: Beyond Systems to People. *Harvard Business Review*, (May-June): 132–142.

Bechhofer, S. et al (2004). *OWL Web Ontology Language Reference: W3C Recommendation 10 February 2004.*

Belbin, R. M. (2000). *Beyond the Team.* Oxford, UK: Butterworth-Heinemann.

Brooking, A. F. (1999). *Corporate Memory: Strategies for Knowledge Management.* London: Thomson.

Brown, J. S., & Duguid, P. (2000). The Social Life of Information. Cambridge, MA: Harvard Business School Press.

Brown, J. S. & Duguid P. (2002). Mysteries of the Region: Knowledge Dynamics in Silicon Valley.

C. & Parcell. G. (2001). *Learning to Fly: Practical Lessons from one of the World's Leading Knowledge Companies.* Oxford, UK: Capstone.

Ian Neoh, S., Yu-N Chean, D. (2003). Knowledge and agent based coalation formation framework for surgical team formation and resource allocation. *ITSIM 2003*, (pp 547-555).

Liebowitz, J., & Chen, Y. (2001). Developing Knowledge-Sharing Proficencies. *Knowledge Management Review*, *3*(6), 12–15.

Little, S., Quintas, P., & Ray, T. (Eds.). (2001). *Managing Knowledge: An Essential Reader.* London: Sage.

Malhotra, Y. (1999). Bringing the Adopter Back Into the Adoption Process: A Personal Construction Framework of Information Technology Adoption. *The Journal of High Technology Management Research*, *10*(1), 79–104. doi:10.1016/S1047-8310(99)80004-2

Malhotra, Y. (2000a). From Information Management to Knowledge Management: Beyond the 'Hi-Tech Hidebound' Systems. In K. Srikantaiah & M.E.D. Koenig, (Eds.), *Knowledge Management for the Information Professional,* (pp. 37-61). Medford, NJ: Information Today, Inc.

Malhotra, Y. (2000b). Knowledge Management and New Organization Forms: A Framework for Business Model Innovation. *Information Resources Management Journal*, *13*(1), 5–14.

Malhotra, Y. (Ed.). (2000c). *Knowledge Management and Virtual Organizations.* Hershey, PA: Idea Group Publishing.

Malhotra, Y.(2000d). Knowledge Management for E-Business Performance: Advancing Information Strategy to 'Internet Time'. *Information Strategy: The Executive's Journal*, 16,4, 5-16.

Malhotra, Y. (2001a). Expert Systems for Knowledge Management: Crossing the Chasm Between Information Processing and Sense Making. *Expert Systems with Applications*, *20*(1), 7–16. doi:10.1016/S0957-4174(00)00045-2

Malhotra, Y. (Ed.). (2001b). *Knowledge Management and Business Model Innovation.* Hershey, PA: Idea Group Publishing.

Malhotra, Y. (Ed.). (2002a). Enabling Knowledge Exchanges for E-Business Communities. *Information Strategy: The Executive's Journal, 18*(3), 26-31, Spring.

Oracle Magazine. (1998). *Knowledge Management in the Information Age*, May. Retrieved 1998 from http://www.oracle.com/oramag/oracle/98-May/cov1.html

Preece, J. (2000). *On-line Communities: Designing Usability, Supporting Sociability.* London: John Wiley & Sons.

Prusak, L. (2001). Where Did Knowledge Management Come From? *IBM Systems Journal, 4*, 1002–1007.

Tsoukas, H., & Mylonopoulos, N. (2004). Knowledge Construction and Creation in Organizations. *British Journal of Management, 15*(1Supplement 1), S1–S8. doi:10.1111/j.1467-8551.2004.t01-2-00402.x

Van de Sompel, H., & Beit-Arie, O. (2001). Open linking in the scholarly information environment using the OpenURL framework. *D-Lib Magazine, 7*(3). doi:10.1045/march2001-vandesompel

Van Wijk, R., Van Den Bosch, F., & Volberda, H. (2003). Knowledge and networks. In M. Easterby-Smith, & M. Lyles, (Eds.) *Blackwell Handbook of Organizational Learning and Knowledge Management* (pp. 428 – 454). Oxford, UK: Blackwell Publishing

Wellman, B. (2001). Computer Networks as Social Networks. *Science, 293*, 2031–2034. doi:10.1126/science.1065547

Wellman, B. (2002). Designing the Internet for a Networked Society: Little Boxes, Glocalisation and Networked Individualism. *Communications of the ACM.*

Wellman, B., Boase, J., & Chen, W. (2002). The Networked Nature of Community: Online and Offline. *IT & Society, 1*(1), 151–165.

Wenger, E., McDermott, R., & Snyder, W. M. (2002). *Cultivating Communities of Practice: A Guide to Managing Knowledge.* Cambridge, MA: Harvard Business School.

Wenke, L., & Stolfo, S. (1998). Data Mining Approaches for Intrusion Detection. In *Proceedings of the Seventh USENIX Security Symposium (SECURITY '98)*, San Antonio, TX.

Zack, M. H. (1999). Developing a knowledge strategy. *California Management Review, 41*(3), 125–145.

Section 6
Information Transmission

Chapter 19
Information Transfer

ABSTRACT

The transfer of live data over the supply chain is challenging. The problem is compounded if multimedia data is involved. The delay in the transmission, packet loss etc will be the cause for concern. In this chapter hierarchical data representation is introduced towards data streaming and better performance.

INTRODUCTION

In the previous chapter, information storage and organization mechanisms are discussed. Finally, the information has to reach the end user or the applications over the available communication channels. Here, the different protocols and techniques for the transfer of the information to the end user are explained.

The source of information, depending up on the end user application, can make use of one of the several available data transfer techniques- Streaming, download etc making use of the available protocols such as file transfer protocol (ftp), hyper text transfer protocol (HTTP). For the applications involving interactive data transfer, the protocol Real Time Streaming Protocol (RTSP) may be used. The download or file transfer can happen as a background process through the available or left out resources. In this chapter, the streaming techniques (U. Horn, B. Girod, 1997) are provided in detail as it has to address real time issues. It requires intelligent data management system based on signal processing techniques. It is expected to be useful in various applications stressed in the chapter including online education, advertisement, video games, video conferencing etc. It is useful especially in the financial organizations, marketing etc. Digital media management system makes use of streaming for corporations, universities, enterprises etc.

DOI: 10.4018/978-1-60566-888-8.ch019

Streaming technologies have become increasingly popular with the growth of internet. It provides a mechanism to share the multimedia files in real-time. Conventional down loading of the files through ftp will have several disadvantages for multimedia data transfers. With ftp, the user has to wait till the huge file gets downloaded on to the machine and then start playing the same. Most of the users do not have access to high speed network to download large multimedia files quickly and support the live audio or video. Streaming technology has made it possible for the client machine to start playing the audio and the video before the entire content has been transmitted and makes the live video transmission possible. The user in general, will not be interested in retaining huge audio and video files on the machine or equipment after using or watching them. The typical example is advertisement. In such cases streaming would be extremely helpful providing a kind of use and discard environment.

In the streaming process, the data transmissions would not be uniform. Some times the transmission rate would be high, calling for the client machine to buffer the data for future use. Some times and quite often, the data rates would be low, making the application to suffer. Hence, appropriate error recovery, starvation and buffer overflow conditions are defined in the standard used for generating the stream.

Video streaming in an enterprise is found to be extremely useful for training, live conference and debate. It gets rid of the parties involved to travel and present physically, saving considerable cost and time over travel. In this chapter, the applications around video streaming would be stressed. The other benefits span marketing, inter company collaboration etc. Today, various collaborative and ERP tools are directly integrated to the streaming tools. I.e. in the same screen of ERP, it is possible to negotiate the data rates and service qualities of the data transfer. An intelligent element would be required to broker and monitor the data transfers in the streaming process. This chapter addresses the problem suggesting a signal processing technique to play the mediating role in multi media streaming.

The video compression standards such as MPEG-4, H.264 the audio compression standards such as MP3, AAC and the streaming standards such as H.323, RTP and RTCP have made it possible to stream the data over the network. To preserve the intelligibility of the data, the textual data is often compressed with a loss less compression standards such as Zlib.

BACKGROUND

There are two techniques for media content transfers: Bulk data transfer through down loading and (live) data streaming from a media source. In bulk transfer, the data movement happens in the background. It generally caters for off-line consumption. Streaming is the only option if the data is to be consumed live. It is also suitable for data transfer to hand held devices. In all these cases, service quality on the data, characterized by the parameters such as delay bound, loss rate etc has to be stringent. Streaming can happen over the protocols UDP, TCP or HTTP.

The platform for data streaming consists of a compression engine and a streaming server. The streams are transferred over the Internet. Good discussion on Data streams is available in (S. Muthukrishnan, 2003). Multimedia data may also be stored as compressed, streaming ready format. However, it is difficult to edit compressed data. For the same reason, it is generally not mixed up with the transport stream. It is maintained as a part of asset management database. For metadata, the general exchange format (GXF) provides a mean to transfer from one system to another. Streaming infrastructure requires the support of multicasting, where by the same information may be streamed to multiple users simultaneously.

Figure 1. Data streaming in a fleet

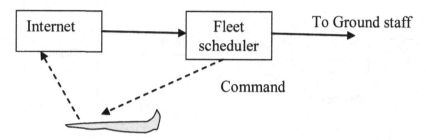

Sample Applications of Streaming

Streaming Media finds place in Business process. It is an effective mode for business applications such as Advertisement, marketing and branding, sales, Training, customer support etc. It generates on line customers. The advertisements could be interactive and placed in important web pages where the hit ratio is high. Figure 1 shows data streaming in a fleet management application.

Streaming from multiple sources enable the customers to have interesting multiple scenes, provide comparison etc. It provides details about the products online and hence improves the business multiple folds. The applications with streaming have entered in to the field of education. Online universities spread the knowledge through streaming. The course materials are being sold online. The servers are capable of handling thousands of transactions and sessions per second. It has thrown out the barriers on geographical boundaries. Students can receive the same quality of education through the Internet as they get in the classroom with a difference that they can get in to the business of studies at leisure, whenever they want.

For the products, customer support is also feasible with streaming. The customer, instead of waiting for time consuming interactive human support, can download a 'faq' kind of clip from the product website that answers most of the queries and provides adequate demonstrations about the product. The faq's are prepared based on the customer queries in the past. Such a support is predominantly required during the initial stages of the product usage such as setup and registrations. Visual demos will be very useful. It saves time and money for both the parties. Technically it is feasible as the same website can support and stream over hundreds of simultaneous sessions, unlike a human operator. However, a good streaming infrastructure, powerful servers and good network bandwidth are required to make it practical. The technique works well for presale demos of the products, providing training for the sales people about the product etc.

Protocol Support

The protocol support for streaming exists from the transport layer onwards. The typical networking standards that support streaming are RTP/RTCP, RTSP (Amir E, 1997). The flow of command and data in these protocols is shown in figure 2. The RTSP basically supports user command flow.

The choice of protocols used for streaming the data over the network depends up on the application in hand and ease of implementation. Each of them will be having its own advantages and drawbacks to support a particular application. There are two popularly used protocol stacks:

Figure 2. command and data flow in streaming

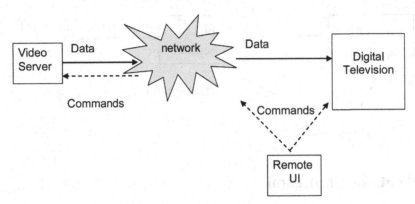

- **Datagram protocol:** In a datagram protocol such as User Datagram Protocol (UDP) the data to be streamed is packetized before transmission. The packets implementing this protocol are not acknowledged by the receiver. As such there is no mechanism to inform the data source about the successful delivery of the packets. With adequate error correction capabilities the consequences of packet loss can be minimized. The protocol is typically used to support the multimedia applications where it is affordable to loose some data packets. The Real-time Transport Protocol (RTP), the Real Time Streaming Protocol (RTSP) and the Real Time Control Protocol (RTCP) running over the UDP are used to support the multimedia applications. In general, firewalls are more aggressive and tend to block the UDP packets than the TCP packets.
- **Connection oriented protocol:** It includes the transport layer protocols such as the Transmission Control Protocol (TCP) that take the responsibility of correct delivering the data packets to the receiver. The receiver has to indicate the delivery of the packet by means of acknowledgement. Packets are acknowledged individually or in groups. If the acknowledgement (for receiving or nor receiving the packets) is not received with in a stipulated time, the source retransmits the data assuming the data packet has been lost during the transmission. This process leads to a lot of retransmissions, often unnecessarily if the acknowledgement is delayed or lost. In addition, certain applications involving audio, video and image can tolerate certain packet loss due to the redundancies associated with the data. The retransmissions also lead to variable delays that may be absorbed by buffering the data.

Unicast versus Multicast Protocol

In Unicast protocol, a separate copy of the data packet is sent from a source to the destination. Although it is straight forward, it results in unnecessary consumption of the bandwidth when the same data is to be sent to the different users simultaneously. This drawback is addressed through Multicast protocol where the data packets get duplicated just before the multiple destinations. The bandwidth and buffer requirement are small as there will be less number of packets in the network at any given point of time. However due to the complexity of its implementation and the investment, it is mostly deployed in proprietary networks such as government organizations and universities, comprising of their own routers and the infrastructure. The servers as well as the routers are required to support the multicast protocol. In general, the packets are blocked and discarded by the firewall.

The information may be streamed over a standard protocol such as Real time protocol RTP. The other similar protocols are H.323, SS7 etc. They provide live updates and support the live video and audio (S. -F. Chang, A. Eleftheriadis, D. Anastassiou, S. Jacobs, H. Kalva, and J. Zamora, 1997). The feedback path protocol such as RTSP associated with the RTP can carry the required feedback information to the streaming server. Accordingly the service quality would be renegotiated or the transmission rate would be re-adjusted.

In the devices that need the transfer of the content directly, getting rid of the server, Peer-to-peer (P2P) protocols are to be implemented. The usage of expensive and resource crunched servers can be avoided. Support for this direct communication among the devices is challenging in terms of the security, technology and the business value. For example, a high-end camcorder can stream video in to a computer through Fire Wire protocol, possibly for several devices at a time. As the streaming of media has become popular creating a large volume of business, many devices and applications demand the same. It results in scaling and Quality of Service issues (Yeadon N, 1996, Yeadon N., Garcia F., Shepherd D. and Hutchison D, 1997). On top of the protocol conformance, the streaming devices have to be interoperable, scalable and support a reasonable quality of service for the flow as well as the quality of experience for the end user (Witana, V. and Richards. A, 1997).

Multimedia Streaming

The encoders and decoders (Codecs) designed to support the Internet traffic require greater bandwidth scalability (M.H.Lee, K.N.Hgan, G. Crebbin, 1996), lower computational complexity to handle real time data, greater robustness for the packet losses and lower encoder or decoder latency for the interactive applications. These requirements call for the design of codecs exclusively to support the internet traffic.

The standard MPEG-4 part 10 or Advanced Video Coding (AVC) will be the popular standard for the delivery of video over the network at low bandwidths (D.M. Monro, H. Li and J.A. Nicholls, 1997). The content created for broadcast and storage applications with standards such as MPEG-2 are not suitable for transfer over the internet although MPEG-2 (Shanwei Cen, Calton Pu, Richard Staehli, Crispin Cowan and Jonathan Walpole, 1995) is scalable and extensible.

There are basically two categories of compression algorithms depending up on the underlying mathematical tool:

1. **DCT based algorithms:** Here the underlying mathematical tool is the Discrete Cosine Transform. One of the major advantages with this approach is that, it is being used in most of the standards and conversion of the compressed archive media such as songs from one standard to other does not require complete decoding and subsequent recoding. The transform is not scalable. It poses a major issue for transcoding (Nicholls, J.A. and Monro, D.M, 1996). Transcoding is often done to alter the bitrates or from one compression standard to another.
2. **Non DCT based algorithms:** Here the compression algorithms make use of a different set of mathematical tools such as sub-band, wavelet etc. The algorithms are scalable. However, they are not extensively used in the compression standards due to their complexity, performance and proprietary implementation techniques. The existing movie and song archives are not in this format and require a transcoding in large scale, that is not attractive for the content providers.

Figure 3. Streaming involving hierarchy of abstraction

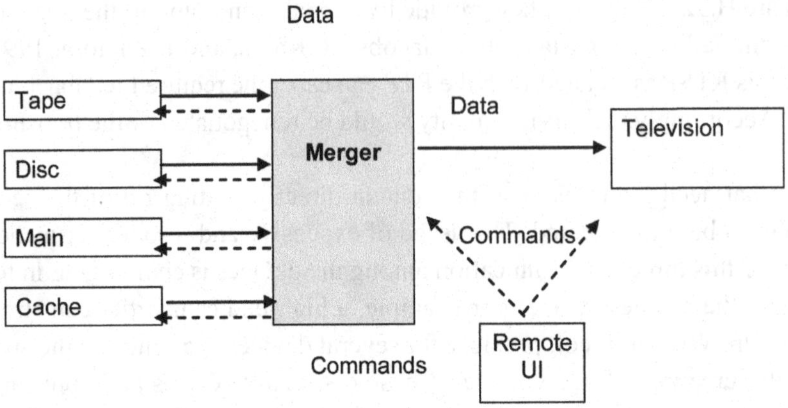

Often, data is required to be generated in the compressed form on the fly adaptively. This is to meet the dynamically available bandwidth.

Hierarchical Data Organization for Streaming

Random access in a stream is not possible unlike conventional database. So, hierarchical data organization is extremely useful in providing the appropriate output and relevant information to the queries. The search engine would be provided with coarse information initially and signaled to wait over a definite time to get more & more details for the query.

Streaming video over Internet will be increasingly used in future. It requires efficient data organization to meet the real time transfer and access goals. The hierarchical data organization provides different right access during the transfer.

The content creation may be linked to streaming by means of abstraction and hierarchical organization of the data. With hierarchical representation of the data in place, a single technology will be able to handle Digital media, entertainment and streaming. The scheme integrates Digital media with entertainment.

When offline browsing of data is to be supported, the content in the local cache needs to be updated or synchronized periodically. Alternatively, an event or change in the content can trigger the synchronization. When a lot of text or content is to be uploaded, the frequency of update is to be minimal. This mechanism may be implemented with hierarchical representation of the information in different resolutions. The streaming involving multiple physical media is shown in figure 3. The hierarchy of abstractions in the data map on to the different physical media. More information in the hierarchy is retained in cache as it requires more bits for representation. The more abstract data is placed in the tape. The reverse is good for memory optimization. A tradeoff between storage and speed are required. The drawback with any database organization in general is that it consumes bandwidth for frequent updates. However, with abstract representation of the data, only the incremental data needs to be transferred reducing the burden.

The data encoding standards in the video camera are required to be designed (G.K. Wu and T.R. Reed, 1996, H.J.Kim, M. Chan and K.N.Ngan, 1996) to support these hierarchical features. The hierarchies result in a queue of queries waiting for results at different abstraction. Multiple queries could be placed active at a time. The queue in the query calls for systematic organization based on the service quality associated with the query, the streaming sequence, levels of hierarchy (J. Y. Tham, S. Ranganath, A. K. Kassim, 1997) etc.

The database is often not fixed. Example: the list of fuel service stations with in a kilometer from a moving car. In that case, the data may be thought of as a moving stream. The unpredictability in streaming calls for the usage of adaptive and appropriate scheduling algorithm in the search engine. The adaptation is required for changing network and streaming conditions. The QoS requirements are met by the underlying scheduling algorithm (S. Paek, P. Bochek, and S-F. Chang, 1995). The appropriate algorithm is chosen dynamically based on network conditions. The scheme is scalable and extensible with scope to add new algorithms.

Dynamic Supply Chain

With the usage of web based SCM, suppliers and manufacturers are integrated in a better way leading to dynamic supply chain. The QoS is used as a criterion for dynamic selection of services. It allows the retailers choose the suppliers and customers to choose the retailers dynamically depending up on the optimal cost and resources. The same is true with the suppliers depending up on the market dynamics. Forecasting is made and the resources are mobilized appropriately. The three QoS matrices important in a supply chain are time, cost and reliability. This is in addition to the data security.

The client places a request for data along with the QoS parameter for which the retailer responds. Prioritization of the clients and suppliers can happen based on the QoS parameter. A database on what type of QoS the supplier supports can be made available for the clients through the web. The retailers often broker this and provide the best supplier and vice versa.

ISSUES AND SOLUTIONS

One of the challenges with the real-time information steaming over the supply chain is to meet the service quality in the limited bandwidth. When the audio/video (Long, A. C., 1996), information is involved or when an interactive session is called for, delay and jitter are to be under control. To make it happen, multitasking is to be supported at the network level.

Packet Drop

In the presence of noise in channels, packet drops will be more. It calls for (Amir E., 1997) retransmission of data that turns out to be expensive. An alternative method is to increase the quantization step based on the feedback from the user terminal. The packet drop rate represents the instantaneous channel status. It provides useful information to control the quantizer step size and consequently the resulting compression and the bit rate.

Data Stream Clustering

Multiple instances of the same software or process is to be running to support some of the applications such as the service replication, load balancing etc. To make it possible, requisite data or service has to be made available in time. The scheduling or attachment of the clients to the appropriate instances of the service calls for intelligent agents such as a feedback neural network. Depending up on the application, when several streams are required at a time, the connectivity, and the switching over to the different streams on the fly is challenging. It creates a scenario similar to a distributed environment. Discussion on clustering of data streams is found in (S. Guha, N. Mishra, R. Motwani, L. O'Callaghan, 2000).

Mobility

Streaming is also possible in mobile environment. The same protocols support the handoff during the mobile user switching over the network boundaries. The transmission temporarily stops during the handoff. It increases fast after the handoff and hence calls for a tradeoff with the quality. However if the buffer is adequately full, the same quality may be retained. Reduction in the cell delay is extremely important is this scenario.

Packet Delay

In spite of adequate buffering of packets initially, up on changes in the network conditions, the stream player empties the buffer. This forces the player to pause for a while until it has buffered enough data.

Data pre fetching is possible based on the access pattern of the user. An intelligent algorithm is used to predict the pattern. New generation of query engines come with built in prediction features. The Stream monitoring helps in acquiring the most recent data. It happens through queries over the running stream of the data. The data acquisition, processing and queries happen continuously rather than getting triggered by events. Forecast of the queue build up is possible only by the continuous monitoring of the stream queue behavior. It is basically used in sensor networks of online monitoring applications.

The quality of service may be fused to stream query engine. The different queries can have different service quality requirements. This is further coupled to different data arrival rates in the stream. More details on the queries are provided in the chapter on information retrieval.

In order to have sufficient data before rendering to the players and to take care of the variable network delay between the data source and the receiver, buffers are used. However it increases the latency.

Real-Time Streaming

Real time streaming of the content such as game requires complex computations. The server has to make considerable analysis on the movements from the end user and stream the right data in the real time. It involves data capture, motion detection, interpolation, prediction, compression, decision making, data packetisation and streaming over the network. The packets streamed have to reach the user without loss, which otherwise kills the user experience of the game. Sufficient band width is required to support this.

Quite often, the audio, video, text etc of a scene is stored in different servers, requiring the appropriate mixing before transmission. Alternatively, they are transferred independently and simultaneously resulting in the over utilization of the bandwidth. UDP protocol is more suitable than TCP to support such application. This is because, in TCP, a data packet, if lost during the transmission, is retransmitted. By the time it happens, its relevance for scene composition and rendering for the user would have gone and the subsequent packets would have already been consumed. Also, the limitations of the human audio visual systems can afford to lose some packets here and there without affecting the quality of the

Figure 4. Cell drop

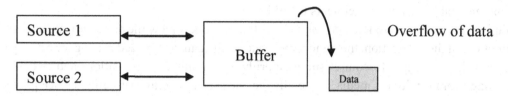

rendered scene.

In the absence of feedback path from the destination to the source through the TCP path, it would be difficult to transfer the network conditions and feedback signals such as the cell drop as shown in figure 4

A neural network may still be used as a predictor with unsupervised learning that does not require a feedback signal for learning.

The Real-time protocols such as RTP, RSVP, etc. are specifically designed for the optimal utility of the network with intelligent scheduling. However they are not efficient for multimedia contents, as it requires real time streaming. It calls for new protocols absorbing the feedback on the network conditions such as predicted cell loss. The protocol has to address the QoS of the stream transferred over the network.

The other interesting solution for all these problems is to increase the compression of the multimedia files with new and sophisticated signal processing technologies. It ensures that, for the acceptable quality, the total data to be transferred over the network gets reduced by a huge factor. With the advances in the processor technology, present day personal computers can afford large computing power. They can afford to run complicated decoding algorithms implemented over real time if the compression ratio can be increased. A temporary solution is to upgrade the infrastructure including the modem, routers, transmission media, servers etc down the line. The graphical analysis of streams and the extraction of parameters for analysis are provided in (S. Guha, N. Koudas and K. Shim, 2001).

The edge servers provide an alternative solution for this. The server is at the edge of the internet. Here, the content to be streamed is placed close to the close to the consumer of the information to avoid the passage of the data packets over multiple routers that require expensive resources to route the packets. The additional advantage is that the speed of streaming is limited only by the processing equipment at the consumer end and not by the network. The agreed quality service can be easily met. To implement this, the web link of the content would be pointing to the URL of the nearest streaming server loaded with the content. It works as a mirror server as the content is copied only once from the internet. For this to happen seamlessly and to support interoperability, standardization of various activities such as the mode and frequency of replication, the mirroring procedure etc is required.

It has been found out that the usage of proxies will not be of much use to speed up the streaming. The mirror servers would not be used effectively. The packets k\likely to get duplicated, leading to congestion.

Multicasting

In a multicast data communication, the duplication of data packets from the source may be avoided resulting in effective utilization of the bandwidth. When one of the data paths or sources in the multicast is congested, it sends the retarding feedback signal to the source. It results in the reduction in the transmission rate making all other recipients to suffer.

The solution is to keep this troublesome branch off the network for a while and duplicate the packets. Once it comes out of the congestion, the same may be included again and placed at a higher priority to allow recovery in the streaming. It requires small algorithms to monitor the transitions and switchover.

In Streaming over the wireless media, especially the one used in wireless surveillance, RF power and the RF bandwidth are the additional constraints. The data streams are prone to RF related issues such as fading, multiple hop, security threats etc. It calls for the usage of compressed signals with adequate burst error detection and correction codes.

Digital Rights

The content streamed over the network is prone for recording and resale reducing the income of the original content creators and the broadcasters in the supply chain of the digital content (McCanne S., and Jacobson V, 1995). Although recording of the content is not intended to be prohibited and can not be prohibited, it has to be streamlined and triggered a considerable debate.

Prevention of recording of the content is nearly impossible. The streaming server virtually loses control over the content once it is put on the medium. However, the broadcasters can declare the copying or unrestricted consumption of the content as illegal. The streaming can start only when the user agrees to a set of conditions in which the rules for the consumption of the content are specified. The legal administration steps in if these conditions are violated, providing some relief for the broadcasters although it is a bit difficult to detect the violations from a large community of the users. The content may be encrypted by the broadcasters before streaming. Even if it is copied, it will not be possible to play or consume the same unless authorization key is available for the decryption of the content. The key is provided for the authorized users for one time or a limited time decryption of the content. The rights enforcement software ensures that, Subsequent usage of the key will not play the content. Broadcasters can also use unpublished data formats that would make sense only in the presence of the key. However, it is easy to reverse engineer these formats, making encryption as the only choice.

FUTURE TRENDS

Streaming Network Model

New network models would be required to simulate the streaming over large networks. The transmission of information through intermediate nodes may be modeled in lines with transmission lines. The capacitance of transmission line is playing the role of differential feedback from the intermediate nodes to the source and the inductance is taking the role of the delay in the transmission. In a transmission line, the inductance and the capacitance determine the degree of power transmission from the source to the destination. It takes a maximum when the impedance at any point turns out to be the characteristic impedance.

In an information system, the delay and the degree of feedback together determine the information flow over the transmission line and it happens to be maximum for a particular choice of these parameters. Thus, the information transfer or information content of the data may be traded with the user feedback

Figure 5. Traffic information feedback

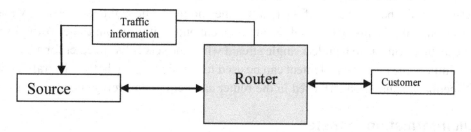

and the decays associated with the transfer of the information. These factors may be considered in the tariff for the information.

In the inverse transmission line model, what gets transferred down the line from the end user of the information towards the data source would be the set of commands. The end user contacts the agent through a series of commands. The agent in turn may contact other middle level resources or service providers and the command sequence travels as a wave. What gets transferred in the reverse direction are the information, the response to the commands and query. Again, the query results and the command structures form a tradeoff for maximum transfer of the information. If the data source is mirrored or reflected, it is as good as providing additional feedback. It would have impact on the delay.

Information Feedback

The data rates and service parameters such as cell drop ratio measured at the user end can provide the valuable feedback to the source to alter the data rates. This is true especially when the data transferred is in compressed form. Integration of the data streaming from different sources poses a tough challenge. It calls for maintaining a fixed ratio (relative service parameter) between the parameters such as bit rate or data loss or delays from different sources. Here, the traffic from each of the sources is predicted and the information is fed back to the source. This feedback signal is used to regulate the flow of the information from each of the sources. Prediction provides adequate time to adjust the rates keeping the quality of service parameters constant. The feedback mechanism is shown in figure 5.

Unlike any other traffic controller, a feedback neural network used in a traffic network for traffic shaping would impart the characteristic properties to the network that is otherwise not possible. Due to the self-similarity property of the estimators of a feedback neural network, the entire network where the neural network is placed would behave as self-similar. I.e. the network or the traffic starts exhibiting the properties of the feedback neural network. Separately, the forward and the feedback flows individually become self-similar to the neural controller. Thus, any changes in the controller would get reflected over the traffic characteristics of the network providing a hold on the network behavior.

The information regarding the network may be sent over the feedback path. The forward path consists of the data streams. A predicted version of the feedback signal would be sent as the feedback signal. This prediction is done to indicate the future status of the network and to take appropriate preventive measures in time. For example, it can predict the overloading of the traffic network or increased cell drop and delay in advance so that the data pumped in to the network may be reduced. It is better to prevent the congestion by adaptively controlling the data rates than getting in to congestion and think of a firefight at that time. A smart algorithm can be used for this prediction. The usage of predicted signal in the place of actual signal can reduce the delay, jitter and cell loss resulting in reduced retransmissions over the network and a better quality of the data for the end user. The cell loss probability may be used as the feedback signal. The prediction is done at the client end as it turns out to be costly for the server. This is because the client has to handle a single stream while the server has to cater for a large number of streams. In addition, the intelligent element can be used for traffic shaping before the traffic gets in to the network. A feedback neural network used in the router can help in enforcing scheduling algorithms.

Push-Pull Information Transfer

In a conventional client server model, whenever the client requests for the data or the updates, the server provides the same. It is also called pull technology. Contrary to this is the push technology wherein the server streams the updates happening in the information for all the clients registered for that information. It happens even without the client asking for the same, once they register for the same.

The client by and large gets reduced in to a dumb browser receiving the updated information. It goes well with the model of unsupervised learning in the absence of a feedback or a request path. Again a neural network may be used to learn the server behavior. This will help in maximizing the information transfer. I.e. it changes the entropy by increasing the order of the feedback. Synchronization problem in this scenario may be addressed with the unsupervised learning. The updating happens either manually or automatically.

Dynamic QoS

During run time, the quality of service of the content and the data transmission rate can change adaptively. The rate of data streaming is dictated by the application, the encoding rate and the available bandwidth. This parameter is negotiated in advance during the start of the streaming session. Feedback path can predict the cell loss rate and the available bandwidth over the channel and transfer this information over the underlying protocol to the source. The source then adjusts the service rate accordingly.

With the advances in the content creation and network management technologies, the content may be created dynamically for streaming, replacing the stored or static content. It helps in providing the latest or updated information.

CONCLUSION

In this chapter,

- The challenges for the multimedia data transfer over the internet are discussed.
- The mechanisms for fast and real time data transfers and the supporting protocols are explained.

Multimedia streaming is challenging especially in the multicasting of live programs. However, when made possible, it provides a wagon of benefits. It has increased the business and profit multifold in service based industries. It has cut down the operational costs of the organizations by cutting down the travel costs and providing live and interactive work environments for conferencing, training, product demos etc. It has made possible for the organizations to interact with the end customers through live video clips. Online learning, collaboration have been made possible with the multimedia streaming

On the down side, it has eaten up a large proportion of the network bandwidth. The real time transmission does not meaningfully get achieved with the protocol TCP for transmission. Intermittent solutions that make the streaming a bit comfortable are provided.

The streaming technologies in future are expected to pave the path for video on demand over the Internet. The focus has begun to shift from the cable to the Internet. The digital set top boxes would have to handle the additional functionalities. The technology of web casting is accessible, affordable and has become a reality for masses. By surfing the web, an end user can access unlimited number of TV channels. The content creators can hit a huge market with the customer able to browse and watch the desired program in leisure. It enables the new electronic gadgets such as video cameras with compression, encoding and streaming as a single product to enter the market. Today, the web channels are becoming far more attractive than the broadcast channels. It is possible to watch the television entertainment serial or details of the news in the late night that has been telecast in the morning.

Surveillance systems require real time streaming of video data. Although the frame rate requirement is smaller, adoption of better compression technologies provide improved spatial and temporal resolutions. The protocols such as RTSP support a feedback path using which it is possible to tilt and zoom the camera for desired resolutions. It is interesting to see that the traffic on the forward direction carried by the RTP is huge and well designed for error handling while the traffic in the feedback path is small, supported by the RTSP and meant for small bit rates.

QUESTIONS

1. What is the difference between streaming and downloading?
2. How does the data organization affect the performance of streaming?
3. Give examples where the data streaming is done over the supply chain.
4. What are the different protocols used for the transfer of the multimedia data over the internet?
5. What are the applications of data streaming?

REFERENCES

Amir, E.(1997). *RTPGW: An Application Level RTP Gateway.*

Amir, E., McCanne, S., & Zhang, H. (1995). An Application Level Video Gateway. *Proceedings of the ACM Multimedia Conference `95*, San Francisco, CA.

Cen, S., Pu, C., Staehli, R., Cowan, C., & Walpole, J. (1995). A Distributed Real-Time MPEG Video Audio Player. In *Fifth International Workshop on Network and Operating System Support of Digital Audio and Video (NOSSDAV'95)*, Durham, NH.

Guha, S., Koudas, N., & Shim, K. (2001). Data streams and histograms. *ACM STOC, 2001*, 471–475.

Guha, S., Mishra, N., Motwani, R., & O'Callaghan, L. (2000). Clustering data streams. In *IEEE FOCS, 2000*, (pp. 359–366).

Horn, U., & Girod, B. (1997). A Scalable Codec for Internet Video Streaming. *DSP'97*, Santorini, Greece.

Kim, H. J., Chan, M., & Ngan, K. N. (1996). Region-based segmentation and motion estimation in object-oriented analysis-synthesis coding. In *Picture Coding Symposium (PCS'96)*, Melbourne, Australia, (pp 589-594).

Lee, M. H., Hgan, K. N., & Crebbin, G. (1996). Scalable coding of sub band images with Quad tree-based classified vector quantization. In *IEEE TENCON'96*, Perth, Australia, (pp 788-792).

Long, A. C. (1996). *Full-motion Video for Portable Multimedia Terminals*. A project report submitted in partial satisfaction of the requirements for the degree of Master of Science in Computer Science, University of California, Berkeley.

McCanne, S., & Jacobson, V. (1995). Vic: A Flexible Framework for Packet Video. *Proceedings of ACM Multimedia `95*.

Mitchell, J. L., Pennebaker, W. B., Fogg, C. E., & LeGall, D. J. (Eds.). (1997). *MPEG Video Compression Standard* (pp.177). New York: Chapman and Hall.

Monro, D. M., Li, H., & Nicholls, J. A. (1997). Object Based Video with Progressive Foreground. In *Proc. ICIP*.

Nicholls, J. A., & Monro, D. M. (1996). Scalable Video by Software. In *Proc. ICASSP 1996*, Atlanta. Chang, S.-F., Eleftheriadis, A., Anastassiou, D., Jacobs, S., Kalva, H. & Zamora, J. (1997). Columbia's VOD and Multimedia Research Testbed with Heterogeneous Network Support. *Intern. J. Multimedia Tools and Applications*, (special issue on "Video on Demand Systems: Technology, Interoperability, and Trials").

Paek, S., Bochek, P., & Chang, S.-F. (1995). Scalable MPEG-2 Video Servers with Heterogeneous QoS on Parallel Disk Arrays. In *5th IEEE Workshop on Network & Operating System Support for Digital Audio & Video*, Durham, NH.

Shen, K., & Delp, E. J. (1998). A Control Scheme for a Data Rate Scalable Video Codec. In *Proceedings of the IEEE International Conference on Image Processing*, Lausanne, Switzerland, (pp. 69-72). Washington, DC: IEEE.

Tham, J. Y., Ranganath, S., & Kassim, A. K. (1997). Highly Scalable Wavelet-Based Video Codec for Very Low Bit Rate Environment. *IEEE Journal on Selected Areas in Communications -- Very Low Bit-rate Video Coding*.

Witana, V., & Richards, A. (1997). A QoS Framework for Heterogeneous Environments. In *DSTC Symposium*, Australia.

Wu, G. K., & Reed, T. R. (1996). 3-D segmentation-based video processing. In *Proceedings of the Thirtieth Annual Asilomar Conference on Signals, Systems, and Computers*, Pacific Grove, CA.

Yeadon, N. (1996). *Quality of Service Filters for Multimedia Communications.* PhD Thesis, Lancaster University, Lancaster, UK.

Yeadon, N., Garcia, F., Shepherd, D. & Hutchison, D. (1997). *Filtering for Multipeer Communications DEMO.*

Chapter 20
Information Transmission with Quality of Service

ABSTRACT

The data being transferred over the supply chain has to compete with the increasing applications around the web, throwing open the challenge of meeting the constraint of in-time data transfers with the available resources. It often leads to flooding of resources, resulting in the wastage of time and loss of data. Most of the applications around the customer require real time data transfer over the web to enable right decisions. To make it happen, stringent constraints are required to be imposed on the quality of the transfer. This chapter provides the mechanism for shaping of traffic flows towards sharing the existing infrastructure.

INTRODUCTION

In the previous chapter, the different techniques for the transfer of the information over a medium are discussed. Often, the data has to reach the end user or the application in right time as well as the real time. It puts a lot of constraints on the quality of service from the network. Here, these techniques are discussed in detail.

The present day internet is being put in to various applications falling under the umbrella of web services. It has thrown open new avenues for web based e-commerce. As an example, it has enabled online booking of flight tickets, online check-in, online clearance of electricity dues etc. In all these cases, the transactions have to happen in real time enabling the end user to interact with the databases. Though the data transfer involved is small, it has to happen in real time, without distortion in the information. It calls for stringent constraints to be imposed on the packet delay and losses. The user experience

DOI: 10.4018/978-1-60566-888-8.ch020

and feedback are given due importance. A mechanism where by the end users' feedback in terms of the service quality would reach the information source is explained in this chapter. The same would be used to adjust the quality of service in the transferred data. It will have profound impact on the resource management in the network.

The quality of service in turn dictates the mode of data transfer. For example, the end user has to wait for several hours to get the next morning news paper. On the other hand, the football match has to be telecasted "live". The interactive speech data has to avoid the satellite channel due to the latency and the cost incurred. A fax data can still use the satellite link conveniently. A twisted pair cable can not support the live video for multiple users. However, it can support file transfers. In this chapter, the different media for the data transfer are explored

Enforcement of service quality over the transfer of the information in a resource-crunched network is a tough task calling for the proposal alternative architecture and designs. One of the solutions for this problem is to classify the data packets based on the priority and discard the one with lower priority if there is a contention for the resources. Alternatively, the service guarantee may be provided on per flow basis. The quality of service (QoS) is satisfied for all packets in a flow with the appropriate reservations irrespective of the priorities of the individual packets in the end to end flow. The per class QoS architecture is simple and goes well with the internet traffic and the architecture.

The excess of one data stream in terms of the Quality of service will have a profound effect on the entire flow with multiple streams, especially when they share the common resources such as buffers. With the techniques explained here, the service parameters of the streams are held nearly constant, in spite of a few bad flows.

The focus of discussion in this chapter is on the data transfers over the contention for physical media towards meeting the service quality and the recently proposed class-based service architectures and the mechanisms to implement the same. The data transfer is involved with in the organization, internet, web services etc. In this chapter, the example of Differentiated Services architecture will be elaborated. The issues associated in the data transfers with stringent quality of service requirements are brought forward and the solutions will be proposed.

BACKGROUND

QoS Architecture

Any solution to achieve the agreed QoS has to consider the statistical properties of the network, Scalable, Practical and measurable, Stress on prevention than cure, learn from the experience, online and adaptive, work with limited information, shall address delay, jitter etc. International Telecommunications Union (ITU) has come out with many proposals to support QoS (R. Guerin and V. Peris, 1999) within the IP network (John Evans, Clarence Filsfils, 2007). The IETF has defined two architectures- the Integrated Services (Intserv) and Differentiated Services (Diffserv) for supporting QoS in the Internet (Lee, Donn, 1999). The definition of service as well as the architecture of implementation is different for them. The diffServ architecture is provide in figure 1

Intserv provides the end-to-end service guarantees on a per flow basis. In the implementation of the Intserv algorithms, each router intercepts and act up on the per flow signaling messages and maintain

Figure 1. Working of DiffServ

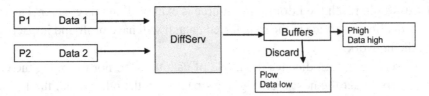

per flow QoS state tables on the control path and thereby achieve per flow classification, scheduling and buffer management on the data path.

The users on the internet running a variety of applications require the support of differentiated services (Vegesna, Srinivas, 2000). Diffserv provides service differentiation among a limited number of traffic classes. It suddenly attains importance during congestion, where the existing bandwidth has to be shared effectively. Further discussion on congestion in TCP is available in (M. Allman, V. Paxson and W. Stevens, 1999). Some applications require consistently high bandwidth calling for stringent restrictions on the packet transfers.

The packets are marked with the priority tag. In the network, the packets are scheduled and routed based on the preference or priority. During congestion, low priority packets are dropped.

Traffic Shaping

The traffic shaping is implemented through a bandwidth broker that monitors the bandwidth allocation to different classes of the traffic and handles new connections based on the policy being enforced. The working of a broker based traffic shaping paradigm is shown in figure 2.

Case Study: DiffServ Architecture

One of the popular architectures to enforce the QoS (Xipeng Xiao, 2008) is the differentiated services, (DiffServ). The DiffServ, proposed by the Internet Engineering Task Force (IETF) for service differentiation on the Internet, enforces the QoS on per class basis. There is ni signaling involved in the DiffServ. There is a weal support for the end-to-end service differentiation or resource reservation. The reservation is handled by a centralized agent called a bandwidth broker. The architecture of a Diffserv is shown in figure 3. Each packet has its associated priority.

Figure 2. Broker based traffic shaping

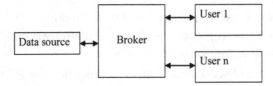

Figure 3. Diffserv architecture

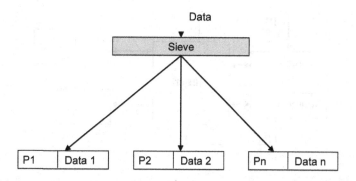

Buffer Management

The DiffServ specifications work with any underlying scheduling and buffer management algorithm, for example, fixed priority scheduling algorithms or rate-based scheduling algorithms including the Class-Based Queuing (CBQ) or weighted fair queuing (WFQ). The aggregation of traffic from multiple sources is shown in figure 4. The information sources get feedback signal from the traffic shaper to control data rate and thereby maintain the QoS.

The implementation technique for the service differentiation is available in (Peter Pieda, Jeremy Ethridge, Mandeep Baines, Farhan Shallwani, 2000).

On the other hand, the Buffer management techniques are dependent on the Service quality differentiations. Quite often it makes use of the backlog controller algorithm that describes when a traffic or packet is to be dropped and the droppe algorithm that defines which traffic has to be dropped.

Active Queue Management

All initial proposals and algorithms used for active queue management (Park, 2000) in IP networks were designed to improve TCP performance, without explicit focus on the service differentiation. One of the early techniques for controlling the congestion is the drop tail queue management. Here packets are dropped upon queue overflow. The problem is the late congestion notification or packet loss. To accommodate the transient congestion periods, queue must be large, thus resulting in increased delay. There

Figure 4. Traffic shaping

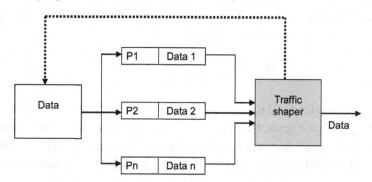

Figure 5. Computation of loss ratio in RED

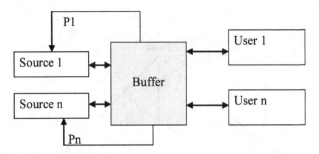

is a bias against the bursty traffic. When the queue overflows, several connections decrease congestion windows simultaneously. Early detection of incipient congestion will be helpful. Some of the techniques used to gauge the congestion are:

- Send control packet to some or all source nodes. However, it requires additional traffic during the congestion.
- Analysis of the routing information. But it may prompt a very quick reaction.
- The probe packets from source to destination. It however, increases the overhead.
- Add congestion information to packets as they cross nodes. It works well for the packet flow of either backwards or forwards.

One of the earlier, yet powerful backlog control algorithms to improve the throughput of the network is the Random Early Detection (RED) (S. Floyd and V. Jacobson, 1997). This algorithm indirectly considers the quality of service of the data. Generally, other algorithms of feedback control are compared with the benchmark results of RED. In RED, the packets are dropped to reduce congestion depending up on the degree of the backlog in the buffer, so that further overloading and chaos are prevented at the cost of a controlled packet loss. In this chapter, the proposed solutions for Resource contention and service quality issues make use of a variant of RED with feedback from the end user of the information to the source of the information. The architecture of RED is shown in figure 5.

Service Differentiation

Providing service-based architecture especially when the players of supply chain pump in data, is a challenging task. The algorithms working on per hop basis find it difficult to arrange for the resources to meet a specified service quality. To make it happen, the available resources are to be shared based on priority.

Physical Medium

There are various means to transfer the data over the medium. It makes use of baseband or band pass communication depending up on the application. In a baseband communication, the digital data is placed on the physical medium such as a cable directly and transferred over a short distance without distortion. However, the data gets attenuated and distorted with distance. Over such a medium, unlike the free

Figure 6. Data transfer over multiple physical media

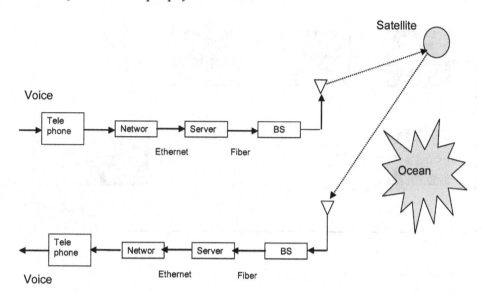

space, addition of new data receivers is not easy. It results in a serious limitation of the scalability. The medium will be assigned to a single source at a time resulting in the reduced throughput. The contention for the medium reduces the transmission capabilities further. These issues are addressed by the band pass communication where several sources can transmit simultaneously over the same channel using modulation techniques.

A combination of several media may be used for data transfer as shown in figure 6. For example, the data from the end user in a wireless LAN first gets in to the fixed network or Access point over the free space and then in to the fixed infrastructure network.

Multimedia Traffic Control

Recently, the data that gets exchanged over the supply chain comes in the form of graphs, audio as well as video. For such traffic, the window control of TCP is not much useful as the time-scale is too short, of the order of RTT. It leads to constantly switch the codecs and visible or audible transitions in the received data. The packets may start or drop below the minimum codec rate. Flow control is not needed since the receiver will need to process the data at the nominal (codec) rate. The TCP reliability mechanism may impart additional delay (> 500 ms) resulting in increased packet loss.

In multimedia traffic, a certain loss rate is tolerable due to the limitations of the human perception. The goal of the traffic shaper is to maintain the agreed loss, delay and jitter tolerance. The focus is to retain the stringent QoS constraints as being applied for the normal data. The congestion control turns in to QoS control. Alternate mechanism are explore to control the data rate based on the congestion status with the

- Usage of multiple resolution/ quantization scale data
- Using more B frames

Figure 7. Multimedia data encoder

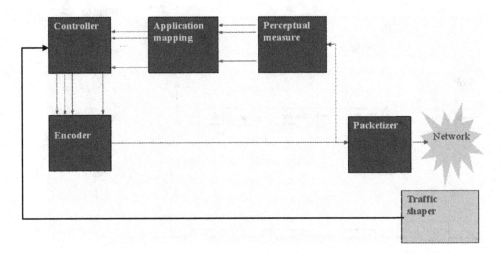

- Knowledge of the resource requirements in advance, reserve the agreed resources and use CBR. CBR decoders may be implemented easily. Predicted feedback signal available at the encoder would be helpful

Figure 7 shows the set up used for multimedia traffic shaping. The bit rate at the encoder may be controlled by varying then quantization step size.

A Frame loss is the indicator for congestion. A frame is assumed lost when:

- The receiver gets a frame whose sequence number is greater than the expected sequence number.
- The receiver does not get any frame within a timeout interval

FUTURE TRENDS

Probabilistic Results

The data transfer both within and outside the organization has increased multiple folds. The enterprises are interested in right-time data than in the real time data. It calls for the support of variable data rates. When the certainty of the data is not known, its probabilistic version has to be made available with the appropriate confidence interval. The generation and subsequent processing of the probabilistic data requires the usage of intelligent elements.

Query Based Business Model

In future, in a straightforward business model, the query time will be linked to the payment. The percentage of the queries that satisfy the QoS constraints is also a quality constraint. It provides constraint for a group of queries or flow. The constraints are either set by the user or made known to him through the broker.

The query time will be linked to the data organization and the degree of information required by the end user. When the data is organized in to the multiple abstract levels, the user can have the freedom of choosing the suitable information at the desired level of abstraction that is meaningful for him. The user will not be interested in too much of the details, but only in the relevant information.

The iterative procedure for query process makes use of user feedback to improve the quality in each of the iteration. The method may be improved by providing historical feedback i.e. the weighted sum of a set of consecutive feedbacks. With this, it would be possible to estimate the user behavior and transfer the matching information subjected to the availability of the resources.

Data Compression

To transfer the data, often data compression techniques are used. The compressed data would be free from redundancies and transfer more information per unit time. However, the de-compressor at the user end has to process this data before use. It requires powerful processors. The present day processor technologies allow the same. Especially when the audio or video data needs to be transferred, compression techniques are used.

The scheme of using compression for the transfer of multimedia data is already in place. Compression has become a must for the transfer of live data such as sports, share market spread sheets etc that also need in-time availability for the end user.

Information Controller

Moving forward, intelligent elements sitting at the end user terminal that control the rate of information transfer are required to be used. In feedback congestion control scheme, a signal proportional to the packet loss is fed to the source as the user feedback signal, according to which the transmission rates get adjusted. It makes the queue to increase slowly and fall off rapidly.

In the XML pipeline language model, there can be a predicted feedback of information at every stage in the pipeline. This feedback would improve the quality of the processing in the pipeline and makes the overall operation fast. Feedback neural network is used to predict the rate of processing and contention for the processing power as a result of existence of the other processes. This shifted and predicted information may be used as the feedback signal.

Network Control

The network is generally modeled as a huge time varying control system with several algorithms and traffic controllers running in the background. A closed-loop algorithm based on linear feedback control theory may be mapped on to solve the non-linear optimization problem of service rate allocation and traffic drops in the congested network. The stability conditions on the feedback loops are important.

For the future network requirements, efficient congestion control algorithms are to be integrated with QoS of the data. In a typical QoS enforcement architecture, the enforcement of the policies happens at every bottleneck node. In the network control approach, the flow or packet differentiation happens over the RTT time scale rather than on the packet-by-packet basis. The control traffic should be very small compared to the data traffic.

The network traffic control makes use of a variety of parameters such as the Proportional Loss Rate (PLR). It indicates the proportional differentiated services and provides the ratio of the loss rates of two successive traffic classes. In relative loss rate (RLR) the ratio is to be maintained constant over a window of time.

The integration of the QoS and the congestion control algorithms happens through the Proportional service differentiation models. The model quantitatively specifies the degree of differentiation between the different classes without speaking about the absolute service guarantees. The constraints specify that the ratios of delays or loss rates of successive traffic classes be roughly constant.

Service Guarantees

The brokers are finding it increasingly difficult to meet both loss rate and the delay guarantee in a flow. Different optimizing schemes are being used in practice. In a typical router per class buffering is performed over the output link and rate based scheduling is used for the traffic control.

The set of guarantees considered for traffic shaping will be a mix of proportional and absolute guarantees. There is no limit on the number of classes that are supported by the traffic. It requires that the algorithms used to implement the service are to be independent of the choice of specific constraints or parameters for each class.

Often, it is difficult to meet all the constraints on the service at a time. When it is required to satisfy the absolute guarantees, the admission control is overlooked. As a result, a set of service guarantees can not be met. For example, it may be impossible to meet both a delay bound and a loss rate bound in a bursty traffic. If it is difficult to meet the predefined service guarantees, some of the constraints are required to be relaxed. Among the priorities, the absolute guarantees are favored over the proportional or relative bounds. In the eventuality of not feasible to meet all the service guarantees, a priority is to be set among the QoS parameters.

Traffic Shaping with Differential Feedback

The present day network traffic is crowded with multimedia payload making the real time delivery a must. This calls for the usage of intelligent elements to adapt to the time varying traffic characteristics and take the decisions quickly. Artificial neural networks provide one such implementation. Though the usage of Artificial Neural Networks (ANN) for this task is not new, their scope is very much limited. Conventional neural network suffers with the drawback of lengthy training period and increased square error. These problems are addressed with a feedback neural network.

The neural network assists to carry out the following functions:

- Reserve the resources (buffer the packets) optimally,
- Improve the throughput for the fixed available resources,
- Modulate the feedback packets of resource allocation and maintenance to reduce the congestion, incorporate long term dependency (and self similarity) in the traffic and thereby decrease the packet loss probability,
- Replace piecewise (or multiple) congestion control algorithms with a single one,
- Better prediction of the traffic trends.

The internet traffic exhibits fractal like property. The currently used models are not able to capture the fractal behavior resulting in the poor analysis and control of high speed networks. The existing traffic shaping schemes that work well under conventional traffic conditions perform less satisfactorily under self similar traffic environment. Self similar models provide a simple and accurate description of the traffic anticipated during the deployment. A feedback neural network models the network traffic as they share many properties in common. It sits in the feedback path providing the control input for the sources of the data to adjust the transmission rate. In effect, it works as a controller.

The problem of traffic shaping is shifted to optimization in the neural network domain. It has been shown that the feedback neural networks have two fold advantages over conventional artificial neural networks- the training iterations are less & the overall error (residual error) gets minimized. The results are more pronounced with increase in the order of the differential feedback from the output to the input of the network.

In the closed loop feedback the destination provides feedback signal to the source through the RED algorithm or otherwise. No assumption is made on the underlying algorithm. The feedback signal is then predicted a few steps in advance and time aligned, providing sufficient time for the source of the data to adjust the data rates. The neural network basically sits as a Quality of Service (QoS) monitor adjusting the rate of source transmissions based on the predicted feedback. The QoS is guaranteed for the fixed network resources with the control of rate of transmission from the source. The variance of queue length and cell loss probability is taken as QoS parameters. Both of them get reduced with the help of a feed back neural network controller.

Simulation results shows that the resources consumed with such a feedback are arbitrarily small attributing smoothening of the traffic with differential feedback. A peak reduction in loss rate by a factor of 40, delay reduction by 50%, queue variance reduction by 1.3 has been observed. Table 1 shows the variance of the queue in one of the simulation experiments. Different number of sources is considered in the simulation with the underlying algorithm of RED to generate the feedback signal. Table 2 shows the performance with different orders of the differential feedback. As the order increases, the delay variance or jitter gets reduced although the gain is marginal after some order of the differential. Packet Loss probability also gets reduced. Maximum buffer size of 200 has been taken for simulation. Traffic from 20ftps running on RED is considered.

Table 1. Performance with RED and the proposed method for different number of sources

No.	Number of sources	Variance with RED	Variance with feedback neural network
1	20	125.2279	111.5828
2	30	134.0159	126.0763
3	40	140.5793	129.6867
4	60	142.8687	111.8134
5	80	177.0254	126.0417
6	100	194.5093	138.2350
7	120	219.2376	151.1265

Table 2. Performance with RED and the proposed method for different orders of feedback

No.	Order of the neural network	Loss probability	Peak delay	Delay variance
1	0	0.5	0.5989	0.0964
2	1	0.14	0.5920	0.0874
3	2	0.1065	0.5920	0.0821
4	4	0.1009	0.5920	0.0724
5	8	0.1009	0.5920	0.0672

Impact of the Feedback Signal on Relative QoS Parameters

In a general scheduling algorithm, the service rate allocations of traffic classes dynamically get adjusted to meet proportional guarantees. The service rate allocation is based on the backlog of the traffic classes at the scheduler. For two classes of traffic with backlogs $B_1(t)$ and $B_2(t)$, at a link of capacity C, a service rate of

$$r_1(t) = \frac{B_1(t)}{B_1(t) + \alpha B_2(t)} C$$

(1)

is assigned to the first class. Here $0 < \alpha < 1$ is the proportional differentiation factor equal to the ratio of the delays of the first class to the delays of the second class. In general the service rate of class i is equal to

$$r_i(t) = \frac{B_i(t)}{\sum_j \frac{s_j}{s_i} B_j(t)} C$$

(2)

Figure 8. Delay versus time plot

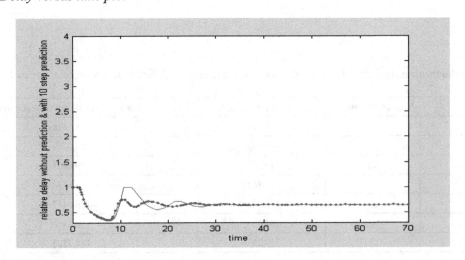

Figure 9. Delay versus time plot

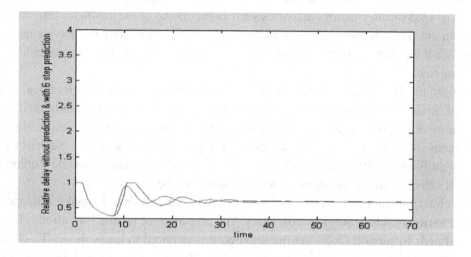

The rate of output is to be less than the channel capacity. I.e.,

$$\sum r_i < C \tag{3}$$

C is the channel capacity. I.e. the available capacity is proportionally shared. This implies that the rates are proportional to the queue lengths. Such a scheme results in more absolute delays though the relative delay constraints are satisfied. This calls for a reduced Q length. I.e. the absolute delay constraints are easily met in additional to the relative delay constraints if the queue lengths are reduced.

Simulation results show that, the relative constraints are better met with a better prediction in the feedback signal, providing sufficient time for the resources to get adjusted. In the experiment, focuses is on the proportional service differentiation, and does not include absolute constraints. A single output link with capacity $C = 1$ Gbps and a buffer size of 8000 locations is considered.

Two traffic classes are assumed. The length of the experiment is 70 milliseconds of simulated time, starting with an empty system. The number of sources active at a given time oscillates between 200 and 550, following a sinusoidal pattern. All sources generate packets with a fixed size of 125 bytes. Here relative loss rate constraint (RLC) is given as 4. The loss rate or the feedback signals are generated in the same ratio. The relative delay gets stabilized faster if more advanced signal is given as the feedback.

CONCLUSION

In this chapter,

- Scalable data organization architecture is proposed to cater for the QoS.
- The traffic shaping algorithms are introduced.
- The models and protocols to implement the QoS in multimedia data transfer are explained.
- The relevance of traffic information feedback from the user end is discussed.

Transfer of information with agreed and acceptable service quality is the topic of discussion for this chapter. The QoS dictates various activities such as the choice of the media for transfer, contention for the medium etc. The rate based congestion control algorithms integrate the service quality and are equipped to face the issues with resource allocation, congestion, scheduling and bandwidth allocation in the emerging networks.

Models of the traffic offered to the network or a component of a network are critical in providing high quality of service. One such model that absorbs the important feature of the multimedia traffic and relating the same with the performance is the traffic correlation. The complexity of traffic in a multimedia network is because of the aggregation of data from a variety of information sources such as video, voice, and data that significantly differ in their traffic characteristics as well as their resource requirements over the network. It calls for intelligent resource management over the network.

Internet architecture supports a variety of services over the network. To make it happen, Internet has to support various kinds of services efficiently. The performance profile for various classes of traffic is to be defined. To support QoS over the internet, it is required to know the traffic characteristics of services that the Internet must support and to develop efficient traffic control mechanisms to match with these characteristics.

The proposed scheme in this chapter is for avoiding congestion collapse and providing QoS in Internet. The characteristics of the proposed scheme are scalable, economic and easy to implement.

QUESTIONS

1. What are the parameters to be considered to meet the QoS in the transfer of the digital data?
2. How do the QoS parameters depend up on the data organization?
3. How does information feedback help in meeting the QoS?
4. What are the unique features of the multimedia traffic shaping?
5. How does the differential feedback help in traffic shaping?

REFERENCES

Bobinsky, E. (2001). Digital modulation techniques [Book Review]. *IEEE Communications Magazine, 39*(6), 24–28. doi:10.1109/MCOM.2001.925668

Clark, D. & Fang, W., (1998). Explicit Allocation of Best Effort Packet Delivery Service. *IEEE/ACM Transactions on Networking, 6*(4).

Dovrolis, C., & Ramanathan, P. (2000). Proportional differentiated services, part II: Loss rate differentiation and packet dropping. In [Pittsburgh, PA.]. *Proceedings of IWQoS, 2000,* 52–61.

Evans, J., & Filsfils, C. (2007). *Deploying IP and MPLS QoS for Multiservice Networks: Theory and Practice.*

Floyd, S. & Jacobson, V. (1997). Random Early Detection gateways for congestion avoidance. *IEEE/ACM Transactions on Networking, 1*(4).

Guerin, R., & Peris, V. (1999). Quality of service in packet networks: basic mechanisms and directions. *Computer Networks, 31,* 169–189. doi:10.1016/S0169-7552(98)00261-X

Jacobson, V., Nichols, K. & Poduri, K. (1999). *An Expedited Forwarding PHB.* RFC 2598

Lee, D. (1999). *Enhanced IP Services.* Indianapolis: Cisco Press. Allman, M., Paxson, V. & Stevens, W. (1999). *TCP congestion control.* Internet RFC 2581, April 1999. Christin, N. Liebeherr, J. & Abdelzaher, T. (2002). A quantitative assured forwarding service. In *Proceedings of IEEE INFOCOM 2002,* (Vol. 2, pp. 864-873), New York, June 2002. Christin, N. (2003). *Quantifiable Service Differentiation for Packet Networks,* University of Virginia.

Padhye, J. Kurose, J. Towsley, D. & Koodli, R. (1999). A model based TCP-friendly rate control protocol. In *Proceedings of International Workshop on Network and Operating System Support for Digital Audio and Video (NOSSDAV),* Basking Ridge, NJ.

Park (2000). *A Study on S e lf - Similarity of Internet Traffic and an Active Queue Management Method for QoS Provisioning in IP Networks.* PhD thesis, Department of Electrical and Electronic Engg. The Graduate School of Yon si University.

Pieda, P., Ethridge, J., Baines, M. & Shallwani, F. (2000). *A Network Simulator, Differentiated Services Implementation.* Open IP, Nortel Networks. Gurin, R., Li, L., Nadas, S., Pan, P. & Peris. V. (1999). The cost of QoS support in edge devices: an experimental study. *INFOCOM'99.*

Vegesna, S. (2000). *IP Quality of Service for the Internet and the Intranets.* Indianapolis: Cisco Press.

Xiao, X. (2008). *Technical, Commercial and Regulatory Challenges of QoS: An Internet Service Model Perspective*

Chapter 21
Information Transmission Security

ABSTRACT

The data transactions over a web based supply chain are prone to security threats as the internet is involved all the way. The internet happens to be an open forum easily accessible to the general public. It is quite possible that the data gets hacked or faked resulting in financial losses. Worse, it may not reach the intended recipient at all, defeating the purpose of the usage of the web. However, it should not be a cause of concern. With appropriate pre processing of the information getting uploaded on to the web, it should be possible to see that the data does not fall in to the wrong hands and reaches the intended recipients. The required tools and techniques are introduced in this chapter.

INTRODUCTION

The previous chapter explained the transfer of the data over different media including the public network. The data over the medium is vulnerable for attacks from the hackers. Here, different techniques to safeguard the content are discussed.

Large numbers of enterprises are now producing a huge quantity of multimedia information in various applications involving advertisement, business updates, marketing updates etc. As the data and business grow, it is required to transfer the information across the organization calling for the foolproof security techniques. As the enterprises turn increasingly mobile, access to the sensitive information would be required only for the appropriate stakeholders from across the globe. Although Industrial wireless transmission has provided the solution, security is always an important issue. Those involving financial transactions need additional care. The solutions make use of encryption and digital signature technology.

DOI: 10.4018/978-1-60566-888-8.ch021

Figure 1. Intrusion of data over physical medium

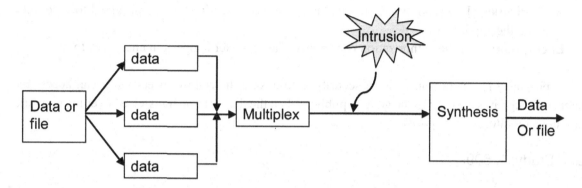

Secure methods are required for the data transfer across the Interactive Internet sites. Internet supports active interactive pages. It poses the risk to the users in the form of encountering malicious code, viruses, tampered code, unknown authors and impersonations. Authentication and encryption hold the key for secure data transmission of code, Email and financial transactions. The websites and portals need to be free from security threats and malfunctions. They are visible to the general public and often targeted for duplications and discretion resulting in losses worth billions of dollars.

The different techniques of providing security for the data transfer are explained in this chapter. The secure transmission is explored with the security risks involved in data transmission, such as eavesdropping and decrypting. It explains how and why secure data channels are established and the ways to prevent or foil attacks on them. It provides useful information for the design of a fully secure system for conveying the information and encryption of data for transmission. This chapter links the degree of transmission security to the data organizations and the underlying encryption technologies. Based on these combinations, a set of secure transmission techniques are presented. The applications include financial institutions, corporations with offices in different geographical locations and the share proprietary information, individuals doing business through the Internet for buying and selling the products, money transfers etc. All of them get involved with the transfer of the information over the information supply chain via the web to cater for the customers.

BACKGROUND

Transmission security (Schneier, Bruce, 2000). is the ability to send data from one computer system to another computer system so that only the intended recipient gets the data. In addition, the data received has to be identical to the data sent. Transmission security gets implemented through secure networks. Any attempt by the intruder to intercept the data stream (Bishop, Matt, 2003) over a fiber through tapping can be more easily detected than a tap into the copper wire. This is because the tap in to fiber damages the network and alters the topology that can be easily detected. The intrusion of data over a physical medium is shown in figure 1. On the other hand, detection of an intrusion that takes place over the air would be nearly impossible.

The security components involved in the transfer of data consists of (Gollmann, Dieter, 1999):

- **Authentication:** The authentication is required to prove the identity of the client and the server.
- **Authorization:** Based on the identity of the client, authorization will be provided to access the data and the applications.
- **Encryption:** After the authorization is provided, data transfer happens in encrypted form.

The purpose of content transmission security is to ensure the rightful users alone can access the content although it is exposed to the general public. When the data is to be transferred over the network, continuous monitoring is required.

Case Study: X.509

It is a standard that binds the public key with a set of attributes such as user name, issuing authority, validity of the key, serial number etc. With the help of the User ID and the password, a machine readable code word is generated for further processing.

X.509 is the standard for providing the digital certificates. The certificate validates the public key used for authentication and identification certificate validates the public key used for authentication and identification of the public key encrypted over SOAP. The certification is prone for attacks with the content being tampered or substituted.

The same public key may be bound to more than one set of attributes leading to that many X.509 certificates. The choice of this certificate depends up on the context of the creation and the usage.

Security Standard

Case Study: XACML

XACML standard ensures the secure transfer of the data over a network. The standard describes the access control policies in a interoperable language so that any device and understand the same. The unauthorized users are prevented from using the data. It has the wide support of OASIS standardization body. The main features of XACML are provided in listing 1.

Listing 1. Features of XACML:

- XACML is written in XML.
- It supports the descriptors of XML. Therefore easy to handle quality of the content described in XML along with the security.
- Scalable and extensible and allows to define new data types and policies in an interoperable way.
- To help programmability, provides a large set of data types, supports mathematical operations, libraries and functions.

XACML has two structural components:

- *The policy language:* It provides the description of the content access restrictions. The description is provided along with the data.

Figure 2. Architecture of public key based decryption

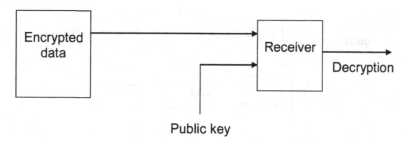

- *The query language:* It encodes the description of the data requests and the response from the database for the same. The user request for the data gets translated in to a construct in XACML language. Based on the access permissions the user enjoys, the data is provided.

Data Encryption

Secure file transfer protocol (SFTP) is used for the secure transfer of the large data files through encryption (R. Housley and P. Hoffman, 1999) and authentication (D. Maughan, M. Schertler, M. Schneider, and J. Turner, 1998). In general, the protocol is popularly used by the organizations interested in transferring large volumes of the data and rarely by the individuals.

As 802.11 follows the open architecture, it is easier for any body to implement the same and dump the data of choice, posing a great security threat (J. Walker, 2000). So, for a secure transmission, 128 byte encryption is used. Today it is difficult to decrypt this data. However, it can not be guaranteed in the future. Statistics shows that, through decryption software, it is possible to decrypt at least 10% of the data with in 24 hours. After learning the loopholes in the security algorithms, the 802.11 security algorithms and standards are consistently improving with stronger keys and algorithms.

In general, for authentication, both public and the private keys are used. (P. Vixie, O. Gudmundsson, D. Eastlake, and B. Wellington, 2000). The working of a public key system is shown in figure 2. Here, before data transmission, the sender encrypts the data using a private key . At the receiver, the sender's public key is used to decode the data. The authenticity of the data may be tested by verifying the hash of the original code matches with the hash of the decrypted code. Encryption is used to transfer digital signatures that are legally valid as much as a hand written signature as far as the document in which the signature is placed is concerned. The signature also means that the data in the file is not changed or tampered with, after the digital signature is placed over the document.

Case Study: SET

In addition to ensuring the secure transmission of code, the safety of the financial transactions is to be ensured by the organizations involved. The SET is a widely used protocol for the bankcard payment. It includes two components: the Secure Transaction Technology and the Secure Electronic Payment Protocol. SET allows multiparty transactions by using the message-based encryption. It supports multiple transports like E-mail, secure interaction etc (D. Eastlake, 1999, D. Eastlake 2000).

Figure 3. Hacking over wireless medium

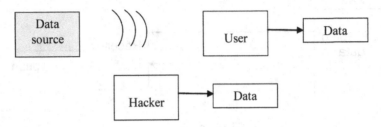

Network Hacking

The best way to test the vulnerability of a system for security threats is to try to hack the system as a part of the test (Anderson, Ross, 2001). The tests span the realistic attacks from both inside and outside of the organization. To carry out the same, the information of the network is to be collected through a PERL script. Vital information on the internal topography, the network hardware, OS, client type and server types are collected. This information is very useful to 'hijack' the network and carryout the attacks. Through the configurations, the hackers can change the access permissions, enter in to the file system, collect the passwords and credentials, all of which are used for hacking at different degrees. Today, tools are available on the internet to crack the passwords.

The data security largely depends up on the security policies of the organization. It is recommended to have periodic internal and external auditing and go for certification. The certificates are issued usually for a short period to make sure that the organization is ready to meet the new security challenges. They are tested with new challenges. However, it is specific to the organization and varies widely across the industries.

Wireless Medium

In a wireless medium, where the hacker uses the radio frequency (RF) channels, frequency hopping technique is popularly used. With some efforts, the hacker can get in to the RF network. First the frequency hopping sequence or pattern of the RF is detected. With some training, intelligent RF receivers can easily do this. With the help a program, the modulation type used with the data may be analyzed and the data packets can be demodulated. Further, by collecting sufficient data, it is possible to get the required information on encryption techniques, compression method etc. With all these information, it is possible to completely reproduce the data from the RF medium.

Often, the hacker will not be satisfied with the recovery of the secure data alone. Attempts would be made to jam the medium or insert malicious data to confuse the intended recipients. To make it happen, the hacker follows exactly the reverse steps with the help of a transmitter. Figure 3 illustrates how hacking happens over wireless network.

Search as QoS Parameter

Feedback neural networks may be used to assist the secure transmission of data. Here the examples of data networks are considered for examining the secure flow of the data. Quality of Service parameters

Figure 4. Broker based data transfer architecture

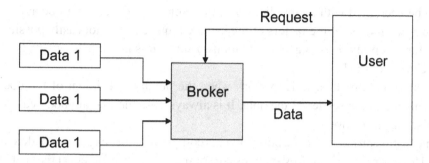

is defined over the flow. The impact of multiple flows with different QoS parameters on the intermediate resources or brokers is examined. A broker based data transfer architecture is given in figure 4. The constraint is to meet these relative service parameters with minimal utilization of the resources and minimum loss or rejection due to non-conformance to these security parameters. It is interesting to observe that the data gets dropped when the security constraints are not met at the broker. The broker can also drop them if the resources are full and no place to hold the data. All these scenarios are to be considered in the simulation before implementation.

The architecture comprises of feed forward and feedback paths. The feed forward path is made up of the actual information or data the flows to the end user from the source depending on the simulation application. The feedback signal is generated with the position and status of the information at the destination that has departed from the source. The feedback neural network will be used as the controller, with in the loop comprising of the source, the forward path, the destination and the feedback path.

A broker-based model may be used to handle the issues arising in the streaming and screen the end user from these issues. The activities involving the QoS, security etc has to be handled by the brokers down the line from the actual data source up to the end user. Each of the brokers acts as a virtual data source for the other broker in the line and they separately meet the service and security constraints. The brokers take the responsibility of meeting the security constraints or parameters.

Encryption of the Data with Keys

In a private encryption, the data to be encrypted undergoes a pre-determined transformation with a key, known to the transmitting and the receiving entities well in advance. A typical transform, also called as ciphering, involves ex-or operation of the data with the key.

The usage of private keys has several disadvantages. If the key is hacked, the hacker will be able to get access to the network completely. Today software modules are available to carry out the same. The secure transmissions require the keys to be available with both the parties to carry out the encryption and the decryption. To exchange the keys, another secure channel is required, which is not logical to afford for several applications.

The problem with the private keys is solved to a great extent with the usage of the public keys. It works on an algorithm that is difficult to reverse. The user first publishes the public key selected carefully, with the assumption that, it is impossible for the hackers to get its prime factors. These factors are known only for the publisher of the key and used for the deciphering of the data. Those who want to send secure data for this user can do so using the public key.

In public key encryption method, encryption can happen without the exchange of the keys. The data to be sent is to be encrypted with the public key of the user. Only the user will be able to decipher the data. To decipher, the unique prime factors of the key are required. It is not easily possible for anybody to get these factors, as it involves huge computations. Hence, it is possible to enable the e-transactions without the exchange of the keys.

Public key encryption method fails to work when the potential recipient of the document has no means to authenticate to the sender of the data. It is always possible that anybody can send the public key under a false authentication.

Since the encryption process with the public keys is computationally expensive, it demands more time and resources. However, the private Key systems are computationally efficient at the cost of compromise in the security. Hence, a combination of the two will be helpful.

Encryption Models

The encryption technique makes use of simple but powerful mathematical models. The user chooses two large prime numbers p and q as the private keys. A variant of their product is published as the public key. It is very difficult to reverse engineer and extract the prime numbers from the public key. The products m and n are generated as

$$m = (p-1)(q-1) \tag{1}$$

$$n = pq \tag{2}$$

An integer e is chosen as the public key exponent such that, $1 < e < m$ with e and m are co-primes. Another integer d is chosen as private key exponent such that,

$$de \equiv 1 \bmod(m) \tag{3}$$

To start with, the message to be encrypted is mapped in to an integer i using a pre selected lookup table or padding such that $0 < i < n$. The integer i get encrypted to c as

$$c \equiv i^e \bmod(n) \tag{4}$$

c gets transferred over the network. Up on receiving c at the receiver, the integer i is deciphered from c using the private key d as

$$i \equiv c^d \bmod(n) \tag{5}$$

Once i is known, the same agreed lookup table or reverse padding can get back the original message. For example, let $p=3$ and $q=5$. This gives $m= 8$ and n = 15. Let e=3. Now 8 is to divide 3d-1. Hence, d takes the value 3.

Choosing the message i to be encodes as 4, the encrypted value c becomes 64 mod 15 or 49. The deciphered value at the receiver is $(49)^3$ mod 15 or 4, which is same as the original data i. Only the authorized receiver is able to decipher, as the value of d is not known to any one else.

ISSUES AND SOLUTIONS

XACML being flexible, allows numerous security policies that compete with each other or overlap. For a system to learn the policies, it takes quite a lot of time. In effect, the redundancies associated with the rules being applied collectively would get eliminated. A set of estimators are required to apply these rules. However, a single estimator, the ideal estimator, can learn all the rules and replace all other estimators. i.e., the network can replace piecewise learning with global learning. With the Bayesian decisions, it is possible to merge the rules or policies optimally. Alternatively, the overlapping rules may be segregated with a feedback neural network as a Bayesian classifier.

For the encryption of the text, the RC4 text-ciphering algorithms are commonly used (O. Goldreich, 2001). Here, ex-or operation is performed over the text to be encrypted and a known key. The secret key used for encryption is unique and known only to the source and the destination. To get back the original text at the destination, ex-or operation is carried out over the stream and the secret key.

Channel Errors

Data transfer over a noisy channel poses a major security issue. Transmission security (W. Diffie and M. Hellman, 1976) also involves error detection and correction in the data while transferring over the channel. The error detection and correction codes call for the increase in the information redundancy in the transfer of the data by sending extra bits that again carry the redundant information. A feedback neural network generates redundancy for the data as the order of the differentials get increased. The planes corresponding to the higher order differentials carrying redundant information may be used for channel coding. In addition to being error tolerant, the hierarchical storage and transmission of data hence does not require additional channel coding.

Intrusion

One of the solutions for preventing intrusion or sniffing of an external unauthorized agency in to a network is to logically divide the network in such a way that, all the secure data as well as the transactions are grouped in to one domain and any intruder on the other side of the network i.e. the other side of the bridge or router would not be able to sniff the network. This technique works only when all the secure transactions are confined to a single physical location.

One of the major security issues in the network is Spoofing. It is the intrusion in to the network through false credentials. In general, Firewall will not allow it to happen and stop the network from getting fooled. The hierarchical storage of data over different storage servers can overcome the Spoofing problem to a great extent. The different abstractions of the data will be stored on machines with different IP address. The intruder will not know the IP address of all the machines. More over, for the intruder, the abstract levels do not make sense. The user application layers take the responsibility of collecting the data from the different machines and integrate them. The data from the missing hierarchies may be recovered with some signal processing techniques. This technique of enhanced security is used to safeguard highly sensitive information from the network and physical attacks.

Figure 5. Recovery of pass word protected file

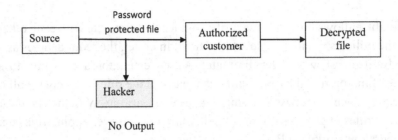

Exchange of Credentials

Private Key

One major issue with the key based encryption is the usage of key itself! The public key may be used to exchange the keys first. Once the keys are known, the private key may be used to encrypt the data. In general, encryption with a private key is less complex implement and consumes less power compared to a public key. Therefore it is used for the encryption of the actual data.

Public Key

More security in the public key transfer may be achieved with the transfer of an integrated signal in the place of the key. The integrated signal happens to be the weighted sum of the different *estimators*. The weights and the individual estimators are known only to the sender of the integrated signal much like the prime factors of the public key. However the difference is that, in the case of computing the prime factors of the large numbers, there is a possibility that a hacker would be successful in computing the factors as the factors are finite and few. However splitting an integrated signal in to its constituent signals is nearly impossible due to infinitely large combinations and choice of the weights.

Password Protection

Anyone sending out the password over the network often does it with clear and readable text, because of which any eavesdropper can easily get the authorization information and misuse the same. The authorized customer would be able to retrieve the file as shown in figure 5

One of the issues with the interactive communication involving the transfer of credentials is the risk of providing both the user name and the password with a very short gap of time. The information poses serious security threat even after the data transactions end. The problem is severe if the data is transferred in plain text format that may be easily intercepted and read.

For secure access of remote resources, the transfer of user name and the password over the network may be carried out through a local workstation that takes the responsibility of screening the credentials. Here the user first logs on to the local work station. The workstation authenticates the user so that the password and the use name are not required to be transferre3d over the network at least in text form. The workstation contacts the remote server which in turn issues a token or ticket. The token contains the encrypted data used to recognize the user of the resource (server). The local work station answers to this token by providing the user information in encrypted form.

First, the local machine identifies and authenticates the user. Then it transfers its credentials to the remote server through a secure key. The server then provides an encrypted ticket to the user. Now, the user will be able to send the answer to the ticket over the network instead of the credentials. In practice, when the user has to access the official documents over a secure net, the user first connects to a local machine that in turn identifies itself to the server containing the sensitive documents. Later, the user name and the password are transferred over a secure ticket for further identification

Secure Socket

Secure socket layer (SSL) is the open standard protocol for the secure transfer of the data between the computers as well as the applications. For example, data transfer between the web browser and the web server. It automatically gets invoked when the URL starts with https://. It is responsible for the encryption and decryption of the data. For the encryption of data, SSL makes use of public key encryption algorithms of RSA. This encryption is transparent to the end user and the applications.

When a web site is protected from SSL, the data of the site is more secure with immunity for hacking and attacks. The web pages may be provides with this security either through a vendor supported program or with in-house development.

Wireless Networks

Wireless networks are more prone to the security threats (Dirk Balfanz, Durfee, G., Grinter, R. E., Smetters, D. K. and Stewart, P, 2004). The physical medium being the open space, is physically accessible for the potential intruders. It is very important, to prevent the medium access by anyone not authorized to access the network. In addition, all the data getting transmitted between the wireless devices are to be encrypted to prevent unauthorized consumption of the information.

In a wireless adhoc network (L. Zhou and Z.J. Haas, 1999, P. Papadimitratos and Z.J. Haas, 2002, P. Papadimitratos and Z.J. Haas, 2003, P. Papadimitratos, Z.J. Haas, and P. Samar, 2002) or a mesh network, there is no centralized server to monitor the network. In such a situation, it is very important that the communication has to happen with adequate security shifting the responsibility on to the individuals.

In a network, a malicious node can congest the network or jam the communication between other nodes. A centralized controlling server will be able to detect such issues and block the access to the erring node. However, such a feature is absent in the adhoc network.

A buffer control protocol running over the adhoc network (M. G. Zapata and N. Asokan, 2002) would be helpful to handle this issue. The protocol is to realize the security policies based on the buffer monitoring algorithms. Any abrupt or unusual changes in the buffer level or routing patterns may be detected easily and the node because of which it happens may be assigned a low priority or discarded eventually.

User Interactivity

Internet supports the active interactive page. They are vulnerable for viral attacks, impersonations, tampered code etc. To ensure the transfer of secure data, authentication and key based encryption are used. It is specifically required for applications such as financial transactions, on-line purchase, code transfer, e-mail etc. A good discussion on internet privacy is available in (Dakshi Agrawal and Charu C. Aggarwal, 2001).

The data authentication procedure for data transfer follows a known protocol realized with the help of the Certificate Authority (CA) system. The body provides a mechanism to verify the publisher's authenticity (J. Feghhi, J. Feghhi, and P. Williams., 1999). The Publishers of information submit the public key of the encryption to the certification authority. The authority publishes this public key of the organization and the same has to be used by the organization to encrypt the content or the code. The same public key is used by the organization until it expires.

The CA issues certificates at different levels for commercial or personal use. For each level, the associated risk is made known. Based on the security information in the certificate, an automated system can accept or reject the transmission of the data. A feedback neural network may be used to map on to the service quality and storage abstractions to these levels.

Removable Media

In addition to the data transfers over the network, removable media are vulnerable for security threat. It is difficult to detect them. The thumb drives, MP3 players etc can be used to drag sensitive data or introduce virus or malicious code in to the system. The best way to overcome this issue is to restrict the usage of portable drives and disable the permissions wherever possible. To some extent, the antivirus software would be useful to fight against the malicious code introduced in to the system.

Internal Security

Web or intranet access from the organization also creates security issues. If the outbound data contains virus it quickly spreads across the organization as well as outside. Quite often, the emails with the attachment of such viruses get sent automatically for all the mail ids in the address book. In addition to consuming the network resources extensively and unnecessarily, it brings in a kind of embarrassment to the organization. Further discussion on secure web transactions is available in (Michael K. Reiter, Aviel D. Rubin, 1998). A proactive solution of blocking such mails and malicious services from the firewall is sought. Often, stringent policies are imposed on the firewall to carryout the same. The firewall also stops un authorized access in to the organization. The official communication is often carried out through the powerful encryption standards and firewall technology supported by a virtual private network (VPN).

Firewall

One of the issues with the firewall is the certification. Today the certification uses known test patterns that keep changing posing new threats for the data and resource security (R. Rivest, 1998). It calls for periodic renewal of the certification to make sure that the firewall is strong enough to support the requirements of the organization in meeting the new challenges.

Although firewall can handle the security threat of direct attack over the network, coming through the modems, there can be issues with physical infiltration through removable media, misuse from authorized users etc. The spread of malicious codes across the organization may be prevented by installing interior

Figure 6. Recovery of compressed file

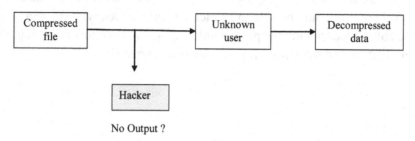

firewall. The issue of authorized user misusing the system can be tackled by enforcing stringent security policies across the organization.

FUTURE TRENDS

The digital information or assets of an organization are largely composed of multimedia data involving video clips, associated and independent audio, spread sheets etc calling for a large bandwidth for the transmission across the organization. The immediate solution to address this requirement makes use of fiber channels that provide large bandwidth and secure transmissions. Hence, research in this area focus on the usage of fiber channels and the improvements in bandwidth technology with reduced signal degradation along the channel.

Security Policies

The security policies themselves come in different levels of hierarchy and abstraction. The policies may be defined in other forms and languages. The inter operability of XACML can take care of this issue. This is true especially when a couple of the data bases have sub policies under the already defined security policy. This results in a hierarchy of heterogeneous policies. When the security policies are too lengthy and too many, a Bayesian estimator may be conveniently used to merge the security policies associated with the data and simplify the subsequent query policies. The hierarchy members can have different levels of security permissions. In addition, the outcome of each rule has to be merged to indicate if the access has to be granted. These two activities may be handled together to save the time and processing power.

The security policies may be associated with the data organized in to abstract levels. The hierarchical permissions map on to the hierarchical organization of the data. In addition, the security QoS parameters will be different at different levels of the hierarchy. Brokers continue to support the stringent security quality constraints.

Data Compression

The data transferred over the Internet (S. Kent and R. Atkinson, 1998, 1998a, 1998b) is often compressed to save the bandwidth and achieve the real time performance. The security aspects may be fused in at the time of compression. There are algorithms that encrypt the data before compression. For example, the intensity of a picture with the superimposed text may be modulated before transmission. Only the end user who is aware of this would be able to extract the text blended with the image. Any intruder in between would be able to decode only the picture unless he is aware of this ciphering and has the valid key in possession. Recovery of such a compressed file is shown in figure 6.

CONCLUSION

In this chapter,

- Various security measures and the associated issues are discussed.
- Popular security standards and protocols are introduced and their implementation techniques are discussed.

Information transmission over the Internet is challenging especially when it comes to the security. To cater for this, various sophisticated algorithms have been developed for the secure information or data transfer. Billions of dollar transaction happens over the network calling for appropriate enhanced security.

QUESTIONS

1. How does firewall help in the enforcement of the data security?
2. What are the steps followed by a hacker in gaining the access to the wireless medium?
3. How does the encryption applied over the stored data differ from the one used for the transfer of the data?
4. What are the steps to be taken for the secure exchange of the credentials over the public network?
5. How does the firewall help in maintaining the content security?

REFERENCES

Agrawal, D., & Aggarwal, C. C. (2001). On the design and quantification of privacy preserving data mining algorithms. In *Proceedings of the twentieth ACM SIGMOD-SIGACT-SIGART symposium on Principles of database systems*, (pp. 247-255). New York: ACM Press.

Anderson, R. (2001). *Security Engineering: A Guide to Building Dependable Distributed Systems*. Chichester, UK: John Wiley and Sons, Inc.

Bishop, M. (2003). *Computer security: Art and Science*. Upper Saddle River, NJ: Pearson Education, Inc.

Eastlake, D. (1999). *Domain Name System Security Extensions*, (RFC 2535). Balfanz, D., Durfee, G., Grinter, R. E., Smetters, D. K. & Stewart, P, (2004). *Network-in-a- Box: How to Set Up a Secure Wireless Network in Under a Minute*. 13th Usenix Security Symposium, San Diego, CA.

Eastlake, D., III. (2000). *DNS Request and Transaction Signatures (SIG(0)s)*, (RFC 2931).

Feghhi, J. Feghhi, J. & Williams, P. (1999). *Digital Certificates*. Reading, MA: Addison-Wesley.

Goldreich, O. (2001). *Foundations of Cryptography* (Vol. 1). New York: Cambridge University Press.

Gollmann, D. (1999). *Computer security*. Chichester, UK: John Wiley and Sons, Inc.

Housley, R. (1999). *Cryptographic Message Syntax,* RFC 2630.

Housley, R. & Hoffman, P. (1999). *Internet X.509 Public Key Infrastructure Operational Protocols: FTP and HTTP*, RFC 2585.

Kent, S. & Atkinson, R. (1998). *IP Authentication Header*, IETF FC 2402.

Kent, S. & Atkinson, R. (1998a). *IP Encapsulating Security Payload*, IETF FC 2406.

Kent, S. & Atkinson, R. (1998b). *Security Architecture for the Internet Protocol*, IETF RFC 2401.

Linn, J. (2000). *Generic Security Service Application Program Interface Version 2,Update 1*. (RFC 2743).

Maughan, D., Schertler, M., Schneider, M. & Turner, J. (1998). *Internet Security Association and Key Management Protocol*, (IETF RFC 2408).

NIST, (1995). *Secure Hash Standard*, (Technical Report FIPS PUB 180-1).

Papadimitratos, P., & Haas, Z. J. (2002). Secure Routing for Mobile Ad Hoc Networks. *Proceedings of the SCS Communication Networks and Distributed Systems Modeling And Simulation Conference (CNDS 2002)*, San Antonio, TX, Jan. 27-31.

Papadimitratos, P. & Haas, Z.J. (2003). Secure Message Transmission in Mobile Ad Hoc Networks. *Elsevier Ad Hoc Networks Journal, 1*(1).

Papadimitratos, P., Haas, Z.J. & Samar, P. (2002). *The Secure Routing Protocol (SRP) For Ad Hoc Networks*, [Internet Draft]. draft-papadimitratos-secure-routing-protocol-00.txt.

Reiter, M. K., & Rubin, A. D. (1998). Crowds: anonymity for Web transactions. *ACM Transactions on Information and System Security, 1*(1), 66–92. doi:10.1145/290163.290168

Rivest, R. (1998). Can We Eliminate Certificate Revocation Lists. *Financial Cryptography, 1465*, 178–183. doi:10.1007/BFb0055482

Schneier, B. (2000). *Secrets and Lies: Digital security in a Networked World*. Chichester, UK: John Wiley and Sons, Inc.

Vixie, P., Gudmundsson, O., Eastlake, D. & Wellington, B. (2000). *Secret Key Transaction Authentication for DNS (TSIG)*, RFC 2845.

Walker, J. (2000). IEEE P802.11 Wireless LANS, Unsafe at any key size; an analysis of the WEP encapsulation.

Zapata, M. G., & Asokan, N. (2002). Securing Ad hoc Routing Protocols. *Proceedings of the ACM WiSe 2002*, Atlanta GA.

Zhou, L. & Haas, Z.J. (1999). Securing Ad Hoc Networks. *IEEE Network Magazine, 13*(6).

About the Author

Manjunath Ramachandra is currently working at Philips, Bangalore. He has about 14 years of industrial and academic experience in the overlapping verticals of Signal processing including Multimedia, information and supply chain management, Wireless/mobile and networking. Research in the same field led to PhD thesis, about 75 international publications, patent disclosures etc. He has chaired about 10 international conferences and Figures in Marquis Who's Who 2008. His areas of interests include Signal processing, database architecture, networking etc.

Index